Michigan

A History of the Great Lakes State

Second Edition

Michigan

A History of the Great Lakes State
Second Edition

Bruce A. Rubenstein
University of Michigan—Flint

Lawrence E. Ziewacz
Michigan State University

Harlan Davidson, Inc.
Wheeling, Illinois 60090-6000

Library of Congress Cataloging-in-Publication Data

Rubenstein, Bruce A. (Bruce Alan)
    Michigan: a history of the Great Lake states / Bruce A. Rubenstein,
Lawrence E. Ziewacz.—2nd ed.
        p.   cm.
    Includes bibliographical references and index.
    ISBN 0-88295-919-0
    1. Michigan—History. I. Ziewacz, Lawrence E. (Lawrence Edward) II.
title.
F566.R8   1995
977.4—dc20   95-4296
                                                                    CIP

Unless otherwise credited, all illustrations are from the Michigan History Division, Department of State.

Maps on pages 3, 14, 38, 55 by Morris O. Thomas

Cover photograph: Mackinac Bridge
Cover design: Jay Bensen

Manufactured in the United States of America
99 98 97 96   2 3 4 5 TS

Contents

Introduction

Writing a state history is generally thought to be a thankless task. Geographic areas complain of being slighted; every city views itself as living in the shadow of the major metropolis; and ethnic groups are perceived as either receiving too little or too much emphasis. Yet, it is these very complaints which make the recitation of a state's history worthwhile. In a very real sense, these voices of discontent are the state's history. Throughout Michigan's existence as a state, the western portion of the lower peninsula and the entire upper peninsula have felt dominated by the power and influence of the eastern lower peninsula, especially Detroit. It is this continuing sense of being neglected which has given rise to movements in the upper peninsula to break away and become a separate state. Moreover, for better or worse, much of Michigan's history is the history of Detroit, and it is understandable that smaller cities should feel frustration as they pale by comparsion to the Motor City. Likewise, even though ethnic groups, both white and nonwhite, have contributed mightily to the state's growth, their contributions have been minimized because of a "melting pot" syndrome which demands that native cultures be abandoned so that everyone can become "American."

While mindful of these past truisms, this book endeavors to present Michigan's history in a different fashion. To be sure, there are the traditional accounts of the impact of the French and British, the rise of the automobile industry, and the tales of lumbering and mining—no story of Michigan would be complete without them. However, this volume intends to go beyond the well-known aspects of the state's development; it intends to tell the story of the people of Michigan. Special emphasis is given to American Indians and their fight to survive in a "white man's world," the struggle for black rights and women's suffrage, and the contributions of white ethnics. Nor is this book intended only to glorify the state, its people, and its accomplishments, for that would be a distortion of reality. Thus, stories are told of Ku Klux Klan and Black Legion violence, the anti-Semitism of prominent Michiganians such as Henry Ford and Father Charles Coughlin, the disregard for civil liberties during the "Red Scares" of 1919-20 and the McCarthy period, and the riots, both racial and otherwise, which have plagued the state since 1837.

Like all states, Michigan has grown because of the boldness, wisdom, strength, and creativity of its citizens. Missionaries, explorers, warriors, statesmen, politicians, inventors, business entrepreneurs, civil libertarians, educators, artists, and laborers in factories and fields have joined to shape Michigan's heritage. This book is their story—the history of the Great Lakes State.

1

The Original Michiganians

For generations, most schoolchildren have been told by well-meaning teachers that their national heritage began in 1492 with Christopher Columbus' discovery of America. In recent years, Scandinavian scholars have objected to this interpretation, claiming that Leif Ericson arrived in North America before Columbus. In an effort to retain their national pride, Italian historians countered by promoting another of their countrymen, Amerigo Vespucci, as the true discoverer of America. European arguments over who discovered the North American continent are interesting, but they ignore a basic fact: non-Europeans lived on the continent for at least fourteen thousand years before any European arrival. Thus, it is impossible for any European nation to claim "discovery." Some scholars refute this argument by saying that Europeans can still boast discovery because they had never before seen North America. The foolishness of this contention was shown in 1975 when an Iroquois college professor from New York boarded a plane, flew to Rome, and upon arrival, announced that because his people had never been to Italy before he was claiming that land for the Iroquois Nation by right of discovery!

Ironically, Indians, so named by Columbus because he was certain that he had landed in India, lived in western Europe long before any Europeans established permanent colonies in North America. English fishermen, working the Newfoundland coast in the early 1500s, captured several natives and took them to England as examples of the "savage inhabitants" of the New World. After a few years, the amusement of viewing Indians diminished and another fishing expedition returned the captives to their homeland. Immediately these Indians spread tales of their adventures and told fascinated friends and relatives of the "world across the sea." English culture and language clearly had intrigued the captives and they taught "white man's words" to their people. Therefore, when the Pilgrims landed at Plymouth Rock in 1620 they were astounded when a descendant of one of those early visitors to England greeted them in English and assured them that others in his village spoke the language fluently. While it would be an exaggeration to say that Indians knew English "fluently," it is fair to say that Europeans do not even have a valid claim to being the first English-speaking residents of North America.

Throughout the years whites have been puzzled as to how Indians arrived on the continent and from whom they were descended. Several far-fetched ideas have been put forth to answer these questions. An early popular theory was that Indians came by ferry from Europe. Disbelievers said that such a hypothesis was ridiculous and that the only logical answer was that Indians were descendants of people from the lost continents of Mu and Atlantis. In the 1600s, Puritans asserted that Indians were descendants of the "Lost Tribe of Israel," who had wandered so long and far that they had been stripped of all godly qualities and had become savage "Children of the Devil." This theory was accepted for over two centuries, although it, like the others mentioned, have absolutely no basis in fact.

By the 1970s, there were two accepted theories on how Indians arrived on the North American continent. Most anthropologists believe that small bands of Indians crossed the Bering Straits from Siberia approximately fourteen thousand years ago. Such a crossing was made possible because during the Ice Age sea levels declined and land bridges were formed linking Asia and North America. Since the continents are separated by a mere fifty-six miles, it is assumed by many anthropologists that ancestors of the modern Eskimo were the first settlers of North America. Many Indians, however, accept a second theory. They believe that the Creator placed them on the continent and that they have always been its inhabitants. Whichever theory is valid perhaps cannot be conclusively resolved. However, one point is indisputable: Indians were the original native North Americans.

The Three Fires

When Europeans first arrived on the North American continent, approximately one hundred thousand Indians, or 10 percent of the total Indian population north of Mexico, lived in the Great Lakes region. Of the several tribes residing in what is now Michigan, the most numerous and influential were the Ottawa, Chippewa, and Potawatomi. These tribes, which originally were united, split sometime before the sixteenth century, with the Ottawa remaining near Mackinac and in the lower peninsula, the Chippewa going west and north into Wisconsin and the upper peninsula, and the Potawatomi moving down the eastern shore of Lake Michigan. All continued to live harmoniously, without defined territorial boundaries, and never failed to recognize their common Algonquian language dialect and culture. They thought of themselves as a family, with the Chippewa the elder brother, the Ottawa the next older brother,

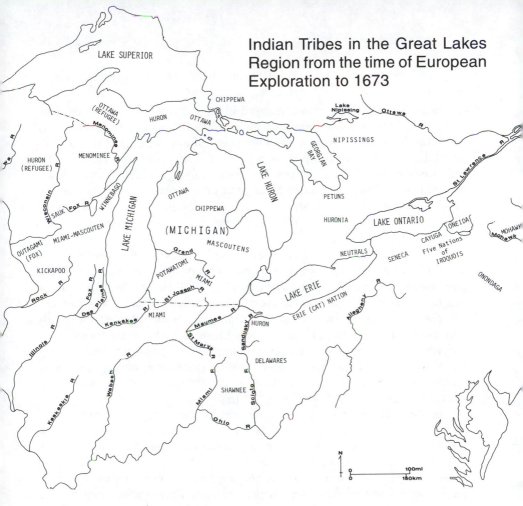

Indian Tribes in the Great Lakes Region from the time of European Exploration to 1673

and the Potawatomi the younger brother, and referred to their loose confederation as the "Three Fires."

The Chippewa, or Ojibwa, who inhabited the northern upper Great Lakes area, were the largest Algonquian tribe, estimated at between twenty-five and thirty-five thousand at the time of white arrival in the New World. In order to survive in their harsh environment, the Chippewa lived in small bands, usually consisting of five to twenty-five families, who could sustain themselves on the available food sources. During the summer, bands moved to good fishing sites and used hooks, spears, and nets to catch whitefish, perch, sturgeon, and other food fish. Men also hunted small game, while the elders, women, and children gathered nuts, berries, and honey. A portion of the gatherings and fish catch was dried and set aside for use in the winter. In the autumn, wild rice and corn were harvested and hunts for large game, such as deer, moose, and caribou, were organized. As the "Hunger Moon" of winter set in, food grew scarce and families shared what little resources they possessed with their relatives. Sharing those items most valuable and scarce was an economic and physical necessity among band-level people in order to survive. In the spring, maple sap was collected, boiled, and made into syrup and sugar for their own use and trade. While

Chippewa in the lower peninsula engaged in limited farming, most of the tribe acquired agricultural staples through trade with the Ottawa and Wyandot.

Like all band-level people, the Chippewa did not possess highly organized political structures. Leadership in their classless society was based on an individual's hunting or fishing skill, physical prowess, warring abilities, or eloquence in speech. Leaders had no delegated power, but maintained influence through acts of kindness, wisdom, generosity, and humility. Positions of leadership always were earned and could not be passed from generation to generation as a hereditary right.

Chippewa social structure centered around approximately twenty "super-families" called clans. Each child belonged to his or her father's clan, and thus clans traced the line of an individual's descent. Furthermore, because marriage had to occur between different clans, a strong intratribal unity was fostered.

The second of the Three Fires, the Ottawa, was estimated to number nearly four thousand at the time of white arrival. Living in bark-covered lodges in the northwestern two-thirds of the lower peninsula, the Ottawa followed a subsistence pattern similar to that of the Chippewa, except that during the summer months they engaged in extensive farming. The Ottawa became known as great traders and their name, Adawe, means "to trade."

Ottawa social and political structures were similiar to those of the Chippewa, as was the Ottawa religion. The religion of the Ottawa and Chippewa was extremely sophisticated. Because Indians had always lived in nature, they thought of themselves as merely one of many elements constituting the environment. The white concept of man being a special creation apart from nature was foreign to every Indian belief of man's role in the universe. They believed that a Great Spirit, Kitchi Manitou, created the heavens and earth, and then summoned lesser spirits to control the winds and waters. The sun was the father of mankind, the earth its mother. Thunder, lightning, the four winds, and certain wildlife were endowed with godlike powers. In the Indians' animistic belief structure any object, especially crooked trees and odd shaped rocks, could possess religious significance.

To Indians, religion was primarily an individual matter. At puberty each child journeyed to an isolated sacred place where a vision was sought through fasting. In most instances, a spirit would appear and grant the supplicant a personal spirit song and instructions for assembling a strong protective medicine bag. This spirit became the person's lifelong guardian, and it was a source of great comfort for the individual to know that a spirit was taking personal interest in his life.

Not all spirits were benevolent. Mischievous spirits, or "tricksters," were ever-present. These demigods were believed responsible for the annoyances of daily life, and all frightening sounds and accidents were caused by these playful, yet malevolent, sprites. Snakes and owls were thought to be earthly forms assumed by evil gods. Man-eating monsters were believed to dwell in certain sectors of the Great Lakes, and no journey was begun without first making offerings to appease them.

The most common offering was tobacco. Manitous, or gods, were said to be fond of this dried leaf and it became the link between mortals and spiritual powers. Before each harvest it was placed on the ground as a gesture of thanks, accompanied with a request for Mother Earth to accept their offer. Tobacco was put on streams to assure plentiful harvests of wild rice and bountiful catches of fish, on graves to placate the dead, and at all holy sites. The Ottawa and Chippewa considered tobacco so sacred that they insisted on smoking it with whites at treaty councils to signify that the accord was sanctioned "in the eyes of the Great Spirit." Later missionaries, however, refused to honor what they considered "savage superstitions" and collected the tobacco offerings for distribution among their half-blood interpreters.

Chippewa and Ottawa religion was a refined system of cultural beliefs, based more on feelings than a formalized creed, which was perpetuated by oral tradition and adapted to fulfill the spiritual needs of its followers. It was no more primitive than the ancient Greek and Roman religion which also used polytheism, legendary cultural heroes, and symbolic rituals to explain the "inexplainable." Indians personified the elements because they were in awe of them and wished to demonstrate to the gods their desire to live in harmony, not competition, with nature. Unfortunately for later Indian-white relations, only the Catholic Jesuit missionaries made any attempt to understand the Indians' feelings toward their environment.

Missionary work among the Indians of Michigan was doomed to ultimate failure because it demanded that Indians undergo a total social and cultural revolution. Missionaries did not separate the concepts of Christianity and civilization. They thereby committed themselves to destroying the Indians' culture in order to save their souls and prepare them for life in white society. When the mass of Indians refused to comply with the wishes of the preachers, churchmen angrily said that their task was hopeless because "when a tribe or nation has reached a certain point in degradation, it is impossible to restore it." In truth, their failure was because of an inability to comprehend the intricate sensibilities of the Indian religion. Consequently, among all aspects of Indian culture, religion best withstood the onslaught of assimilation.

Like other Great Lakes Indians, the Ottawa believed that the most important social custom was reciprocity. This was basically the idea of doing something for someone, or giving them something, with the expectation that they would do something in return. There were three types of reciprocity practiced among the Indians. First was general reciprocity. This was usually done between close relatives and assumed a balanced exchange. The distinguishing feature of this type of reciprocity is that part of the transaction could be based on future considerations; that is, one person would do something immediately and trust the other party to do something of equal worth for him in the future. The second type was balanced reciprocity. This was the most common form and consisted of a straight trade of goods and services assumed to be of equal value. Such a trade was made between distant relatives, or nonrelatives, who were not as well known to each party. The final type was negative reciprocity. This was extremely rare and occurred when one party knowingly attempted to cheat the other. When word spread of such behavior, the guilty party was ostracized from future trading functions.

Europeans never fully understood reciprocity because in its broadest sense it implied sharing as a way of life. The root difference between the races in this respect is that Europeans, who believe in private property, hoard in expectation of gaining increased profits. Indians, by contrast, do not believe in private property, but rather have only communal and personal property. Communal property belonged to the band as a whole. Personal property belonged to an individual and was understood to belong to that person, but could be borrowed by anyone. In other words everyone in a community had access to everyone else's materials. Likewise, it was unthinkable in Indian society, before white contact, for one person to have two of an item while another person had none. It was understood that everyone would share. Reciprocity and sharing was the heart of Indian economic and social organization.

The third major tribe was the Potawatomi, who received their name from the Chippewa term "Potawatamink," which means "people of the place of the fire." Because they were primarily an agricultural people, this name probably derived from their practice of burning grass and brush to clear fields for cultivation.

Potawatomi life, like that of their kinsmen, followed the rhythm of the seasons. During the summer, they formed large villages, usually near fertile lands along rivers and streams. Women planted corn, squash, beans, melons, and tobacco, while the men took to the forests and waterways to hunt and fish. In the fall, final harvesting was made and the villages were moved into the heart of the forests where winter hunting would be best and protection from winter winds was afforded by the trees. In the spring, maple sap was collected for use as sugar.

The most noteworthy aspect of Potawatomi social structure was the practice of polygamy. If a man married women from different clans, the union joined not only the individuals but also their entire clans. Marriage thus brought together large numbers of people as a family unit. Since it was considered essential to have as many relatives as possible to survive and care for each other in times of need, this practice was extremely beneficial.

Potawatomi culture, like that of the Ottawa and Chippewa, had well defined roles for every member of society. Men were expected to hunt, fish, trap, trade, and defend the tribe. Women farmed, cooked, sewed, made camp, and raised children. Youngsters were taught to respect their elders and gain wisdom from them. Having been raised amid an atmosphere of love and respect, Indians perpetuated a society based on strong family ties.

Effects of White Contact

European arrival in the Great Lakes area during the seventeenth century led to gradually increasing disruptions in the comparatively stable Indian culture. Initial changes were not great, but as contact became more prolonged and intense, its effect on Indians was pronounced. Material culture was the first aspect of Indian life to undergo alteration. European trade goods quickly brought the substitution of iron knives and axes for those of stone. Iron farm implements replaced ones made of wood. Iron and brass arrowheads took the place of those from chipped stone. Brass kettles displaced native pottery vessels, and ultimately guns replaced bows, arrows, and lances.

By the mid-1700s, Michigan's Indians were almost completely dependent upon European trade goods. Many Indians no longer made their own tools, utensils, or weapons, and, as a result, native skills in handicraft gradually diminished. Economic dependency altered the Indian's relationship to the environment by disrupting the traditional subsistence hunting and gathering pattern. Because Indians could not obtain European merchandise without supplying furs, which had become the established medium of exchange, they placed an ever-increasing emphasis on hunting and trapping. Even agricultural bands turned to the forests to provide them with currency to purchase white trade goods. No longer was the food quest the dominant reason to hunt and no longer was the balance of nature an important consideration. The overriding goal then had to be successful commercial hunting—the increasing slaughter of animals for their pelts. As the fur supply dwindled in their home area, many Indians ventured beyond their own territory into that of their enemies. Often these dangerous treks took them so far from their camps that they could bring back only the furs, while leaving the once invaluable meat behind to rot. Many risks were taken in order to assure continued favor of the white traders.

Eventually, white contact caused changes in the Indian political structure. The traditional classless society with leaders who led by example was transformed into one with powerful chiefs holding well-defined positions of authority. Whites expected Indians to have leaders with power to speak for an entire band. To satisfy this expectation, and to expedite trade and treaty making, chiefs were voluntarily granted by their followers previously unknown amounts of responsibility. White contact even resulted in the creation of the position of "trading chief," whose sole function was to negotiate trade agreements for his band.

Introduction of whiskey among the Indians by European traders also had a marked impact upon their culture. Henry Rowe Schoolcraft, a lifelong observer of Michigan's Indians, wrote that "whiskey is the great means of drawing from him [the Indian] his furs and skins." The sad result was that Indians often would even sell their personal and family possessions to buy alcohol. Schoolcraft further believed that the introduction and use of alcohol, along with white-induced diseases, idleness, and a lack of food, accounted for the Indians' gradual population decline. His observation was accurate, as these forces reduced the number of Indians in Michigan to an estimated eight thousand by 1900. Clearly, Indian involvement in the fur trade started a dramatic, and disastrous, change in native culture.

Effects of Assimilation

In the decade following the Civil War, Michigan's Indians experienced a rebirth of cultural pride. During the first seventy years of the nineteenth century Michigan's Indians had ceded their land to the federal government by treaties, accepted missionaries, and welcomed settlers. They had dealt with whites in good faith and sought to live harmoniously with them. By 1870, however, Indians began to reassess their relationship with whites. They noted that in return for their friendship, government officials had refused to protect them from timber thieves and speculators. Indian agents often used their position to defraud, rather than protect, their wards. Missionaries, who had promised to educate Indians and prepare them for life in white society, often had proved to be false friends, involved in graft and land frauds. Settlers, forgetting the aid given them by Indians in the past, began to depict Indians as obstacles to civilization and progress. Bitter memories of this type of white injustice and ingratitude made Indians resentful of all attempts to assimilate them into a society they had grown to consider corrupt and treacherous. Indian hatred of whites grew in proportion to the increased numbers of fraud and swindles perpetrated upon them. Although they were too poor and ignorant of their rights to protest actively against white treachery, Michigan's Indians were determined to do more than suffer in stoic silence. Most resolved that they would never totally abandon their native heritage and become "red white men." White culture would be adopted only as it became necessary for survival.

Oblivious to rising Indian hatred, Indian Department officials noted only the superficial change occurring in the Indians' way of life. They claimed that Indian willingness to accept private property, wear white-style dress, attend Christian churches, learn English and arithmetic, and work at "white man's labor" was proof that Indians were eager to abandon their old ways and become civilized. Michigan's Indians were touted by department officials in the 1870s as being contented, prosperous "models of assimilation."

Department officials were incorrect, however, as the state's Indians were

Indian
Land
Cessions.

Treaty of
La Pointe
1842

Treaty

of

Cedar Point

1836

Washington
1836

Treaty
of

Saginaw

Treaty

of

1819

Treaty
of

Detroit

Chicago

1807

1821

Carey Mission
1828

Chicago
1833

Foot of the Rapids
1817

Greenville
1795

Indians ceded their land to the United States government by a series of treaties. This map shows how the federal government obtained title to Michigan from the state's original owners.

not "models." They attended Christian churches not because they believed that Christianity was a superior religion, but rather to placate their Methodist Indian agents, receive food, shelter, and clothing, and partake in social gatherings and festivals. They went to "white schools" to learn basic skills in order to survive in communities filled with people eager to cheat them. White-style dress was accepted partly because it was received as gifts and partly because it was not perceived as a threat to native culture. Some worked at "white industries" because they needed money to feed and clothe their families, but most chose labor which involved their native skills of hunting, fishing, forestry, and manufacture of artifacts. What federal officials thought was a willingness to assimilate was, in reality, an attempt to preserve Indian culture while living in white society. Indians accepted elements of white culture to supplement, not supplant, their native beliefs.

Michigan's Indian residents desired only equality from their white neighbors. They wanted fair treatment under the law, wages comparable to those paid whites, and, most of all, they wanted to share in the freedoms promised all Americans in the Bill of Rights. Indians neither possessed religious freedom nor received due process of law. Despite theoretical "full equality" granted by the 1850 state constitution, Michigan's Indians, by virtue of their race, religion, and economic condition, were second-class citizens. At the turn of the twentieth century, the state's Ottawa, Chippewa, and Potawatomi would have been satisfied with "separate but equal" status, as they believed that their lives would be improved isolated from the evils of liquor, moral debauchery, disease, and corruption associated with white society.

Sincere friends of the Indians tried to assist them but were thwarted by state politicians and judges controlled by lumber and railroad interests. To most whites, Indians were not human beings, but obstacles to economic growth for the state. Accordingly, avarice took precedence over humanitarianism, and the state's Indians continued to be denied both moral and legal justice.

The poverty of rural Indians in modern Michigan is evident by this typical home in the upper peninsula.

Indians in Modern Michigan

During the twentieth century, Michigan's Indians have fared little better. Following World War I, American industry boomed and income soared, but Michigan's Indians did not share in the prosperity. Because they were not white, they were not hired to work in the automobile plants and other related industries—industries which needed workers so urgently that they recruited them from other states! In desperation, many Indians decided to become "white," to give up their cultural heritage and try to conceal their Indian blood simply to obtain a job and survive. Even this has failed, however, for a study made for Governor Milliken in 1970 related that poverty was still the rule among Indian households, especially in rural areas.

In 1970, nearly 40 percent of Indian households earned less than the national poverty level of three thousand dollars and 29 percent of rural families brought home less than one thousand dollars. In rural regions much of the low income level is because of a high number of retired persons living on Social Security, but omitting these people from the survey leaves almost 40 percent of the rural households earning less than three thousand dollars. This economic plight grew worse, as the 1980 census revealed 49 percent of Michigan Indian households were near or below the national poverty line, compared to the state average of 11 percent.

Much of the poverty is a direct result of extremely high levels of unemployment among Indians. Approximately 25 percent of heads of Indian households in 1970 were out of work, and among those heads of households under thirty-five years of age the figure increased to 39 percent. Most of this was because of a lack of training and education. Indian children in Michigan in 1970 had a 60 percent drop-out rate from high school. Some left school because they felt alienated, others left because they did not think that a "white education" would benefit them, and still others left because they had to help support their families. Despite the various reasons, they did not receive a diploma, and without at least a high school degree the only jobs available are low paying, unskilled, manual labor.

Poverty directly creates another problem—poor health. Among unemployed heads of households nearly 30 percent reported a physical disability which restricted the types of labor they could do. Poor health affects the entire household of poverty-stricken people, and the very young are especially hard hit. Infant mortality, which was twenty per one thousand among the general population in 1970, reached ninety per one thousand among Indians, and 16 percent of all urban Indian families interviewed for the governor's survey claimed to have lost a child within one year of its birth.

Another problem Indians face is how to get to a potential job. Among employed Indians in 1970, nearly 40 percent had to travel more than five miles daily to get to their place of work and 75 percent of these people owned an automobile which was in good operating condition. However, 60 percent of the unemployed Indians did not have access to an automobile and could not get to a job even if one were offered.

Yet another reason for high unemployment among Indians is the lack of available child care. Nearly 20 percent of Indian heads of households in 1970 were women. However, a mother could not accept a job if she had to pay a babysitter because there was no one available to care for her children. Consequently, many women remained on Aid to Dependent Children or welfare.

In May 1979 another wave of anti-Indian sentiment surged through Michigan when Federal Judge Noel Fox issued a decision reaffirming the rights of the state's Indians, as set forth by an 1836 treaty, to fish on the Great Lakes. The Department of Natural Resources and the state's sport fishermen protested the decision on the incorrect assumption that it granted Indians unregulated and unlimited fishing, a practice which could quickly deplete the lakes. Many upper peninsula residents, especially near Sault Ste. Marie, threatened physical violence to stop Indian fishermen.

Virtually all of the fears of sport fishermen were unwarranted. Judge Fox's decision did not permit unregulated fishing, but rather instructed Indians to work with the Department of the Interior to establish mechanisms for self-regulation, management, and enforcement. Moreover, Indians were commercial fishermen, and it would have been contrary to their best interests to overfish the lakes. Nevertheless, conservation groups kept up their relentless criticisms.

In an attempt to quell the unrest, in 1985 a fifteen-year plan for joint use and management of the Great Lakes was agreed upon by the federal government, the state of Michigan, and the Indians. The treaty waters of Lakes Superior, Michigan, and Huron were divided into three management zones with defined uses, fishing techniques, and allowable catch limitations. Indians were granted exclusive rights to commercial fishing on the lakes, and in return they consented to relinquish claims to certain sectors of the lakes and not to do commercial fishing in designated sport fishing areas. As well, Indians pledged both to use trap, rather than gill, nets in selected areas so that sport species of fish could be released safely and to avoid totally fishing in trout rehabitation areas.

Another positive economic advance for the state's Indians was casino gambling. Beginning with a single Indian-owned casino at Sault Ste. Marie on July 4, 1984, reservation casinos expanded rapidly during the following ten years. In 1993 Michigan's eight Indian casinos represented a $70,000,000-a-year industry which offered not only employment for Indians but also respect from the business community and the promise of a better life for their children. The Sault Ste. Marie Chippewa, for example, spent $2,700,000 a year in casino profits on tribal social programs and set aside another $5,000,000 in a tribal trust fund. In 1993, Governor John Engler signed a compact with the state's seven tribes, clearing the way for discussion of Indian-operated off-reservation casinos in Detroit, Flint, and Port Huron. Thus, for the first time since the arrival of Europeans, Indians have hope for economic independence; yet, more must be done.

In the face of such obstacles as racial discrimination and stereotyping, the plight of Michigan's Indians, who, according to the 1990 census number 55,638 or .06 percent of the state's population, will not be easy to alleviate, but it can be accomplished. Throughout the state, Indian community action groups are dedicating themselves to support for improved educational opportunities. In the United States, in order to succeed, an education is an absolute necessity. Educated people receive better jobs, have better health, and enjoy the fruits of society. Education is the key which will unlock the chains of centuries of repression for Michigan's Indians. There is no other acceptable alternative.

For Further Reading

Several excellent works have been published describing Indian customs, religion, and way of life. Among the most readable and informative are W. Vernon Kinietz, *The Indians of the Western Great Lakes, 1675-1760* (Ann Arbor: University of Michigan Press, 1940) and *Chippewa Village: The Story of Katikitegon* (Bloomfield Hills: Cranbrook Institute of Science, 1947); George I. Quimby, *Indian Life in the Upper Great Lakes* (Chicago: University of Chicago Press, 1960); Robert E. and Pat Ritzenthaler, *The Woodland Indians of the Western Great Lakes* (Garden City: Natural History Press, 1970); Charles E. Cleland, *A Brief History of Michigan Indians* (Lansing: John M. Munson Publication, Michigan History Division, Michigan Dept. of State, 1975); R. David Edmunds, *The Potawatomis: Keepers of the Fire* (Norman: University of Oklahoma Press, 1978); and Edmund J. Danziger, Jr., *The Chippewas of Lake Superior* (Norman: University of Oklahoma Press, 1978).

Specialized topics concerning Indian life are covered in Gertrude Kurath, *Michigan Indian Festivals* (Ann Arbor: Ann Arbor Publishers, 1966); Frances Densmore, *Chippewa Customs* (Washington: U.S. Government Printing Office, 1929); and Bruce A. Rubenstein, "To Destroy a Culture: Indian Education in Michigan, 1855-1900," *Michigan History*, LX (Summer 1976).

Early efforts to depict Indian life are always interesting, but must be read with care, as their scholarship is often faulty. The three best and most accurate accounts written in the nineteenth century are Henry Rowe Schoolcraft, *Personal Memoirs of a Residence of Thirty Years with the Indians on the American Frontier . . . 1812-1842* (Philadelphia: Lippincot, Grambo & Co., 1845); William W. Warren, *A History of the Ojibway Nation* (Minneapolis: Ross and Haines, 1957 reprint); and Andrew J. Blackbird, *History of the Ottawa and Chippewa Indians of Michigan* (Ypsilanti: Ypsilanti Job Press, 1887).

Among the most recent accounts are Charles E. Cleland, *Rites of Conquest* (Ann Arbor: University of Michigan Press, 1992), which offers a detailed general history of the state's Indians, and Edmund J. Danziger, Jr., *Survival and Regeneration* (Detroit: Wayne State University Press, 1991), which sets forth the struggle of Detroit's Indian residents during the twentieth century.

New France in the Great Lakes Region

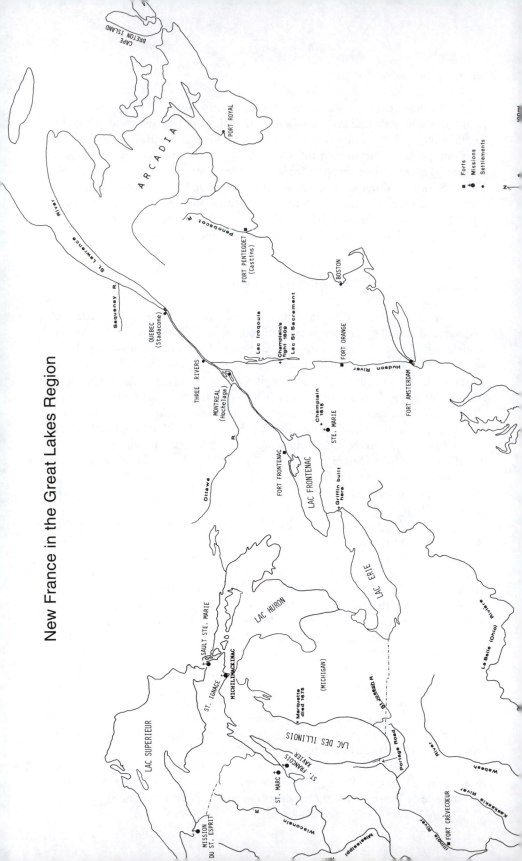

CAPE BRETON ISLAND

ARCADIA

PORT ROYAL

St. Lawrence River

Saguenay R.

QUEBEC (Stadacone)

THREE RIVERS

MONTREAL (Hochelaga)

Ottawa R.

FORT PENTEGOET (Castins)

Penobscot R.

BOSTON

Lac Iroquois
Champlain's fight 1609
Lac St Sacrement

FORT ORANGE

Hudson River

FORT AMSTERDAM

Champlain 1615

STE. MARIE

FORT FRONTENAC

LAC FRONTENAC

Griffin built here

LAC ERIE

SAULT STE. MARIE

LAC HURON

ST. IGNACE

MICHILIMACKINAC

(MICHIGAN)

Marquette died 1675

LAC SUPERIEUR

St. Joseph R.

Portage Road

LAC DES ILLINOIS

ST. FRANCOIS XAVIER

ST. MARC

MISSION DU ST. ESPRIT

Wisconsin R.

Mississippi R.

FORT CRÈVECOEUR

Illinois River

Kankakee River

Wabash River

La Belle (Ohio) River

■ Forts
● Missions
· Settlements

N

100 mi.

2

The New Acadia

France, Europe's wealthiest and most populous nation, did not enter the race for new lands until 1522. Prior to that time, France's economic and political interests remained centered in the Mediterranean area. Spurred by accounts of Magellan's success in circling the globe, the French sought to become the first European nation to discover the shortcut to the spice-rich Orient. In 1523 Giovanni de Verrazano, an Italian navigator, sailed under the French flag and explored the North American coast from Virginia to Newfoundland, but reported that he could not find a passage to the East.

French motivation for discovery and exploration in North America was predicated primarily on finding both a short route to the Orient and great amounts of precious metals. These motives, which remained constant during much of the French presence in North America, help to explain most of the differences between the French and English colonization efforts. No English colony was founded to secure a passageway to the East while the French constantly kept probing the interior regions in an effort to find such a route. French efforts were also aided by geography. While the English remained clustered along the Atlantic coast, barred from westward expansion by the seemingly impenetrable Appalachian Mountain Range, the French faced no such obstacle. Following the St. Lawrence River to the Great Lakes, French voyageurs and explorers used highways of rivers to advance rapidly into the interior of North America.

Eleven years after Verrazano's voyage, Jacques Cartier made the first of his three ventures to the New World in search of the "Northwest Passage" to China. While sailing into the Gulf of St. Lawrence, he encountered Iroquois Indians whom he assumed had had previous meetings with whites because upon his arrival they displayed furs to trade and hid all their young women. Returning to France, Cartier received financial backing for another voyage. On this second trip, in 1535, Cartier revisited the Iroquois village of Stadacona (Quebec) bringing with him two sons of Chief Donnacona, whom he had taken with him to Europe on his previous voyage. From Stadacona Cartier was eager to make his way down the St. Lawrence to the Indian village of Hochelaga (Montreal). Fearing that his people would lose a portion of the French trade if such a trip was made, Chief Donnacona warned Cartier that he would freeze to death amid the ice and snow of Hochelaga. Undeterred, Cartier sailed north to Hochelaga, which proved to be a village of approximately fifty lodges, surrounded by vast cornfields. These Indians told Cartier of a great river to the West where people lived who wore European clothes and used tools of gold and silver.

Pleased with this knowledge, Cartier returned to Stadacona, but, having grown suspicious of Donnacona, the French leader decided to construct a fort at the present site of Quebec City. Having done so, Cartier and his men prepared to meet their first Canadian winter. Fierce, howling winds, subarctic temperatures, and blinding blizzards caught them unprepared, however. Starvation, exposure, and scurvy resulted in the loss of twenty-five men, and the toll might have been even higher had not Indians shown the whites how to prepare a tea, from the bark and pine needles of white cedars, which was rich in Vitamin C. In the spring, Cartier sailed for France, taking with him Donnacona and several other Indians, none of whom would ever return to their homeland.

Although many Frenchmen were interested in Cartier's discoveries, internal political problems and religious strife prevented him from obtaining immediate support for a third voyage. Finally, in 1540, King Francis I decided to establish a permanent French colony in Canada. Because Pope Alexander IV in 1493 had divided the non-Christian world into spheres belonging to either Spain or Portugal, Francis needed an acceptable rationale to receive the church's blessing for his enterprise. Citing the need to Christianize savages in the New World, the king selected Jean Francois de la Rocque, Sieur de Roberval, a noted soldier and court favorite, to head the next expedition to the New World. Cartier was to accompany him as master pilot and guide. The church sanctioned the voyage, but since Roberval was Protestant, Francis' sincerity in wishing to propagate the Catholic faith is dubious.

The king opened the treasury and lavish funds were provided to amass ten ships, several hundred soldiers and sailors, trained craftsmen, livestock, and supplies. Recruitment of volunteers proved difficult, however, and expedition leaders had to resort to combing prisons to fill their manpower needs. In May 1541, Cartier, with five ships, set sail for North America, but because of a shortage of supplies and weapons, Roberval did not depart for another year. Upon arriving in Canada, Cartier erected another fort near Stadacona. On this occasion his men discovered what Cartier believed were diamonds and gold. Quickly he dispatched two ships to France to inform the king of his great discovery.

Cartier and his men endured another difficult winter, suffering both from nature and constant harassment from hostile Indians seeking revenge for their missing chief. Fearful of being overrun by the Indians if they remained, Cartier and his men sailed for France in the spring. Reaching St. John's in Newfoundland, he encountered Roberval, who ordered him to return to Stadacona. Inexplicably, Cartier disobeyed this order and continued to France, leaving Roberval to conduct all further explorations.

Roberval then founded a colony near Cape Rouge, which he said was "a convenient place to fortify ourselves in, fitted to command the main river, and of strong situation against all our enemies." Severe weather, scurvy, and constant Indian hostility, however, forced Roberval to return to France just as Cartier had done earlier.

This entire expedition was a failure. No passage to the East was discovered and Cartier's gold proved to be nothing more than iron pyrite and his diamonds mica. All Cartier had given France was a new saying, "as false as Canadian diamonds!" The only thing which made the trip worthwhile was that Cartier did discover the Ottawa River, which would later become the French highway into the North American interior.

Internal religious struggles again dominated French politics and the government turned its attention from settling the New World. Attempts by French merchants in 1580 to organize expeditions to North America proved disastrous because of competitive rivalries, and eventually the French government, following the precedent of the English, resorted to chartering private companies to promote settlement and trade, with emphasis on the latter. Beginning in 1588 France once again was involved in commercial and colonization efforts in Canada.

Samuel de Champlain

Samuel de Champlain was truly the "Father of New France." Born in 1567, Champlain fought courageously under the banner of Henry of Navarre during the French religious wars. After the Treaty of Vervins brought peace with Spain in 1598, Champlain sailed for the Spanish and spent three years in New Spain, gathering valuable knowledge of the New World. Later he returned to France and wrote a narrative of his adventures, which established his reputation as an explorer and cartographer.

In 1603, the Sieur Pierre du Guast, Sieur de Monts received from the French government a ten-year monopoly on trade and settlement in Canada, provided that he settle sixty persons there. In 1604, de Monts set sail with Champlain as his cartographer, and the following year they established France's first permanent settlement at Port Royal, which would become the capital of Acadia. Unfortunately, Port Royal was too near New England and was virtually indefensible. As well, French merchants had convinced the king to reinstitute free trade and in 1607 de Monts lost his monopoly.

Undaunted, de Monts commissioned Champlain to explore the St. Lawrence region for settlement possibilities. In 1608, Champlain founded a colony at the site of Cartier's outpost near Stadacona. From this base Champlain launched

This seventeenth century sketch depicts Champlain defeating the Iroquois in 1609. The European concept of superiority is evident as Champlain is almost singlehandedly fighting the foe.

a systematic program of explorations of the continent's interior and established the framework for Indian relationships that determined French and Indian alliances until the end of the French presence in North America. What made Champlain truly extraordinary, however, was his vision of Canada's future. He sought to create not merely a fur post, but rather a strong permanent colony populated by enterprising settlers. His plan put him in direct opposition with private companies who sought only profits from the fur trade and feared that large numbers of settlers would ruin their industry.

In 1609, Champlain and two companions aided a party of Huron warriors in a battle against a band of Mohawk, who belonged to the powerful Iroquois Confederation. Three Mohawk were slain and a dozen captured and tortured to death. Because the French had been friendly with enemies of the Iroquois in earlier years, this action solidified Iroquois hostility toward the French.

Champlain undertook further explorations along the St. Lawrence in hope of both finding the elusive "Northwest Passage" and encouraging other Frenchmen to plunge even deeper into the interior. That he succeeded in his latter goal is demonstrated by the 1622 expedition of Etienne Brule. Brule, who had spent several years living among the Huron, and a companion canoed to the present site of Sault Ste. Marie, where they viewed the rapids through which Lake Superior empties into Lake Huron. Twelve years later, again under the auspices of Champlain, Jean Nicolet became the first white man to traverse the Straits of Mackinac, follow the shore of Lake Michigan, and arrive at Green Bay. His voyage was a personal disappointment, however, as he had been told by Indians that his course would lead him to "stinking water." Nicolet interpreted this to mean the briny Pacific Ocean, which, if true, would mean that he had found the inland route to the Orient. Unfortunately, he discovered only the less than fresh waters of Green Bay. He did, however, deeply impress the Indians who came to meet him, as he was attired in a colorful silk robe which he had donned in anticipation of landing in Cathay.

Missionaries and Their Activities

Missionaries played an instrumental role in French exploratory efforts. Recollect priests under Father Joseph LeCaron performed missionary work among the Huron at Quebec as early as 1615. Ten years later the Recollects invited the Jesuit order to assist them in their work. All missionary activity ceased in 1629 with the English capture of Quebec, but it began anew in 1633 when Champlain arrived bringing two hundred settlers and four Jesuit priests to re-establish the colony which he had founded twenty-five years earlier. Jesuits gradually expanded their work among the Huron and made their headquarters at Sault Ste. Marie.

The course of French missionary activity was dramatically altered by the Iroquois wars which began in 1646. For nearly two decades French settlements along the St. Lawrence had been harassed by the Iroquois, but the greatest conflict was between the Iroquois and their Indian neighbors. In a series of devastating raids, the Huron, who had assisted the French in the fur trade, were crushed by the Iroquois in 1649 and driven from the Great Lakes region, while the Erie and Petun were virtually exterminated. Many eastern tribes fled west to escape the Iroquois fury. In so doing, they forced indigenous western tribes such as the Saux, Fox, Mascouton, and Potawatomi to relocate farther west.

Not only Indians perished by the Iroquois tomahawk as numerous French missionaries suffered torture and death. Among such martyrs were Fathers Jean de Breboeuf and Gabriel L'Alemant. Breboeuf especially suffered horrible torture. The Iroquois slung red-hot tomahawks over his neck and fastened a bark belt around his waist and ignited it. When the priest continued to pray, his lips and tongue were cut off. He was then scalped while still living, and after his death his heart was cut out and devoured in honor of his bravery. In 1653, Iroquois brutality against the French and their Indian allies was finally stopped when a coalition of Ottawa and Chippewa defeated a large body of Iroquois near Sault Ste. Marie at a site still known as Iroquois Point.

The Crown Takes Control

In 1661 the Crown's colonial policy underwent a drastic revision. King Louis XIV, imbued with a desire to make France the dominant European power, personally assumed control of governmental affairs. He then decreed New France a royal colony and cancelled all existing trading charters. His chief minister, Jean Baptiste Colbert, shared the king's vision of expanded French power through the acquisition and exploitation of colonial possessions. Not only did Colbert seek to import furs, but also he sought to institute a full mercantile policy. His goal was for New France to provide naval stores and timber for the mother country, while foodstuffs and barrel staves from Quebec would be sent to the French West Indies in return for rum, molasses, and sugar. In short, France was to create a colonial economic policy similar to England's successful "triangular trade."

To assure the achievement of these goals the government established new political structures for the colony. The central body was to be the Sovereign Council. This group was composed of the royal governor, who was in charge of the army and Indian affairs, the intendant, who controlled internal and financial matters, and a bishop, who was in charge of ecclesiastical affairs. Other council members included a record's clerk, attorney general, and five (later increased to twelve) councilors, who represented the interests of the merchants. Initially the governor appointed the councilors, but beginning in 1675 their commissions came directly from the king, thereby assuring their complete independence from the governor. In practice the real power rested with the intendant and in time he tended to exert more authority, while the council as a whole limited itself to judicial matters.

Jean Talon—"The Great Intendant"

The first, and perhaps greatest, of New France's intendants was Jean Talon, who arrived in Canada in 1665 charged with the responsibility of expanding the colony's population and making it economically self-sufficient. One of his first projects was the revision of the seigneurial system. Previously the Crown had granted land to nobles or seigneurs who had sworn an oath of loyalty to the state. In return for the land, usually a narrow strip leading back from a river, the seigneur promised to erect a manor house, encourage tenants to settle upon the land, provide a flour mill, and dispense justice. The Crown ultimately concluded that this policy was a failure because the seigneurs received more territory than they could possibly convert into farmland. Thus, the Crown removed the seigneurs from their role as emigration agents and relegated them to the position of "making land grants and adopting concrete measures to develop their estates." Talon also claimed for the Crown some of the previous grants made to defunct charter companies and divided these lands into numerous seigneuries three to six miles wide and six to nine miles in length, usually with frontage on either the St. Lawrence River or one of its tributaries. These new landowners possessed social prestige, but lacked political power since each of the new divisions was under the domination of the military.

No systematic settlement plan could be initiated until the Iroquois threat was removed. Consequently, one of the first moves instituted by the Crown was to dispatch hundreds of regular troops, including the crack Carignan Salieres regiment, to quell the Indian uprising. Although initial military campaigns proved either disastrous or inconclusive, continued military pressure, combined with losses sustained from a smallpox epidemic, forced the Iroquois to sign a peace treaty in the summer of 1667.

Once the Indian menace had been removed, at least temporarily, Talon sought to stimulate immigration from France both by offering free land and transportation to Frenchmen willing to settle in Canada and by giving special land grants to soldiers willing to remain in North America after the expiration of their tour of duty. As well, nearly a thousand "King's daughters," orphan girls and daughters of poor families, were imported and, according to one source, "the fattest went off best, upon the apprehension that these being less active, would keep truer to their engagements, and hold out better against the nipping cold of the winter." Even over one thousand criminals were added to the immigration list. To further stimulate marriage and procreation, Talon placed penalties on bachelors and provided tax relief and "baby bonuses" to those who married and had large families.

After 1675, few immigrants arrived from France, since the Crown began to fear the effects of populating New France at the expense of Old France. Nevertheless, Talon's policies brought about an enormous population increase. In 1666 there were 3,200 people in New France; by 1673 the population had more than doubled to 6,700. The population continued to grow steadily, even without official Crown support, and by 1750 it had reached 76,000.

Before Talon returned to France in 1672, he introduced such new crops as flax and hemp and imported quality livestock so that New France's agricultural volume and quality was significantly improved. Shipbuilding was encouraged and trade with the West Indies was fostered. Yet Colbert's plan for a diversified colonial economy failed because Crown grants to colonial industries ceased in 1672, and without this source of financial support, they could not survive. Thus, much to Colbert's disappointment, fur trading remained the economic staple of New France. In fact, with the quelling of the Iroquois, new lands opening, and the setting of beaver pelt prices by ministerial decree, the fur trade became even more lucrative and appealing, and it grew at an astounding pace.

Talon and the West

Colbert desperately attempted to restrict the fur trade because he feared that it would eventually draw away all the healthy young men of the colony from their farming endeavors. Seeking to restrain expansionist tendencies, Colbert informed Talon that "it would be better to restrict oneself to an amount of land that the colony would be able to sustain on its own, rather than to embrace too vast an area whereby one would perhaps one day be obliged to abandon a part with some reduction of the prestige of His Majesty and of the State." Canadien voyageurs and Talon largely ignored Colbert's admonitions and edicts aimed at keeping Canadiens within settled areas. The lure of profits and an exciting life proved irresistible to young Frenchmen. Clad in colorful shirts, gaudy sashes, and festooned caps, these voyageurs sailed the lakes and rivers in birchbark canoes, living both with and like Indians. Talon overtly violated Colbert's instructions by encouraging exploration and sending groups to the West and North to search for minerals and a passage to the western sea. In 1669 a party under the command of Adrian Jolliet was sent to explore the copper regions of Lake Superior. The men returned via a lower lake route, passing through the St. Clair River, Lake St. Clair, and Lake Erie, which opened an alternative to the established Ottawa River-Lake Huron passage. On their homeward voyage, they encountered a party of Frenchmen which included Rene Robert Cavelier de La Salle and Fathers Francois Collier de Casson and Rene de Brehant. Using information furnished by Jolliet, the priests proceeded to Sault Ste. Marie, while LaSalle chose to explore the Detroit region to the south.

To consolidate French claims to western lands, an expedition under the command of Simon Francois, Sieur de St. Lusson, arrived at the Sault. On June 14, 1671, with representatives of fourteen Indian tribes in attendance, St. Lusson planted a cross and post bearing the Royal Seal. In the name of the king of France he claimed possession not only of Sault Ste. Marie but also Lakes Huron and Superior and "all countries, rivers, lakes, and streams continuous and adjacent there unto; both those which have been discovered and those which may be discovered hereafter, in all their length and breadth, bounded on one side by the seas of the North and West, and on the other by the South Sea."

The Revival of Missionary Activity

The Iroquois onslaughts of 1648-49 that had virtually annihilated the Huron forced French missionaries temporarily to abandon their work. In 1660, Pierre Esprit, Sieur de Radisson, brought information to Montreal that Huron survivors had moved to the western shore of Lake Superior. His information was sound, as following the Iroquois defeat in 1653, he, accompanied by Medart Chouart, Sieur de Groseilliers, made several trips to the Michigan-Wisconsin area. Radisson

In 1671, Sieur de St. Lusson arrived at Sault Ste. Marie and claimed the region for the king of France.

and de Groseilliers sought unsuccessfully to convince French authorities to establish permanent trading posts and missions in the Canadian North. Strangely, French authorities ignored their reports concerning the feasibility of trading posts; ironically, however, the English were much impressed by them and as a result created the Hudson's Bay Company. Their accounts did inspire Father Rene Menard, a former missionary to the Huron, to accompany a fur-trading expedition to the West in order to reestablish contact with his former charges. Because of ill health, Menard did not expect to return alive, but his mission was deemed so important that in the autumn of 1660 he left Montreal to journey to the upper peninsula. In the winter he arrived at L'Anse, having endured a trek plagued by storms, hunger, and Iroquois attacks.

In March 1661, Menard, along with several fur traders, made his way to Chequamegon, near the present site of Ashland, Wisconsin. The Indians living there were not Huron, but while Menard was there, a Huron arrived and told him that his people lived farther inland and were dying of famine. Hearing this, Menard and a young assistant set out several months later to find the Huron camp. During their quest Menard and the youth became separated and Father Menard was never seen again.

It was not until 1665, after the French had quelled another Iroquois uprising, that Father Claude Allouez was able to retrace the steps of Father Menard. Allouez accompanied an, Ottawa trading party which arrived at Chequamegon October 1, 1665. Learning nothing about the fate of Menard, Allouez founded a mission at La Pointe du Saint Esprit, where he labored several years. While there he heard many stories of a great river, located a six-day journey to the West, which was said to empty into the sea. Allouez sent this information to his Jesuit superiors, which prompted them to expand their missionary endeavors. Another priest was sent to aid Allouez and in 1668 Father Claude Dablon arrived at the Sault to head the Ottawa mission. Later that same year (1668) Father Jacques Marquette was ordered to Chequamegon and Allouez was dispatched to the Green Bay region. From Green Bay, Allouez moved to the Illinois country and then ended his days ministering to the Miami and Potawatomi of the St. Joseph Valley in southwestern Michigan. He died in 1688, at the age of fifty-eight, and was buried near the present site of Niles.

Pere Marquette

Father Marquette was born in 1637 and hoped to be a missionary in the Orient. His Jesuit superiors deemed otherwise, and in 1666 he found himself in Canada. In 1668, after two years at the Sault, he succeeded Allouez at Chequamegon. While there, Marquette immersed himself in Illinois Indian lore, learning the language, and studying the geography of the area. Like Allouez, he had heard· tales of a great river flowing north to south and he desired to investigate its existence. In 1671, hostilities between the Sioux and Huron forced Marquette to flee with his followers to the safer confines of Mackinac Island. Soon afterward he moved across the Straits and built a mission on the upper peninsula side. The dream of finding the "Great River" still haunted him and was his foremost desire.

Unknown to the Jesuit his prayers were to be answered. Intendant Talon commissioned Louis Jolliet, Adrian's younger brother, to seek "the great river called Michissipi and which, it is believed, discharges itself into the sea of California." A former Jesuit who had drifted away from religion and into the fur trade, Jolliet consulted with Father Dablon who suggested that Marquette be included in the exploration party. Jolliet acceded to the request, and when

Jolliet arrived at St. Ignace in December 1672, Marquette was overjoyed to learn that Dablon had ordered him to accompany the expedition.

In May 1673, Jolliet, Marquette, and several voyageurs sailed off in two bark canoes. They crossed Lake Michigan, reached Green Bay, floated up the Fox River until they had to portage to the Wisconsin River, followed it to the Mississippi, and then took that river to the point where it converged with the Arkansas River. At that point they determined that their route was not the longed-for passage. On their return Marquette stopped at Green Bay while Jolliet proceeded to Montreal to relate his adventures. In 1674 Marquette made a second voyage to visit Indians in Illinois. During his return he became ill and died in the spring of 1675. He was buried near the present site of Ludington, but two years later Christian Indians removed his remains and reburied them at his mission at St. Ignace.

La Salle and Frontenac

Robert Cavelier, Sieur de La Salle, was born in 1643. The son of a wealthy merchant family, he received a Jesuit education, left France for Canada in 1666, and arrived in Montreal where his older brother was a priest. At that time Montreal was on the edge of the frontier and the Sulpitian Order, to which La Salle's brother belonged, held seigneurial rights to a huge amount of land. The Order was eagerly dispensing grants so that outlying settlements would develop to serve as a shield for Montreal against Indian attacks. La Salle became owner of a large tract of this land, located just above the Lachine Rapids eight miles from Montreal. He soon became bored with farming and his imagination was fired by Indian legends about a "Vermillion Sea," which he assumed had to be the Northwest Passage. He sold his property and, in 1669, embarked upon a journey to the Great Lakes region.

La Salle's wanderings into the interior of North America convinced him that the Mississippi River flowed neither into the Gulf of California nor the Pacific Ocean, but rather into the Gulf of Mexico. He believed that a fort at the mouth of the Mississippi would protect it from both the Spanish and English. Furs could then be shipped in safety down the river and thence by sea to France.

Eventually La Salle found a sympathetic benefactor in Louis de Buade, Comte de Pallerau et de Frontenac, a former soldier, courtier, and man of vision who dreamed of building an empire in the New World. Having squandered his fortune in France, Frontenac, as a reward for the past service to the Crown, was sent to Canada in 1672 to serve as its governor. He quickly perceived that furs provided a light, valuable export for New France and, contrary to instructions from the Crown, established a policy encouraging both fur trade and western exploration.

To help protect the budding French fur trade in the Great Lakes area, Frontenac erected a fort at the eastern end of Lake Ontario. The purpose of this outpost, named Fort Frontenac, was to block Iroquois invasions and to gain a share of the trade which would ordinarily have enriched Dutch and English merchants of New York. As his men prepared to build the fort, Frontenac addressed several hundred Iroquois warriors whom he had summoned to a council:

Children, Mohawks, Oneida, Onondagas, and Senecas. I am glad to see you here where I have had a fire lighted for you here, to smoke by, and for me to talk to you. You have done well, my children, to obey the command of your Father. Take courage; you will hear his word, which is full of peace and tenderness. For do not think that I have come for war. My mind is full of peace, and she walks by my side. Courage, then, children, and take rest.

The Indians provided no opposition and Frontenac was convinced that his eloquence had won them over. The real reason for their acquiescence, however, was that they were engaged in warfare with the Andastes and Mohegans. The Anglo-French war against the Dutch had prevented supplies from reaching their Dutch allies in Albany and therefore the Iroquois were forced to trade with the French to acquire arms and ammunition.

Colbert opposed construction of Fort Frontenac because he wanted Canada's population to be concentrated in villages and towns and its economy to be based on industry and agriculture rather than furs. Frontenac, however, viewed agricultural colonists in the St. Lawrence Valley as a foundation from which to conduct the fur trade. As a result, when he returned to France to obtain a grant of nobility and request ownership of his fort, Frontenac gave full support to La Salle, whom he saw as a man sharing his own vision for New France.

La Salle received a seigneury at Fort Frontenac, and, in return, he promised to repay the king for the cost of the post, support a garrison equal to that of Montreal, build a colony, provide at least twenty laborers, and erect a church when the number of inhabitants reached one hundred. As might have been expected, La Salle, with his primary interest in trading, did little to fulfill his pledge.

Frontenac's, and then La Salle's, ownership of Fort Frontenac stirred a storm of controversy as Montreal merchants denounced the trading monopoly held by the post and Jesuits opposed further endeavors to penetrate into the western interior. This sense of hostility heightened in 1676 when another outpost was constructed, without Crown permission, at Niagara.

Not satisfied with his initial success, La Salle returned to France in 1677. With the support of Frontenac and his court friends, La Salle received Crown permission to explore the Mississippi River Valley to determine whether it provided a passage to the Pacific Ocean. In return for financing the journey,

La Salle was allowed to erect a series of forts at the base of Lake Michigan and along the Illinois and Mississippi rivers. He was specifically forbidden by the Crown, however, to trade with the Ottawa, who furnished the majority of furs to Montreal merchants. To the ire and consternation of Montreal businessmen, La Salle, again with Frontenac's blessing, violated the provisions of the agreement. The true purpose of Frontenac and La Salle had always been to establish fur-trading posts in the West from which pelts could be shipped down the Mississippi River to New Orleans and then either to France or the Caribbean, thereby eliminating lengthy canoe trips and portages to Montreal and Quebec. Frontenac further aided La Salle by forbidding everyone, even those with trade permits, from doing business in La Salle's territory. With this support from his friend, La Salle had secured a trade monopoly.

In early 1679, La Salle authorized Henri de Tonty, a former Sicilian soldier of fortune known as "Iron Hand" because of an artificial limb made of that metal, to lead a party of men in a trading expedition among the Illinois Indians. Meanwhile, La Salle established a shipyard above Niagara Falls, where he began construction of the *Griffon,* so-named because at its prow was carved a figure representing that mythological half-lion, half eagle. The ship set sail across Lake Erie and reached the Detroit River on August 7, 1679. According to Father Louis Hennepin, a Recollect priest who accompanied La Salle, sights along the voyage were spectacular.

The country between those two lakes from Lake Erie to Lake Huron is very well situated and the soil very fertile. The banks of the strait are vast meadows and the prospect is terminated with some hills covered with vineyards, trees bearing food fruit, groves and forests, so well disposed that one would think Nature alone could not have made, without the help of art, so charming a prospect. The country is stocked with stags, wild goats, and bears, which are good for food and not fierce as in other countries. . . .

The forests are chiefly made up of walnut trees, chestnut trees, plum trees, and pear trees, loaded with their own fruit and vines. There is also abundance of timber fit for building; so that those who shall be so happy to inhabit that noble country cannot but remember with gratitude those who have discovered the way thither.

On Lake Huron the ship nearly capsized, but it withstood the stormy sea and reached St. Ignace. After the party rested a few days, the *Griffon* set sail for Green Bay, where it was loaded with furs and dispatched by La Salle to return to Niagara. On this voyage, however, the *Griffon* was lost in a storm and presumed sunk. (It is thought that the discovery of a vessel's remnants in 1957 about two miles northwest of Tobermory at the tip of the peninsula separating Lake Huron and Georgian Bay may be that of the *Griffon.*)

While waiting for the *Griffon's* return, La Salle continued his journey into the Illinois country, where he built a fort at Lake Peoria in the winter of 1680. News of the loss of the *Griffon,* which was to have brought supplies for him and his men, forced La Salle to abandon plans for further exploration. He and his party trekked across Michigan back to Fort Frontenac. This incredible journey of one thousand miles began in March 1680 and ended with their arrival on May 6, 1680.

Despite the advice of friends, La Salle returned to Fort Miami, near the present site of St. Joseph, in November 1681. From there he set out with a party of fifty-one French and Indians to explore, at his own expense, the Mississippi. His quest was successful, and on April 9, 1682, he claimed the mouth of the Mississippi and all lands in the Mississippi Valley for France.

Upon returning to Quebec to report his activity, La Salle discovered that his benefactor, Frontenac, had been recalled and that the new governor agreed with Montreal merchants who opposed further trade expansion in the West. La Salle then returned to France, where he received permission from the king to found a colony at the mouth of the Mississippi River and to locate forts at strategic points along the waterway. Unfortunately for La Salle, following his return to the New World, he was assassinated by several of his men on March 19, 1687, and his quest for fabulous wealth was left unfulfilled.

Robert Thom painted this scene of LaSalle and the *Griffon* at St. Ignace in 1679.

The importance of La Salle and other early French explorers cannot be minimized. Their expeditions brought the Great Lakes region into the realm of the white man's world. Michigan's coastline was explored, its peninsulas were traversed by foot, and important forts were constructed at St. Joseph, St. Ignace, and Sault Ste. Marie. The Great Lakes and Mississippi Valley were placed under French domination, and this created a territorial rivalry with England which continued until the French were forcibly driven from the North American continent in the French and Indian War.

As previously noted, Frontenac had been removed from power in 1682 because of his constant disputes with the Sovereign Council, clergy, and intendant over such matters as using brandy in fur trade and for acting "completely contrary to the royal edicts, decrees, and proclamations." A year before his ouster Frontenac had been issued a warning from the king:

I admonish you to banish from your mind all the difficulties that you have created so far in the execution of my orders; to behave with good-natured moderation towards all the inhabitants; to strip yourself of all personal animosities which up till now have been almost the sole incentive of all your actions; nothing being more inconsistent with the duty you have to discharge for me in the position you hold. . . . I see clearly everything gives way to your private enmities; and that which concerns my service and the execution of my orders is rarely the sole motive of your action.

Frontenac protested his innocence, but the crux of the problem was that he repeatedly had refused to accept the concept that Colbert and the king had designated the intendant to control the Sovereign Council, not the governor general. When Frontenac caned and imprisoned the son of the intendant, he created an untenable situation and both Frontenac and the intendant were removed from office.

Frontenac's successors as governor, Lefebure de Le Barre and the Marquis de Denonville, turned their attention to trying to control the Iroquois who were being urged by their English allies to make war upon the French. Denonville, in particular, pursued an aggressive policy to quell the Indian uprising by allowing the Jesuits to build a mission near Niles, directing Daniel Greysolon, Sieur de Duluth, to erect Fort St. Joseph at the present site of Port Huron in order to halt English fur traders from reaching Fort Michilimackinac by water, and ordering an expedition against the Iroquois in the summer of 1687. None of these measures proved successful and in 1689 at La Chine, outside of Montreal, the Iroquois boldly massacred two hundred French. In addition, formal warfare between the English and French was declared both on the European continent and in North America. This conflict, known as King William's War, was the first of four outbreaks of hostilities between the two European powers over North America.

Faced with a desperate situation in 1689, King Louis XIV was compelled to reappoint Frontenac as governor of New France. Frontenac had repeatedly told the king that he alone possessed the knowledge and decisiveness necessary to deal effectively with the Iroquois, since they knew and feared him. However, Frontenac's initial attempts to treat with the Iroquois ended in failure and resulted only in earning him the contempt of the friendly Ottawa who felt that he was betraying them. Iroquois war parties continued to attack settlements around Montreal, striking quickly and then disappearing into the surrounding forests. In reaction to these assaults, in January 1690, Frontenac dispatched parties of voyageurs and Indians to attack New York, in hope that the English arms and ammunition traffic to the Iroquois could be stopped. Although Albany was the original target, Schenectady became the focus of the attack. In the initial onslaught sixty residents perished. In later years, an English resident recalled that "the cruelties committed at said place no person can write nor tongue express; ye women big with child ripped up and ye children alive thrown into ye flames, and their heads dashed in pieces against doors and windows."

The success of this attack encouraged Frontenac to launch similar ones against New England. The attacks renewed the confidence of the French inhabitants and their Indian allies, but did not seriously damage the English warmaking ability; in fact, they may have merely served to goad the English into stronger counter-efforts. Subsequently, an English fleet sailed up the St. Lawrence River and prepared to put Quebec under siege. The approach of winter and of reinforcements from Montreal enabled the French to repel the attack and the fleet withdrew to Boston. Small skirmishes were conducted by both sides but neither the English nor the French possessed the superior numbers needed to hold their gains.

In 1697 the Treaty of Ryswick was signed which ended the war. Without their English allies, the Iroquois conducted continued sporadic warfare against the French until 1701 when a peace treaty was negotiated. This agreement removed the Iroquois barrier which had prevented French penetration into Michigan and the West, and opened the way for increased French exploration.

Cadillac and Frontenac

Despite the war with England and the French government's continued opposition to French traders going west, Frontenac never wavered in his support of increased trade and expansion. In 1694 he appointed Antoine de la Mothe Cadillac as commander of Fort Du Buade, located at the juncture of the straits between the upper and lower peninsulas. A professional soldier, charming, unscrupulous, and eager to exploit the fur treasure of the West, Cadillac eagerly accepted the position. During his three years at that post, he managed both to amass a small personal fortune and earn the enmity of Jesuits who opposed his liberal distribution of brandy to Indians. Cadillac defended himself on this charge by stating that brandy was "the only drink capable of aiding them to digest the fish and bad food on which they are compelled to live" and that a "drink of brandy after the repast seemed necessary to cook the bilious meats and crudities which they leave in the stomach." He further maintained that, without the medicinal benefits of brandy, sickness among Indians would have been more prevalent. When a Jesuit, unconvinced by Cadillac's arguments, demanded that Cadillac obey both the orders of the government and God, the commandant reported that he made the following reply:

I told him that his talk smelt of sedition a hundred yards off and begged that he would amend it. He told me that I gave myself airs that did not belong to me, holding his fist before my nose at the same time. I confess I almost forgot that he was a priest, and felt for a moment like knocking his jaw out of joint; but thank God, I contented myself with taking him by the arm, pushing him out and ordering him not to come back.

Concerned that the western fur posts served no useful military purpose and contributed to the surplus beaver supply which was driving prices drastically downward, in 1696 the French Ministry issued an edict stating that all western posts were to be abandoned and no further western travel permits were to be issued. Frontenac bitterly protested this policy, arguing that abandoning the posts would result in France's Indian allies joining the English and Iroquois to receive trade goods. Because of the protests by Frontenac and fur traders, the government reconsidered its position and allowed the posts to be regarrisoned, but it still maintained that neither fur trading nor travel permits would be allowed. As usual, Frontenac largely ignored this order and trade goods were sent westward. Montreal merchants, seeing that the governor ignored the edict, did likewise. Thus, once again, a governmental order to limit trade proved unenforceable.

Frontenac continued to serve until his death in 1698. A man of charm and flamboyance, Frontenac adroitly turned his office into a source of great power and private gain. He was a maverick, who was never able to accommodate himself to superior authority and administrative bureaucracy which sought to restrict his policymaking authority. Despite his independent attitude and defiance, the French government sorely missed his leadership ability in the years following his death.

After the temporary closing of Fort Du Buade, Cadillac returned to France to try to convince the king of the need to construct a fort on the river between Lakes Erie and St. Clair, which could serve as a fortress against English incursions. In 1698 Cadillac managed to persuade Count Pontchartrain, the minister in charge of colonies, of the need for such a post and argued that it would cost the government nothing since he would support it from the proceeds of the fur trade. Receiving the required authority, Cadillac returned to Canada, set out from Montreal with one hundred soldiers and workmen, and arrived at the mouth of the Detroit River July 24, 1701. Immediately a post was constructed and named Fort Pontchartrain in honor of their benefactor. That autumn, the wives of Cadillac and Alphonse Tonty arrived. Cadillac believed that the presence of women would help allay any fears of the pro-French Indians that the post would not be permanent. Cadillac's venture was so successful that by 1705 so many Indians had abandoned the Michilimackinac region and moved to Pontchartrain that the Jesuits had to close their mission at St. Ignace.

Cadillac hoped to make the permanent settlement complete through construction of churches, schools, and hospitals. He also sought to enlarge the population through intermarriage with Indians, which he was convinced would assure Indian loyalty and friendship as well.

Not only was Cadillac a military commander, but also he was a seigneur, which meant that he could perpetuate in the New World the concept of feudalism which was becoming extinct in the Old. Cadillac granted land in a truly feudal manner. Grants were "ribbon farms" which fronted the river and usually were 400-600 feet wide and 1½-3 miles in length. Habitants who received property were required to give Cadillac the "customary prerequisites and emoluments." Cadillac controlled the gristmill, all commerce and trade, and a monopoly on the sale of gunpowder and alcohol. He also issued all licenses for fur trading.

Unfortunately for Cadillac, Fort Pontchartrain did not grow rapidly. By 1708 there were only sixty-three permanent residents. Only two hundred acres of the garrison were cultivated and the colony's domestic livestock consisted of a dozen assorted cattle and a "single, forlorn horse." The difficulty was that young Frenchmen preferred the quick profits of the fur trade to the hard toil of a humble farmer.

Various accusations hurled by his enemies made Cadillac's command a stormy and turbulent period. He supposedly "maintained a haughty and defiant attitude" toward his administrators and charged exorbitantly high prices for liquor—allegedly seven times the price in Montreal. Of course, the clergy disliked him because of his use of liquor in the fur trade. An official sent from France to investigate the charges against Cadillac concluded that they were substantive and commented: "I was able to observe that de la Mothe . . . was generally hated by all the French and Indians. . . . I can assure you my Lord that this aversion was not without cause, he is not hated for nothing. The tyranny that he maintains over them both is sufficient to warrant it." Finally, in 1710, Cadillac was removed from command and sent to Mobile, but he was ordered to leave his property and wealth at Pontchartrain.

Shortly after Cadillac's departure, Pontchartrain was nearly destroyed by Indians. Cadillac had invited the Fox Indians of Wisconsin to live at the post, but the new commander informed them that they were no longer welcome. Undaunted, the Fox remained, but the traditional French allies, the Ottawa

In this painting, Robert Thom captures the joyful emotion created by the arrival of the wives of Cadillac and Tonty at Fort Pontchartrain.

and Chippewa, demanded that the newcomers be expelled. Forced into a precarious situation, the French attacked the Fox, who fought back valiantly and nearly burned the fort before being forced to retreat. Many Fox were captured and tortured by the Ottawa and Chippewa, and those who escaped returned to Wisconsin as implacable enemies of the French.

In 1714 the market for furs began to grow again. To capitalize on the new demand the French expanded their operations in Michigan. A new fort was constructed at the present site of Mackinaw City to replace the earlier one at St. Ignace. Trade flourished because the post was conveniently located at the juncture of three lakes, which made it an easy rendezvous point for Indians. The erection of an outpost at the Straits coincided well with the established French policy of maintaining western forts, Indian friendship, and trade at a minimum cost to the Crown.

By 1755 New France comprised a vast expanse of territory spanning from the Gulf of St. Lawrence to the Gulf of Mexico. At either end lay strong defenses, but the middle was weak. In an attempt to correct this weakness, a string of forts was erected from Lake Erie to the Ohio River. In Michigan, a new garrison was constructed at the Sault to control all fur trade passing through the upper and lower Great Lakes. Thus, the three major French posts in Michigan possessed a common characteristic: they were strategically located where large bodies of water were connected by rivers or straits, so that anyone traversing the Great Lakes area by water, either for trade or military purposes, had to come under French scrutiny.

End of the French Empire

While England and France had been at war three times during the years 1689-1748, the Michigan region had never been seriously affected, but this changed with the outbreak of the Seven Years' War, or French and Indian War as it was known in North America, in 1756. War between these longtime rivals seemed inevitable since both were seeking to exploit the valuable fur trade in the Lakes area. Yet, their economic designs were greatly different. Since France was primarily interested in trade, she sent to North America mostly trappers who had little interest in locating suitable sites for permanent settlements. By contrast, England sought to tame the American wilderness, put the land to the plow, and create colonies which would be secure homes for women and children. Consequently, by 1750, while the French claimed for themselves all Canada and the territory between the Allegheny Mountains and the Mississippi River, their total population in that area was barely fifty thousand. At the same time, the British colonies, despite a small territorial holding, possessed a population of over 1.5 million men, women, and children. To the British, western expansion was an absolute necessity both for increased trade and living space.

Realizing the potential weakness in their hold on North America, the French government appointed Comte de la Galissoniere governor of Canada with specific orders to strengthen French power. To do this, the new governor dispatched Celeron de Blainville and two hundred soldiers to the Ohio Valley in 1749. The purpose of the expedition was to drive out British traders and persuade the Indians to remain loyal to the French. Most tribes received the French with formal courtesy, but some assumed a hostile attitude and proudly displayed British flags and proclaimed their friendship to King George. After burying lead plates and nailing metal plaques to trees as tangible proof that the region belonged to the king of France, de Blainville returned to Canada and was forced to admit to the governor that overall his mission had failed to accomplish either of its intended goals.

In 1752 Galissoniere was replaced by the Marquis Duquesne. Upon taking office, Duquesne's first priority was the destruction of the Miami village of Chief La Demoiselle, or "Old Britain" as he was popularly known, who had demonstrated a warlike attitude toward de Blainville. The governor commissioned a half-blood trader, Charles Mouet, to gather a force of Indians from Sault Ste. Marie, Michilimackinac, and Detroit for the purpose of assaulting the enemy camp. The attack was made with such thorough brutality that not only was the village destroyed, but also Chief La Demoiselle was killed and eaten by the victorious Indians. Duquesne then ordered forts to be erected at strategic points along a line from the end of Lake Erie to the forks of the Ohio. In 1753 Forts Presque Isle, Le Boeuf, and Venango were constructed, and the following year Fort Duquesne was built at the junction of the Allegheny, Ohio, and Monongahela rivers.

The British colony of Virginia, which by charter claimed ownership of the Kentucky region, was alarmed by the construction of these French posts. Governor Robert Dinwiddie, Daniel Boone, Patrick Henry, and other prominent Virginians who had heavily invested in land speculation in the Kentucky area were determined to drive the French out. Dinwiddie sent Lieutenant George Washington with a small detachment of men to Fort Le Boeuf to request French withdrawal. Failing in this, he was to remove the French by force. Washington's overtures were rebuffed and after a brief, bloody skirmish, he was forced to retreat to a hastily constructed stockade, aptly named Fort Necessity. He was soon overwhelmed by an army from Fort Duquesne and forced to surrender. Humiliated by this defeat, which proved colonial inability to remove the French from the West, Dinwiddie requested Parliament to send British regulars to accomplish the task.

In March 1755, General Edward Braddock, with 1,500 soldiers, arrived in Virginia to begin a campaign against the French. Braddock's mission was doomed to failure from the outset. Braddock refused to heed advice from colonial military men, whom he considered untutored in the art of war. Upon learning that his objective, Fort Duquesne, was located one hundred miles to the west and that there was no easy route through the dense forest separating it from Virginia, the general determined to construct a road to facilitate his march. This decision resulted in his soldiers becoming fatigued from construction work which made them unsuited for battle. They also lost the element of surprise as the noise of the road building reached French ears long before the army arrived. The consequence was a disastrous encounter on July 9, 1755, in which 330 French and Indians, many from Michigan, attacked the British army at dawn and killed Braddock and 977 of his command.

By the close of 1755, the French seemed to have a firm hold on North America, as they controlled the trade, forts, and Indians, while the British were disorganized and leaderless. However, the French were still greatly outnumbered and could not risk attacking the British colonies to secure a final victory. The French hope was to forestall British entry into the West for so long that Parliament would decide that occupation of the area would be too costly in money and lives and abandon all claims to it.

In 1756 the tide of the war changed with the selection of William Pitt as England's prime minister. Pitt's policy was to place bold, young men in command of British forces and to open fronts against the French in Europe, India, and the Caribbean. He thought that by turning the struggle into a world war, the French would be forced to concentrate less on North America, which in turn would enable the colonists to gain a victory for themselves. Slowly, British armies under the command of Lord Jeffrey Amherst drove the French back toward their supply base at Quebec. When General James Wolfe defeated a French force under General Louis Montcalm on the Plains of Abraham outside Quebec in September 1759, French rule in North America was over.

When the news of the French surrender reached Michilimackinac, that post's commandant immediately abandoned the fort and fled to New Orleans to avoid being taken prisoner by British troops. On November 29, 1760, Captain Francois de Bellestre formally surrendered Fort Pontchartrain to British forces led by Major Robert Rogers, thus ending French rule in Michigan. Ironically, although the French had had a lengthy tenure in Michigan they founded only a scattering of settlements and left the interior of the territory virtually untouched. Other than a few place-names, the French left a pauper's legacy to the territory.

For Further Reading

Louise P. Kellogg's *Early Narratives of the Northwest, 1634-1699* (New York: Barnes and Noble, 1945) provides a complete background of European exploration in Michigan during the seventeenth century. The following works in the Canadian Centenary Series provide extensive and exhaustive background of French colonial efforts in North America. They include: (1) Marcel Trudel, *The Beginnings of New France, 1524-1663* (Toronto: McClelland and Stewart, 1973); (2) W.J. Eccles, *Canada Under Louis XIV, 1663-1701* (Toronto: McClelland and Stewart, 1964); and (3) G.F.G. Stanley, *New France, 1744-1760* (Toronto: McClelland and Stewart, 1968). Louise Phelps Kellog, *The French Regime in Wisconsin and the Northwest* (Madison: University of Wisconsin Press, 1925) has significant coverage of French activities in Michigan. W.J. Eccles, *The Canadian Frontier, 1534-1764* (New York: Holt, Winston, Rinehart, 1969) is an excellent and readable survey which deals heavily with French efforts in early Michigan. George S. May and Herbert J. Brinks, *A Michigan Reader, 11,000 B.C. to A.D. 1865* (Grand Rapids: William B. Eerdmans Pub. Co., 1974) contains a number of excerpts from both primary and secondary sources concerning the French and British periods of Michigan. W. J. Eccles, *Frontenac, the Courtier Governor* (Toronto: McClelland and Stewart, 1965) is a detailed and rich account of this important administrative officer of New France and useful background articles. Certainly Francis Parkman's works are rich narratives which students would still find interesting. These would include: *La Salle and the Discovery of the Great West* (rev. ed., Boston: Little, Brown, & Co., 1906); *A Half Century of Conflict* (rev. ed., Boston: Little, Brown,

& Co., 1922); and *The Jesuits in North America in the Seventeenth Century* (rev. ed., Boston: Little, Brown, & Co., 1922). George T. Hunt, *The Wars of the Iroquois* (Madison: University of Wisconsin Press, 1940) presents a concise portrait of the economic motivation of the Iroquois wars. Howard Peckham, *The Colonial Wars, 1689-1792* (Chicago: The University of Chicago Press, 1964) is a clear survey of the warfare although there are some errors. Yves F. Zoltvany, "New France and the West, 1701-1713," *Canadian Historical Review,* XLVI (December 1965), 301-322 is a detailed explanation of French western policy and the underlying factors that shaped that policy. S. C. Mitchell, "La Mothe Cadillac, A Stormy Figure of New France," *Bulletin of the Detroit Historical Society,* IX (1955) gives the background of the controversial founder of Detroit. Harry B. Ebersole, "Early French Exploration in the Lake Superior Region," *Michigan History,* XVIII (1934), 121-134, concentrates on the Michigan activities of the French explorers. Eugene T. Peterson, *France at Mackinac, 1715-1760* (Mackinac Island: Mackinac Island State Park Commission, 1977) is a useful paperback which emphasizes French life and culture during the French occupation.

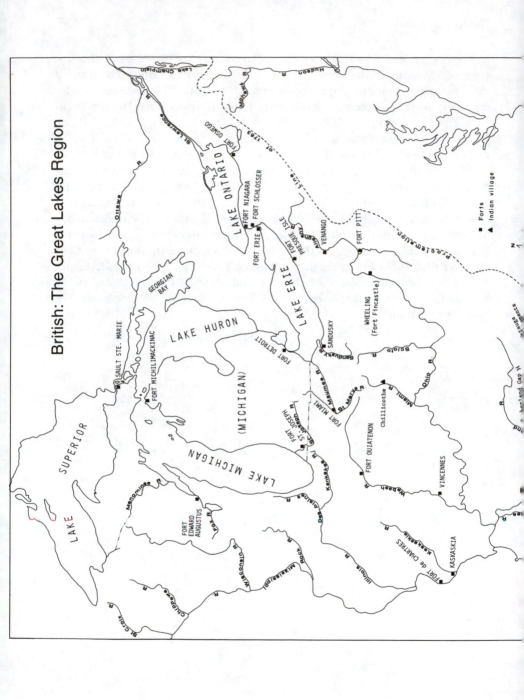

British: The Great Lakes Region

3

Under the Union Jack

After winning control of North America from the French and adding all Canada and the territory east of the Mississippi River, except Spanish Florida, to its empire, the British government had to face the responsibility of governing and protecting the region, as well as dealing with its Indian inhabitants. While the former would be costly in terms of men and money, the Crown had every reason to believe that the latter would be accomplished with relative simplicity. Most Indians appeared willing to abandon old ties with the French and become allied with their former British enemies. This apparent fickleness was actually a reflection of the Indian view of survival in a world increasingly filled with white interlopers—always try to be allied with the group which was the most powerful and delivered the most trade goods. In this instance, however, the transfer of loyalty seemed more sincere because during the French and Indian War British agents had promised both to expand trade with the tribes and to continue the established French policy of distributing food, guns, ammunition, and liquor. Indeed, Indians had good cause to expect that they would prosper from an alliance with the victorious British.

Indian expectations were dashed when the Crown appointed Lord Jeffrey Amherst governor general of British North America. The new governor was unimaginative, fussy, ill-tempered, and totally lacking in respect for both Indians and American colonists, whom he considered crude, uncivilized, and savage. Since the British, at the time of assuming control of North America, had no official Indian policy, the task of creating one fell to Amherst. To assist him, the governor summoned Sir William Johnson, head of the Northern Indian Superintendency since 1756. Johnson, who had a deserved reputation of being a respected, trusted friend of Indians, proposed that the government abide by all promises made during the war and that licensed traders be allowed to visit Indian encampments and sell merchandise at a maximum profit of 67 percent.

Amherst angrily rejected Johnson's suggestions and informed the superintendent that his administration sought economy and discipline. He said that he did not care about either French precedent or earlier British pledges. Under the new regime Indians would receive only a small amount of clothing, a very limited supply of guns and ammunition, and no food or alcohol. This policy was based on the governor's belief that alcohol made Indians uncontrollable and gifts of food made them lazy and unwilling to hunt and fish. Gift giving was also abolished, as Amherst considered it nothing more than expensive bribery to maintain friendship. Johnson tried to explain to Amherst that Indians considered gift giving and sharing as tokens of goodwill and would interpret the ending of such a policy as an act of hostility, but the commander was unmoved. To assure that his policies would be enforced, he decreed that all trade with Indians be done within British forts, under the watchful eye of Crown authorities. Amherst then ordered Johnson to meet with the Indians and inform them of this new policy.

Disappointed and convinced that the new program would cause warfare, Johnson called a council with the tribes of the Great Lakes region to meet at the mouth of the Detroit River, September 9, 1761. On that date he told the assembled chiefs and headmen that they had a "chain of friendship" with the British, and, to prove their British Father's sincerity, he pledged that no more Indian land would be taken except that necessary for expansion of commerce. He closed the council without mentioning the new policy because he feared

Fur trading at Mackinac is portrayed in this Robert Thom painting.

instant death if he did. The following day the Huron, Ottawa, Chippewa, Pota-watomi, and Wyandot reassembled and promised their loyalty to the Crown. Johnson ended the meeting by distributing all the remaining gifts he possessed. He believed that this would be the last peaceful offering, and, despite lacking permission from Amherst, he sought to close it in the traditional symbolic act of friendship.

Pontiac's Uprising

Throughout 1762 Indians living around Detroit began to understand the impact of Amherst's policy even though it had never been formally explained to them by the British. French traders and trappers told Indians that the British were withholding food, clothing, guns, and ammunition in an effort to weaken the tribes preparatory to a war of extermination. To strengthen the credibility of their claim, the French asked the Indians whether or not they were welcome at British posts, if gifts were still being given and rewards offered for the return of prisoners, whether trade prices were reasonable, and if the British showed any sign of needing Indians militarily in the future as they had in the past. In each instance Indians admitted that their reply had to be negative. The French told them to resist the British until an army sent by their French Father arrived to restore conditions to those of earlier times. The "chain of friendship" with the Crown was broken.

Early in the spring of 1763 a Delaware Indian known as the Prophet began to preach to his followers that whites had brought evils to Indian society. Prostitution, alcoholism, and reliance on European manufactured goods all resulted from contact with whites. He urged Indians to free themselves from the influence of Europeans and return to their native culture. Deeply moved by these speeches, several bands of Huron, Potawatomi, Seneca, Delaware, and Ottawa living near Detroit began passing war belts. The Prophet, however, was a spiritual, not military, leader. The honor of guiding the fight for freedom went to Pontiac, an Ottawa chief who lived on the Canadian side of the Detroit River opposite Belle Isle.

Upon assuming leadership, Pontiac told his followers that the Delaware Prophet had made a fundamental error. There would not be a war against all white men, but rather only against the hated British; the French were their friends and would help them.

On May 5, 1763, Pontiac convened a council on the banks of the Ecorse River and told the assembled chiefs of his plot to seize Detroit. According to the plan, on May 7 Pontiac would take sixty men and seek an audience with the commander of Fort Detroit, Major Henry Gladwin, to discuss Indian grievances. Under their blankets would be tomahawks, knives, and sawed-off muskets. Other Ottawa adults, both men and women, also carrying concealed weapons, would follow, and all would await a signal from Pontiac for the attack to begin. Huron and Potawatomi warriors would be stationed along paths leading to the post to prevent any outside assistance for the fort.

Pontiac's plan did not work because Major Gladwin received warning of it on May 6. Romantic legend has it that he was told by an Indian woman named Catherine who had once made him some moccasins. In a not-so-romantic vein, Gladwin could have been informed by blacksmiths who had helped saw off Indian rifles, a soldier who had lived with the Indians, or an Indian spy. However, general credence is given to the story that Angelique Cullier dit Beaubien, whose father was a friend and confidant of Pontiac, revealed the plot to Gladwin in order to save the life of her fiancé, James Sterling, a Detroit merchant. Whatever the source, Gladwin quickly had to devise a plan to save his 120-man garrison from annihilation. He ruled out confronting Pontiac and refusing to admit him to the post because the Indians would simply leave and try again at a later date. Likewise, he could not surprise Pontiac and his men and capture them because he had neither adequate detention facilities to house the prisoners nor enough provisions to feed them. His only option seemed to be to try to bluff Pontiac into thinking that an attack would be futile.

On May 7 Pontiac and his men arrived at Detroit and were admitted into the post. The chief expressed surprise at seeing the fort completely prepared for an attack. Gladwin assured Pontiac that the post was always on the alert for assaults from hostile Indians, but friendly ones like Pontiac had nothing to fear. Sensing that he had lost his advantage, Pontiac made a lengthy speech on the shortcomings of British policy and left without signaling for the attack.

Furious over his failure, Pontiac called another council and announced that he would put the post under siege until the promised French army arrived. Siege trenches were dug with aid from French traders and Pontiac instituted a campaign to try to frighten Gladwin into surrendering by threats of starvation, capture, and torture. Gladwin was not moved by these threats because he knew that the Indians would not risk incurring heavy casualties by a frontal assault and that starvation would be impossible since the rear of the post was on the Detroit River which enabled the sloops *Michigan* and *Huron* to furnish him both men and supplies from Fort Niagara. The major's only concern was that Pontiac might use fire-arrows and burn the fort. However, this was never considered by Pontiac because he wanted to capture the military supplies within the post before destroying it. Only once did Pontiac use fire, but it was directed in a futile attempt to remove the supply ships in the Detroit River and not at the fort itself.

Shortly after the siege began Gladwin received aid from an unexpected source. Several bands of Potawatomi and Huron defected and made a secret agreement with Gladwin whereby he would give them a full pardon and supplies if they would return to the Indian ranks and try to further undermine Pontiac's support. Gladwin's confidence grew even more upon learning that the French

A lacrosse game, depicted in this Robert Thom painting, was the ploy which enabled Indians to attack Fort Michilimackinac.

had finally surrendered and the Seven Years' War was officially ended. No French army would arrive to help Pontiac.

While the siege at Detroit continued, Indians, using strategy patterned after Pontiac's unsuccessful plan, ravaged British posts throughout the Great Lakes region. On May 16, Fort Sandusky fell with no Indian casualties. Fort St. Joseph (Niles) fell May 25, and two days later Fort Miami (Fort Wayne, Indiana) was seized. On June 1, Fort Ouiatenon (Lafayette, Indiana) was lost by the British. The most significant Indian triumph came on June 2 at Fort Michilimackinac. The post commander, Captain George Etherington, had been told that an Indian attack was forthcoming, but he disregarded the warning. On June 2, a group of Indians requested permission to play a game of lacrosse outside the fort in honor of the king's birthday. In the midst of the game the ball fell near the open gate of the fort. The Indians, ostensibly in pursuit of the ball, raced toward the entrance of the fort where they were furnished weapons which had been concealed under blankets worn by Indian women who were spectators at the game. Twenty-seven whites were killed and seventeen captured, including Alexander Henry, a young British merchant, who later wrote a journal recounting the attack and his experiences as a captive.

These Indian victories infuriated Amherst and he gave serious consideration to plans to distribute smallpox-infested blankets among Indians and to set loose hordes of starving dogs on Indian villages. Neither of these plans was put into operation as in mid-October the siege of Detroit was lifted. Pontiac's followers said that they could no longer endanger the welfare of their families by not hunting for food and making provisions for the winter. Even Pontiac admitted that his cause was lost when he finally learned from the French commandant of Fort Chartres in Illinois that the struggle between the French and British was over. On October 31, Pontiac went to Detroit to officially announce the lifting of the siege. He was not a beaten man, however, and in a show of bravado he told Gladwin that he hoped the commander would forget the "bad thing" of the past five months because he was willing to forgive Gladwin for his transgressions.

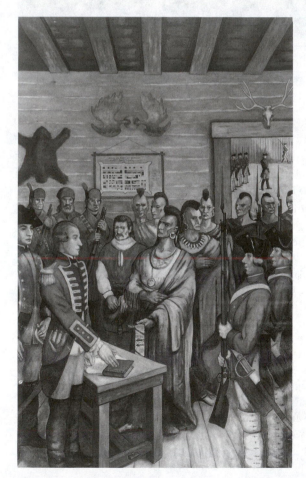

Unable to attack Fort Detroit by surprise, Pontiac presented a list of Indian grievances to the post commander, Major Henry Gladwin.

Defeat was a bitter blow for Pontiac. He could not understand how his old friends, the French, could ally themselves to the British merely for trade, and he was convinced that his Indian allies had deserted him simply because he had not gained a quick victory. Never did Pontiac realize that by keeping the siege, even though victory was impossible, he was inflicting suffering and starvation among his people.

In October 1764, Colonel John Bradstreet held a council with the Ottawa, Chippewa, Miami, Huron, and Potawatomi in which the Indians agreed to acknowledge the British king as their Father, and, in return, the British pledged to pardon Pontiac and remove illegal settlers from Indian territory. To encourage the Indians to abide by this agreement, a force of British soldiers under the command of Colonel Henry Bouquet was sent to Detroit from Fort Pitt.

In 1766 Sir William Johnson hosted a meeting of Ottawa, Huron, and Chippewa at Oswego, at which their chiefs and headmen, including Pontiac, agree to conform to the stipulations of the 1764 agreement. Resigned to life amid the British, Pontiac returned to the Illinois region where he was assassinated in 1769 at Cahokia by an Illinois Indian to avenge Pontiac's murder of an Illinois chief.

Proclamation of 1763

On June 8, 1763, in an attempt to avoid further Indian unrest in the new western holdings, the Earl of Shelburne, head of the British Board of Trade, offered a proposal for governing the area. In October the Crown implemented his report, which became known as the Proclamation of 1763. According to its provisions, all settlement beyond the Appalachian Mountains was prohibited and any Indian land east of those mountains could only be sold to settlers by authorized British officials. As a result, a large region, including Michigan, was left as permanent Indian territory and remained under military rule until the passage of the Quebec Act in 1774.

In England this policy angered a great many people and pleased very few. Fur-trading companies wanted the area to remain undeveloped so that their business could continue undisturbed, but they demanded guaranteed right of entry into the area. Land speculators and developers demanded that the territory be opened for immediate settlement, regardless of Indian claims or potential danger. Philanthropists argued that the region should belong exclusively to its Indian owners, while clergymen and imperialists argued the necessity of spreading English civilization to every inhabitant of the new empire.

Colonial response was equally negative. Traders often refused to obey either British law or officials, and resisters at Detroit proudly dubbed themselves "Liberty Boys." Other traders complained that since the Proclamation retained Amherst's prohibition on the use of liquor in trade and insistence on all trading being done within British posts, French traders of Spanish Louisiana, who paid higher prices for furs and dealt directly with Indians in their villages, would have a great advantage. Only after petitioning Governor Guy Carleton, who had taken office in 1767, did British traders gain permission to roam at will in pursuit of fur-trading business. In 1768 individual colonies regained control of Indian affairs, which they had lost in 1756 to Crown-appointed superintendents, and supervision of trapping and trading grew lax. This condition remained until the Quebec Act gave the provincial government power to control Indian-white commerce.

Michilimackinac and Major Robert Rogers

In 1766 Major Robert Rogers assumed command of Fort Michilimackinac from Captain William Howard, who had been commandant since 1764. The new commander was no stranger to Michigan and the Northwest, as he had previously served with the Royal Rangers during the French and Indian War, accepted the French surrender at Detroit, and helped to relieve the Indian siege of that city.

Rogers was always on the verge of achieving great glory and fame, but he never reached his goal. While in the Royal Rangers, he came under the influence of the governor of North Carolina, Arthur Dobbs, who convinced him of the existence of a water route across the North American continent. In trying to prove this theory, Rogers suffered heavy financial losses and, upon leaving the army in 1765, was sent to a debtor's prison in New York. After serving two years, he returned to England where he published two well received books, *The Journals of Major Robert Rogers* and *A Concise Account of North America,* which enabled him to become financially solvent. In an attempt to capitalize on his literary success, Rogers petitioned King George III for monetary support to conduct another search for the fabled Northwest Passage and the River Ouragon. The king refused the request but did authorize Rogers' appointment as commander of Fort Michilimackinac. Ever optimistic, Rogers assumed that his appointment was made as a prelude for the granting of his exploration request.

Upon accepting his command, Rogers wasted little time in implementing his plans. He had earlier convinced James Tute, a former comrade in the Rangers, and Jonathan Carver, a mapmaker and surveyor who desired to chart the western territories, to participate in his scheme. In mid-1766 Rogers ordered Carver and Tute to begin separate explorations and then meet at St. Anthony's Falls from which they would continue in a joint expedition. Tute was inexplicably delayed and it was not until April 1767 that he reached the rendezvous point. The two men then explored as far as the Chippewa River on the western end of Lake Superior. Exhausted, they returned to Grand Portage where Rogers had promised there would be supplies awaiting them. At that site they found no supplies, only a letter from Rogers directing them to continue their mission. Fatigued, disappointed, and angry, they disregarded this order and returned to Fort Michilimackinac. Carver later published a book on his experiences which became so popular that it was printed in six languages and had thirty editions.

Rogers, unfortunately, was not enjoying similar success. To supplement his income, he traded with Indians on his own authority and used rum to enhance his bargaining power. Both these practices, however, had been forbidden by General Thomas Gage, commander of British forces in North America. Rogers further irritated Gage by petitioning the British government to make Michilimackinac a separate province with himself as governor. Gage commissioned Lieutenant Benjamin Roberts to investigate Rogers' behavior, an act which ultimately resulted in violent disagreements between the two officers. In 1767 Rogers was accused by his former secretary, Nathaniel Potter, of plotting treasonous activities with the French. He was arrested and sent to Montreal in chains. After being acquitted of all charges, he returned to England only to be thrown once again into debtor's prison. During the American Revolution he came back to North America and offered his services to both sides but neither was interested. Rogers then returned to England, where he lived in poverty and obscurity until his death in 1795.

The Quebec Act and the American Revolution

In 1774 Parliament passed the Quebec Act. American colonists considered it one of many "Intolerable Acts" aimed at limiting their freedoms, but in reality it was merely another experiment to find a suitable administrative structure for the North American empire. Provisions of the act included: (1) all territory between the Illinois and Ohio rivers was added to the Province of Quebec; (2) land claims of other colonies to areas south of the Ohio River and east of the Allegheny Mountains were severely restricted; (3) civil governments were to be provided western regions, with French law the basis for all but criminal codes; (4) Roman Catholicism was given legal protection; (5) lieutenant governors were to be assigned by the governor of Quebec for Michilimackinac, Detroit, Vincennes, and the Illinois settlements; and (6) each of these four jurisdictions would have a court comprised of two American and one Canadian judges, with defendants having the right of direct appeal to the British Privy Council.

At the outbreak of the American Revolution in 1775, of the four proposed jurisdictions only Detroit had an established government. Henry Hamilton, who had fought with General Wolfe on the Plains of Abraham, was appointed lieutenant governor of Detroit, but before he left Quebec war began and an American army advanced on Montreal. To avoid capture, Hamilton disguised himself as a French habitant and traveled safely through the American lines, arriving at Detroit November 9, 1775. His good fortune was in marked contrast to that of his fellow governor, Patrick Sinclair, who was to command Michilimackinac. A retired officer who had served with Amherst during the French and Indian War, Sinclair received his appointment April 7, 1775 and hastened to America only to be seized by New York authorities and returned to England. It was not until 1779 that he finally reached Michilimackinac and assumed his post.

Although Michigan's efforts in the Revolution are not commonly known, for as one scholar has said "there were no Minutemen at Belle Isle and no militia men from the Irish Hills," the area did play a significant role because Detroit was the heart of British power in the West. Indian attacks on American settlements to the east, south, and west were launched from Detroit, and Indians from as far as Kentucky trekked to that post to receive guns, ammunition, and supplies.

Hamilton won Indian loyalty through lavish gift giving, prolific distribution of rum (in 1779 he ordered 17,502 gallons to be shipped to Detroit), and payment of bounties for American scalps. This latter practice earned him the nickname "Hair-buyer." It is, however, unfair to single out Hamilton for this dubious title since purchasing scalps was common British practice during the Revolution; in fact, the foremost practitioner of this tactic was not Hamilton, but rather "Gentleman John" Burgoyne. General Horatio Gates was so appalled by the widespread use of bounties that he wrote George Washington that in his estimation "all is now fair with General Burgoyne, even if the bloody hatchet he has so barbarously used should find its way into his own head." Both Burgoyne and Hamilton ceased buying scalps when they discovered that their Indian allies were scalping British loyalists, as well as rebels, to collect bounties.

Members of the Continental Congress immediately realized that the frontier would never be secure as long as Detroit remained in British control, but they never could raise sufficient men and money to initiate a western war front. Finally, Governor Patrick Henry, of Virginia, whose state charter claimed ownership of northwestern Ohio, Indiana, Illinois, and Kentucky, authorized twenty-six-year-old Colonel George Rogers Clark to raise an army and drive the British from the Great Lakes region.

Clark's plan was to march his 127-man force and attack the villages of Kaskaskia and Vincennes in Indiana and then move against Detroit. On July 4, 1778, Clark and his men captured Kaskaskia, encountering little resistance, and soon afterward a small part of his command, led by Captain Leonard Helm, seized Fort Sackville outside Vincennes. Local French residents readily took an oath to support the American cause, as did several local Indian bands who were impressed by Clark's bluster, confidence, and distribution of presents. When Hamilton learned of Clark's victories, he mounted a counteroffensive. Leaving Detroit on October 7, 1778, with an army of 243 British regulars, loyalists, and Indians, he recaptured Vincennes in mid-December and forced the residents to sign an oath of allegiance to the Crown. In response, Clark made a surprise attack on Vincennes February 25, 1779, retaking the city and making Hamilton a prisoner. Because of his infamous reputation, Hamilton was sent to Virginia for punishment. The new governor, Thomas Jefferson, wrote Washington asking what should be done with the prisoner. The general replied that execution was warranted, but since that was forbidden by the rules of war, imprisonment for the duration of the conflict should be his fate and Jefferson agreed.

Upon hearing of Hamilton's capture, Colonel Arent De Peyster, a poet, squirrel breeder, and former commandant at Michilimackinac assumed leadership at Detroit. Both he and his successor at Michilimackinac, Major Sinclair, hastily prepared for an assault by Clark's army. De Peyster ordered another fort built on the high ground behind the city and Sinclair moved his garrison from the mainland to Mackinac Island, believing that only an enormous force, with naval support, could seize that location. Such precautions proved unnecessary as the Virginia legislature failed to provide Clark with the reinforcements and supplies needed to march upon Detroit. Nonetheless, Hamilton's capture and the seizure of Vincennes greatly weakened Indian loyalties to the Crown, and the Ottawa, Chippewa, Potawatomi, and Wyandot adopted a policy of neutrality. Without Indian assistance British possession of, and power in, the Lakes region was tenuous at best.

Diminished British strength in the west was evidenced during the final four years of the war. In early 1780, British forces were repulsed at St. Louis and Cahokia. In February 1781, a small force of Spanish, French, and Indians seized Fort St. Joseph (Niles), looted it, and then abandoned it within twenty-four hours. During the occupation a Spanish flag was raised, giving Niles the distinction of being the only Michigan city ever to have the banners of four nations—England, France, Spain, and the United States—fly over it. In 1782, Captain William Caldwell set out with a company of loyalists and Indians to attack Kentucky settlements, but after several initial triumphs he was forced to withdraw before an onslaught of several hundred Kentucky riflemen.

When the war ended in 1783, the Americans occupied Kentucky and the Illinois country, while the British maintained physical possession of Michigan. Had the Treaty of Paris allowed each side to maintain territory held at the close of hostilities, Michigan would have remained legally British. However, the treaty stipulated that the British-American boundary should follow the middle of the Great Lakes, which gave Michigan to the United States. The British steadfastly refused to abandon their posts at Detroit and Michilimackinac, arguing that to do so would open the region to massive Indian depredations, but, in reality, they were simply trying to maintain their lucrative fur-trading enterprise. Moreover, the British knew that they had no cause to worry because the fledgling American government was too weak to risk another war to drive them out of the Northwest.

Michigan was kept under martial law until 1787 when it was declared to be part of Hesse, one of the four English-speaking districts of Canada. At that time Michigan residents were given the right to have their own sheriffs and courts.

Four years later Parliament divided Canada into upper and lower provinces. John Graves Simcoe was appointed lieutenant governor of Upper Canada, which included Michigan and most of English-speaking Canada. He then divided his province into counties from which delegates would be elected to a provincial assembly. In 1792 William Macomb, Francois Baby, and David W. Smith were elected to the assembly representing Essex and Kent counties (Detroit) and Alexander Grant was appointed to Simcoe's council. Under Simcoe's rule, English civil and criminal law was supreme, and in 1794 an act was passed abolishing the Court of Civil Jurisdiction in the District of Hesse and replaced it with the Court of King's Bench for the Province of Upper Canada.

Michigan did not long remain part of Upper Canada. International problems with Spain and France, declining numbers of fur-bearing animals, and a general realization that ever-increasing numbers of American settlers were making it virtually impossible for a continued hold on the Northwest, made the British government amicable to a plan to end its occupation of American soil. Accord-

The pomp, ceremony, and pride involved in raising the American flag for the first time at Fort Detroit is captured in this painting by Robert Thom.

ing to the terms of the Jay Treaty of 1794, England agreed to abandon its forts in the Northwest by June 1, 1796. On July 11, 1796, thirteen years after the Treaty of Paris was signed, Captain Moses Porter raised the Stars and Stripes over Detroit for the first time. British rule in Michigan had at last come to an end.

For Further Reading

Louise Phelps Kellogg, *The British Regime in Wisconsin and the Northwest* (Madison: University of Wisconsin Press, 1935) provides much information about British activities in Michigan. Nelson V. Russell, *The British Regime in Michigan* (Northfield, Minnesota: Carleton College Press, 1939) is a comprehensive examination of the British in Michigan. *Mackinac History, A Series of Informal Vignettes* is a set of leaflets produced by the Mackinac Island State Park Commission to provide useful information in regard to life at Mackinac Island during the period. Brian Leight Dunnigan, *King's Men at Mackinac: The British Garrisons, 1780-1796* (Mackinac Island: Mackinac Island State Park Commission, 1973) is a well illustrated and brief description of the British military. David A. Armour (ed.), *Attack at Michilimackinac* (Mackinac Island: Mackinac Island State Park Commission, 1971) is a condensation of Alexander Henry's journal. David A. Armour, *Treason at Michilimackinac: The Proceedings of a General Court Martial Held at Montreal in October 1786 for the Trial of Major Robert Rogers* (Mackinac Island: Mackinac Island State Park Commission, 1967) is a useful primary source for the study of one of the more colorful commanders at Michilimackinac. George S. May (ed.), *The Doctor's Secret Journal* (Mackinac Island: Mackinac Island State Park Commission, 1960) is an edited version of a journal kept by Dr. Daniel Morison, a surgeon's mate at Fort Michilimackinac from 1769-1772, which contains interesting and humorous insights into social life and activities at the post. Francis Parkman, *The Conspiracy of Pontiac* (rev. ed., Boston: Little, Brown, & Co., 1922) is still readable, but Howard Pekham, *Pontiac and the Indian Uprising* (New York: Russell and Russell, 1970) and W. R. Jacobs, *Indian Diplomacy and Indian Gifts: Anglo-French Rivalry Along the Ohio and Northwest Frontier, 1748-1763* (Stanford, California: Stanford University Press, 1950) are more factual sources on this topic. Walter T. Havighurst, *Three Flags at the Straits* (Englewood Cliffs, N.J.: Prentice-Hall, 1966) provides a very readable account of the forts at Mackinac. William R. Riddle, *Michigan Under British Rule: Law and Courts, 1760-1796* (Lansing: Michigan Historical Commission, 1926) is a comprehensive and legalistic monograph which is particularly informative on the legal difficulties during the uncertain 1783-1796 period. N. Franklin Hunt, "Growth of Legal Action

During the British Military Rule at Detroit, 1760-1774," *Michigan History,* XL (December 1956) is a good synthesis of the topic. Wayne E. Stevens, "The Michigan Fur Trade," *Michigan History,* XXIX (December 1945) is a useful and readable survey of Michigan's most important commodity during this period. Myles M. Platt, "Detroit Under Siege," *Michigan History,* XL (December 1956), 465-497, is an account of Pontiac's attack on Detroit.

4

Wilderness Politics and Economics

Soon after signing the peace treaty with England in 1783, which, in effect, ended the American Revolution, Congress passed a series of laws establishing governance for the newly acquired lands in the Great Lakes area. In 1784 an ordinance, written in part by Thomas Jefferson, provided, in vague terms, for creation of as many as ten new states in the Northwest, each of which would be admitted to the Union as a complete equal with existing states as soon as its population reached that of the least populated state already in the Union. This law proved to be unworkable however, because it failed to provide procedures by which territorial governments could be organized. The following year another ordinance was passed resolving the questions of survey and sales. Prior to entry by settlers all public land had to be surveyed and divided into townships, each six miles square. Every township was then subdivided into thirty-six sections, each containing 640 acres, with sales from section sixteen reserved for support of schools. Half the townships were to be sold whole at public auction in New York City and the remainder were to be disposed of by section, with the minimum bid set at one dollar per acre. The third law passed by Congress was the Ordinance of 1787, which replaced the Ordinance of 1784 and made precise provisions for creating governments in the Lakes region. This document consisted of three sections. The first established a "Territory North West of the Ohio" which could eventually be carved into not less than three nor more than five territories. Section two defined a three-stage evolution from territorial status to statehood. In the first stage all power rested with a governor, secretary, and three judges appointed by Congress. When the adult population reached five thousand, the territory entered its second stage. At this time a legislature could be elected, but it had to share its authority with a Council of Five selected by the governor and Congress. Also, the legislature was empowered to elect a nonvoting member to serve in the national House of Representatives. The final stage was attained when the territory's total population reached sixty thousand. Congress then allowed the convening of a convention for the purpose of drawing a constitution preparatory to a formal request for admission to the Union as a state. The third section of the Ordinance contained a Bill of Rights guaranteeing the residents of the Northwest Territory freedom of worship, jury trial, habeas corpus, sanctity of contracts, proportional representation, privileges of the common law, and the banning of slavery forever.

In 1800 the Indiana Territory was formed, which consisted of all land in the Northwest Territory west of Ohio and the western half of Michigan. In 1805, two years after Ohio achieved statehood, Congress created the Michigan Territory. When Indiana and Illinois became states in 1816 and 1818, respectively, all remaining land in the Northwest Territory became part of the Michigan Territory.

William Hull, a fifty-two-year-old former Revolutionary War general from Massachusetts, was appointed the first governor of the Michigan Territory and Stanley Griswold, a former Connecticut minister, was made secretary. Selected as judges were Frederick Bates, who had lived in Detroit since 1797, Samuel Huntington, chief justice of the Ohio Supreme Court, and Augustus E.B. Woodward, a friend of Jefferson and an idealist who shared his fellow Virginian's dream of man's ultimate perfectibility in an imperfect world. Unfortunately, Huntington declined to serve, which left Michigan with only four officials for nearly one year. As soon as another judge, John Griffin, of Virginia, was selected, Bates resigned, and once again the government was split between two New Englanders and two southerners. It was not until 1808 that a third judge, John Witherell, of Vermont, was chosen and the deadlock broken. Amid such confusion it is small wonder that the government accomplished little.

In defense of the territorial officers, it must be noted that during the years 1805-12 Michigan was still overrun with disloyal British fur traders and over 80 percent of its five thousand residents were French-speaking inhabitants of the Detroit region who cared little about the success of the new government. Moreover, since Michigan was isolated from the normal paths of westward expansion, lacked sizable amounts of surveyed land for settlement, and was beset by rumors that it was little more than a remote mosquito-infested swamp whose climate was unsuited for civilized people, the territory's prospects for growth seemed dim.

The War of 1812

With the declaration of war against England in 1812 Michigan's future was dramatically altered. Because of its strategic location at the mouth of the Detroit River, whoever controlled Detroit controlled not only the Great Lakes but also the entire Northwest. Unfortunately, Governor Hull proved to be totally unfit for the crucial role which the war thrust upon him.

As governor, Hull had accomplished little except to negotiate a treaty in 1807 with the Potawatomi, Chippewa, Ottawa, and Wyandot in which the

Indians ceded the southeast quarter of the lower peninsula to the United States in return for $10,000 in merchandise and annual payments of $2,400 for an unspecified number of years. Most of the governor's time had been spent engaging in various banking and business schemes calculated to make him wealthy. Never did he prepare his command for a possible outbreak of hostilities. Even after the army of William Henry Harrison, governor of the Indiana Territory,

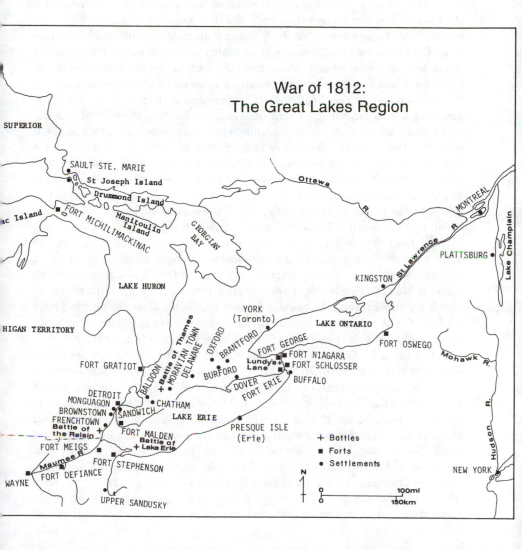

War of 1812:
The Great Lakes Region

defeated the followers of the Shawnee Chief Tecumseh at Tippecanoe in 1811 and discovered British manufactured arms in the Indian village, Hull did not strengthen his post. When war was officially declared on June 18, 1812, Hull was made commander of the armies protecting the Northwest frontier, and his authority extended to Fort Michilimackinac in the north, Fort Dearborn (Chicago) in the west, and Fort Wayne, Indiana, in the south. The fate of the entire northwest rested with the governor of Michigan.

On July 9, Hull received orders to lead his 2,200-man army across the Detroit River and attack the British outpost at Fort Malden. Three days later, without waiting for carriages to transport the artillery necessary for a successful assault, Hull invaded Canada, established a command post at Sandwich, Ontario, and ordered carpenters to build the required carriages. While the wagons were being constructed, Hull issued a proclamation offering protection to all Canadians who took an oath of neutrality and promising death and devastation to those who refused. Many took the oath, and a surprising number of Canadian volunteers deserted the British army to join with the Americans. On July 18, Colonel Henry Proctor, British commander at Malden, reported that desertion was so great that his garrison was defended by only 400 soldiers and 270 Indians led by Tecumseh. Meanwhile, Hull's carpenters had completed their work but Hull, much to the dismay of his junior officers, did not advance. On July 28, the governor learned that Fort Michilimackinac had fallen to the British and he feared that within days Indians would be "swarming down in every direction." In an effort to save the inhabitants of Fort Dearborn from what he believed to be certain slaughter, Hull ordered the post evacuated and its residents taken to Fort Wayne. Tragically, as the small troop of sixty-six men, nine women, and eighteen children marched toward their destination, they were set upon by over four hundred Potawatomi and all were either slain or taken prisoner. News of this disaster reached Hull at Sandwich, but still he refused to strike at Malden. Finally, on August 5, Hull announced to his officers that an assault on Malden would be suicidal because during the delay the post had been reinforced and soon thousands of Indians would arrive to further strengthen the garrison. Three days later the American army withdrew to Detroit.

On August 15, General Isaac Brock, who had arrived less than a week earlier with additional soldiers for Malden, sent Hull a demand that he either surrender Detroit or risk total annihilation. The governor refused to submit and British shore batteries at Sandwich opened fire. The next day Hull learned that more than seven hundred British soldiers, with artillery, had crossed the Detroit River and that six hundred Indians under Tecumseh were within two miles of Detroit. Again Brock asked Hull to surrender. Fearing that he was significantly outnumbered and that Tecumseh's warriors would massacre the entire post, Hull agreed to capitulate, telling his officers that he was "impatient to put the place [Detroit] under the protection of the British" who could stave off the "thousands of savages around us." Later that day, August 16, 1812, to the disgust of his command, William Hull, without ordering a shot in resistance, turned the post over to the British and once again the Union Jack fluttered proudly above the fort's walls.

Later that year Hull was exchanged for thirty British prisoners of war, and in 1814 he demanded a military inquiry into allegations that his conduct had been improper. A court martial was held, and, after hearing testimony from Colonel Lewis Cass and other junior officers at Detroit, the panel found Hull guilty of cowardice, neglect of duty, and unofficerlike conduct. He was sentenced to death, but President James Madison remitted his sentence because of his past record of heroism during the Revolution. Whether or not Hull was a coward is debatable, but without question, his indecisiveness had given the British a stranglehold on the Northwest.

Concerned that the loss of Detroit meant not only the loss of the Northwest but also the entire war, Madison desperately ordered Governor Harrison to recapture Detroit and invade Canada. Harrison and his army marched against British positions in Indiana and Ohio, and their determination to crush their foe was made even greater when they learned of the American defeat at the River Raisin, near the present site of Monroe. More than five hundred Americans had been captured during the struggle, eighty of whom were too seriously wounded to be moved. In an act of deliberate savagery, British officers left the wounded, all of whom were Kentucky militiamen, to be guarded by Indians drunk with British rum and angry over the loss of so many of their brothers during the battle. When the officers left the camp, the Indians killed every wounded soldier. "Remember the River Raisin" soon became the American battle cry.

Harrison's advance was stalled in Ohio at Fort Meigs (Toledo) until Lieutenant Commander Oliver Hazard Perry defeated the British fleet on Lake Erie, September 10, 1813, and cut off the British supply route. When Harrison received Perry's message that "We have met the enemy and they are ours. . . ," he knew that the British could no longer hold Detroit. Colonel Proctor, commander of Detroit, fully realized his predicament and in late September 1813 ordered all public buildings in Detroit burned and the city evacuated.

Fleeing with his army into Canada, Proctor ordered the destruction of all public buildings at Sandwich and Malden. Relentlessly Harrison pursued the retreating British army, finally catching it near Chatham, on the banks of the Thames River. In the ensuing battle, Harrison gained his greatest triumph. The American army lost seven killed and twenty-two wounded, while the British had twelve killed, thirty-six wounded, and over six hundred taken prisoner. Moreover, the brilliant war chief Tecumseh was slain, thereby removing the only effective Indian leader; following his death, Indian enthusiasm for battle waned. Most important, however, was that Detroit was again in American possession.

In 1814 the British government, faced with the fact that total military victory was nearly impossible to attain, agreed to a negotiated peace. With the signing of the Treaty of Ghent, December 24, 1814, hostilities ceased. For Michigan, the war brought about several significant results. First, it proved to be the last time Indians fought against whites in Michigan. Second, it marked the end of British hopes of ever regaining possession of Michigan. Third, Michigan was now open to settlement by families who had previously avoided the region because of Indian and British unrest. Finally, the War of 1812 was the last time the United States fought against England and thus efforts could be made to shore up American relations with Canada.

The Continuing British Threat

Even though the British were out of Michigan after 1814, their influence over the territory's Indians remained. By encouraging Indians to continue their annual treks across Michigan to British outposts at Malden, Drummond's Island, and Manitoulin Island to receive gifts of food, liquor, guns, ammunition, and trinkets, the British maintained their control over the bands while forcing the American government to concentrate on the possibility of a British-supported Indian uprising.

Because of their willingness to spend between £4,000 and £11,000 annually on gifts to Indians, British influence over the Michigan tribes was not easy to eradicate. In 1816 Congress passed an act forbidding foreigners from engaging in fur-trading activities in the Northwest and ordered that only trappers licensed by the American government could enter the area. This law was impossible to enforce and British traders continued to hunt the deer, beaver, bear, otter, raccoon, muskrat, fox, and marten which thrived in Michigan's abundant forests and streams.

Of all the territory's residents, none expressed more concern over the British and Indian threat than Lewis Cass. Appointed governor in 1813, Cass was embarking on a political career which would include distinguished service as a United States senator, secretary of war, secretary of state, ambassador to France, and Democratic candidate for President. Cass believed that the only permanent solution to the problem was removal of all the territory's Indians west of the Mississippi River. Until that lengthy process could be completed, he convinced Congress to authorize construction of a cordon of forts strategically located along routes used by Indians in their treks to British posts. A show of American force, the governor thought, might weaken Indian loyalty to the British.

Another of Cass's ideas for undermining British influence was "scientific exploration." Under the governor's direction in 1820 the North Western Scientific Expedition was organized ostensibly to explore little known regions along Lake Superior and to trace water links between Lake Superior and the Mississippi River. The true purpose of the journey was to meet Indians, purchase land from them, and determine the strength of British trading interests in the upper peninsula. In June 1820, a forty-man expedition reached Sault Ste. Marie and negotiated a land-cession treaty whereby the American government was permitted to construct a post, Fort Brady, at that site. Despite encountering intense Indian hostility, Henry Rowe Schoolcraft, Indian agent at the Sault and an ardent ethnologist, considered that the journey had been a success:

The transit of the mission through those remote regions, and the intercourse had with the numerous and powerful tribes inhabiting the country, has been calculated to produce a feeling of amity or good will towards the United States, which cannot fail to be productive of the most beneficial consequences; and our visit—our presents—and our speeches—in which we have declared to them the friendly and philanthropic views of the Government, will long be remembered. Upon the whole, the intercourse we have held with them will have a powerful tendency to break down the shackles of British influence, and to lift from their eyes the deceptive veil which has heretofore rendered them blind to their own best interests.

No matter what the cost, Cass was intent on opening Michigan to safe entry by American settlers.

The American Fur Company

While the American government was encountering difficulty winning Indian trust and gaining a proportionate share of the Great Lakes fur trade, private enterprises, such as the American Fur Company, were enjoying notable success. The American Fur Company, founded in 1808 by the German immigrant John Jacob Astor, immediately challenged the British North West Company for supremacy in the Michigan fur trade. Organizational ability, political influence with powerful American and British leaders, and a keen sense of how to trade with Indians made Astor the unquestioned champion of fur trading. His company's trade goods, which included firearms, knives, hatchets, ammunition, tobacco, liquor, wampum, silk, Irish linen, foodstuffs, blankets, gold and silver jewelry, and chocolate, were of superior quality, often manufactured in England, and were greatly desired by Indians. Moreover, most of his nearly three thousand employees were British and French Canadiens who had worked the region for years, knew the Indians, and had often intermarried with them. Astor was so successful that by 1828 his company controlled 95 percent of the territory's fur trade and had established posts at Mackinac, Detroit, Sault Ste. Marie, St. Joseph, and in the Kalamazoo, Grand, Saginaw, and Muskegon river valleys. Astor, much more than the American government, pursued a policy which was aimed at winning over Indian loyalty to the United States.

By the late 1820s the "golden days" of the Michigan fur trade were past. Keen observers realized that by 1790 the fur traders' frontier had left lower

Michigan and that by 1820 it was leaving the upper peninsula and moving west into the Red River region of Canada for beaver and the Great Plains for buffalo. Because of Michigan's strategic geographic position, however, its importance in the northern fur trade did not measurably decline when trapping diminished. Detroit and Mackinac remained major clearing houses and shipping depots for the American Fur Company even after Astor sold his interests in the business in 1834. The Panic of 1837 severely damaged the fur industry, and finally in 1854, the American Fur Company closed its only remaining post, at Mackinac, and the era of international fighting for furs from the Great Lakes was officially ended.

Toledo and Statehood

Following the opening of the Erie Canal in 1825, removal of the British threat, and establishment of peaceful relations with the Indians, Michigan's population soared from 8,500 in 1820 to 31,000 in 1830. By 1833, the territory had more than the 60,000 residents required for Congress to authorize a constitutional convention, but Congress refused to permit this step. Michigan's admission to the Union was being delayed not by insufficient population but rather by an unsettled boundary dispute with Ohio.

The area in question was a 468-square-mile wedge, five miles wide at the Indiana border and eight miles wide at Lake Erie. Ever since Ohio petitioned for statehood in 1802, the two antagonists had claimed the so-called Toledo Strip and each presented maps and survey reports to substantiate its position. The problem of ownership arose because when Ohio wrote its constitution it agreed to set its northern boundary along a line established by the Ordinance of 1787. However, a proviso was added that if that line, which was imprecise as to its exact location, failed to include the mouth of the Maumee River for Ohio, a new boundary had to be set giving that area to the Buckeye state. When the Michigan Territory was created in 1805, Congress ignored the proviso in the Ohio constitution, abided by the Ordinance Line of 1787, and awarded the region to Michigan. Ohioans were enraged and the seeds of future warfare had been planted.

In 1832 Congress ordered another survey to determine the exact Ohio-Michigan border. Two years later the results of the survey were submitted to Congress—the disputed area clearly belonged to Michigan. Because Ohio was already a state, with voting power and the ability to trade support on key legislation with other states in Congress, while Michigan, as a territory, could offer nothing in return for support of its claim, congressmen joined their Ohio colleagues in denouncing the survey as inaccurate. In December 1834, the Michigan legislature, in a spirit of conciliation, urged Congress to appoint a three-man commission to negotiate a settlement of the dispute, but the governor of Ohio, Robert Lucas, refused to participate, saying that there was nothing to negotiate.

Stevens T. Mason, Michigan's twenty-three-year-old "Boy Governor," realized that Congress would not authorize a call for a constitutional convention and therefore, following a precedent set by Tennessee in 1795, he ordered the legislature to call a convention without permission from Washington. In response to Mason's action, the Ohio legislature passed a law reaffirming their state's jurisdiction over the Toledo Strip. Mason then urged the Michigan legislature to pass the "Pains and Penalties Act," which imposed a maximum fine of $1,000 and/or a maximum of five years at hard labor upon any Ohio "trespassers" found in the disputed area. War had begun!

Throughout the next several months the actions on the part of both sides were ludicrous. In early April, Governor Lucas visited the region and announced that elections for the legislature would be held there to demonstrate Ohio's possession of the territory. Mason then ordered strict enforcement of the "Pains and Penalties Act." A Monroe County deputy sheriff went to Toledo to arrest any Ohioans there, which proved to be only one in number, while an "army" of thirty Michigan volunteers raided Perrysburg and captured nine members of an Ohio survey party. In mid-July the "Wolverines," as Michiganians had been dubbed by Ohioans who likened them to that "vicious, smelly, ugly northwoods animal," had scored another bloodless victory when two hundred soldiers invaded the deserted city of Toledo. Thrilled by these triumphs, Michigan residents proudly sang a ballad, entitled "The New Cock Robin," extolling the justice of their cause:

>"And who would cut up Michigan?"
>"I," says Governor Lucas
>"What I undertook is
>to cut up little Michigan."

>"And who has bid him do it?"
>A million freemen
>(Counting women and children)
>" 'Tis Ohio bids him do it."

>"And who rings the bells of war?"
>"I," says Gen'l Bell
>" 'Tis I that rings the bell.
>Ding, dong goes my bell of war.

>"And what is all this bother for?"
>For Port Lawrence? no.
>For Vistula? not so.
>Both died of ague last year.

>But out of their graves there did spring
>A little mushroom
>Of sickliest bloom
>Which botanists call Toledo.

> The flower is Ohio's no doubt,
> 'Tis Buckeye in breed,
> She scattered the seed:
> Then let Gov. Lucas transplant it.
>
> But the swamp where it grew is not here.
> Then let him beware
> How he runs up a fence there,
> He will find other strings than mosquito's.

Meanwhile, in May ninety-one delegates had assembled at Detroit to write Michigan's first state constitution. Based on several existing state constitutions, this document was a study in brevity and simplicity. Included were a bill of rights, creation of an office of Superintendent of Public Instruction, establishment of a two-house legislature with senators serving two-year, and representatives one-year, terms, and stipulation for two-year terms for governor and lieutenant governor. In an attempt to shorten ballots, all offices, including the judiciary, except those of state legislators, governor, and lieutenant governor, were to be filled by gubernatorial appointment. Michigan was ready and waiting for statehood.

In Washington, President Andrew Jackson was furious with Michigan and his fellow Democrat, Governor Mason, and on August 28, 1835, he removed Mason as acting governor. His replacement, John S. "Little Jack" Horner, of Virginia, was not well liked, and in November, Michigan voters first exercised their constitutional right to vote for governor and elected Mason. At this election voters also chose Isaac Crary to be representative to Congress, and the legislature named John Novell and Lucius Lyon to be United States senators. Congress, however, refused to seat them.

In March 1836, the House Judiciary Committee, which had been studying the Michigan admission bill, reported that in order to gain statehood Michigan had to cede the Toledo Strip and agree to accept the upper peninsula in return. On June 15, 1836, Congress voted to admit Michigan to the Union as soon as the territory agreed to congressional terms. Accordingly, the Michigan legislature called for delegates to meet in Ann Arbor in September to vote on the congressional dictum. At that gathering the proposal was defeated 28-21 on the grounds that Michigan would be humiliated if it accepted the dictate of an Ohio-influenced Congress.

Governor Mason, knowing that only as a state could Michigan effectively continue to challenge Ohio's claim to the disputed region, asked for a reconsideration of the vote. In December, another convention was held in which it was argued that it was better to lose face in order to secure the advantages of statehood than to continue "an idle, an unprofitable, a hopeless contest for a boundary, . . . a boundary which is assuredly and forever lost to us." The convention, moved by logic and a promise of massive amounts of federal funds for internal improvements if Michigan entered the Union immediately, reversed itself and agreed to the proposal of Congress. On January 6, 1837, by a vote of 25-10, the United States Senate admitted Michigan to the Union, and on January 25 the House of Representatives concurred by a vote of 132-43. On January 26, 1837, Michigan was officially proclaimed the twenty-sixth state.

Ironically, even though by acquiring the upper peninsula Michigan gained over nine thousand square miles of unequaled mineral and timber land, it still sought revenge. In 1889 the Michigan legislature unsuccessfully requested congressional ordering of a new survey. In 1915, 1922, 1932, and 1945 surveys were commissioned by both state legislatures for determining ownership of property for taxation purposes, but the question of the Toledo Strip remained. In 1966 Michigan filed suit in federal court to reclaim Toledo. The suit was dismissed, but to many Michiganians the struggle over the Toledo Strip will never end until Michigan receives what rightly belongs to it.

For Further Reading

Several works deal with early American land policy: among the best are Roy Robbins, *Our Landed Heritage* (Princeton: University of Princeton Press, 1942) and the excellent, though dated, volume by Payson Treat, *The National Land System* (New York: E. B. Treat & Co., 1910). Early attempts at settling Michigan are recounted in C. M. Burton, "Detroit in the Year 1832," *Michigan Pioneer and Historical Collections*, XXVIII (1897-1989); George Fuller, "An Introduction to the Settlement of Southern Michigan from 1815-1835," *Michigan Pioneer and Historical Collections*, XXXVIII (1912) and "Settlement of Michigan Territory," *Journal of American History*, II (1915), and Andrew Perejda, "Sources and Dispersal of Michigan's Population," *Michigan History*, XXXII (1948).

Government during the territorial years is discussed in Timothy Sherer, "The Resistance to Representative Government in Early Michigan Territory," *The Old Northwest*, V (1979) and Frank Woodford, *Mr. Jefferson's Disciple: A Life of Justice Woodward* (East Lansing: Michigan State University Press, 1953).

Michigan's role in the struggle with England is described in Fred Hamil, *Michigan in the War of 1812* (Lansing: Michigan Historical Commission, 1960); Alec Gilpin, *The War of 1812 in the Old Northwest* (East Lansing: Michigan State University Press, 1958); and John G. VanDeusen, "The Detroit Campaign of General William Hull," *Michigan History*, XII (1928). The life of Cass is told in glowing terms by Frank Woodford in *Lewis Cass: The Last Jeffersonian* (New Brunswick: Rutgers University Press, 1950).

Ida Johnson, *The Michigan Fur Trade* (Grand Rapids: Black Letter Press, 1971—a reprint of a 1919 publication) still stands as the standard work on its topic. K. W. Porter, *John Jacob Astor: Businessman* (Cambridge: Harvard University Press, 1931) is the most complete work on the American Fur Company.

The struggle for Toledo is humorously recounted in Sister Mary Karl George, *The Rise and Fall of Toledo, Michigan* (Lansing: Michigan Historical Commission, 1971). Kent Sagendorph relates the story of Michigan's "Boy Governor" in *Stevens Thompson Mason, Misunderstood Patriot* (New York: E. P. Dutton, 1947).

5

Challenges of Statehood

As a territory, Michigan had remained relatively unexplored and unexploited. Protected on its flanks by the stormy and uncertain waters of the Great Lakes, the territory seemed remote and inaccessible, far from the mainstream of western expansion. Michigan's reputation as a land of swamps and sickness whose very name was synonymous with "ague, fever, and chills" served as a further deterrent to growth.

Despite these handicaps, Michigan's early years of statehood saw an enormous population increase. During the 1830s a flood of immigration sent the population soaring to over 212,000—the greatest growth for any state or territory during the decade. By 1850 Michigan had nearly 398,000 residents, of whom 14 percent were foreign-born.

Two developments in transportation had a profound impact on the state's population explosion. First, in 1811 Robert Fulton sailed his new invention, the steamboat, and within seven years the *Walk-in-the-Water* was plying the Great Lakes between Buffalo and Detroit. Although this first lake-steamer was wrecked in a storm three years after its launching, others soon followed, bringing new settlers to Michigan. Second, in 1825 New York's Erie Canal was completed, stretching 350 miles from Albany, on the Hudson River, to Buffalo, on Lake Erie. Its opening meant that potential settlers living in New England and New York could make much of their journey inland by water and that Michigan products would have an easier access to Eastern markets.

Most settlers poured into the rich fertile lands of the two southern tiers of counties, which were readily reached both by water and the Territorial and Chicago Military Roads. In terms of population, the three largest counties in 1837 were Wayne (23,400), Washtenaw (21,817), and Oakland (20,176). Jackson, Calhoun, and Kalamazoo counties also had substantial populations because of the presence of treeless farmland, called by settlers "prairies," which could be immediately plowed and planted. Settlement beyond the fourth tier of counties was sparse because of poorer soil, dense forests, harsher climate, and inadequate inland travel arteries.

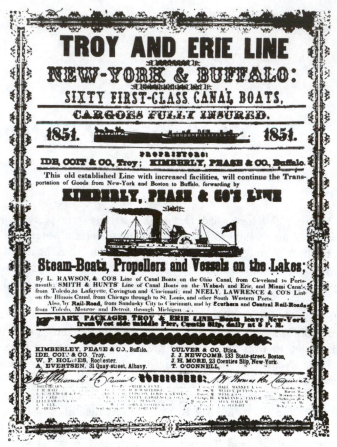

By 1851 steamboat travel was becoming common on the Great Lakes.

Prior to the Civil War most of Michigan's residents were New Englanders who had hoped to transplant their culture and customs to their new western home. Vermontville, whose name indicates the origin of its founders, is an excellent example of the immigrant desire to retain a grasp on the past, even if that hold were as slender as a reminiscent name. Many immigrants came to Michigan from western New York. Upon arriving in Michigan, settlers from Genesee County quickly named their new home after their old. Even these New Yorkers can be considered, in a broad sense, to be New Englanders since they were mostly descendants of New England soldiers who had received land in New York as payment for their service in the American Revolution. All brought with them the Yankee traits of industry, thrift, religious zeal, reformism, and interest in education. Other newcomers came from Ohio and Indiana and established homes primarily in the southwestern part of the state. Since many of these settlers were of southern origin they provided a distinct contrast to New Englanders, and, as a result, two differing political and social cultures were created within the state.

While new settlers were primarily agriculturalists, their interest was in growing cash crops of wheat and corn, not merely in subsistence farming. Wheat soon became the principal commercial crop. If measured by quantity grown, however, corn was the leader because it was used not only for food but also for liquor. Likewise, rye and barley were raised in sizable amounts for both flour and distillery purposes. Oats and hay were grown for feed, but their bulk made them too expensive to haul to market for sale.

Internal Improvements

To exploit potential agricultural markets in the East, South, and West, improved transportation links with other states, as well as development of dependable transportation and communication networks within Michigan, were a vital necessity. Consequently, the immediate priority of the governor and legislature became development of internal improvements.

For precedent, Michigan looked to the achievements of other states. New York had become the nation's foremost commercial state primarily because of its program of internal improvements, especially the Erie Canal. Pennsylvania and Maryland had authorized expenditure of millions of dollars for roads and canals. By 1837, Ohio, Illinois, and Indiana had improvement programs, with the latter's being referred to as the "Mammoth Bill" because it totalled $13 million.

In 1837 only the state government possessed current and potential fiscal resources to finance mass public improvement programs. Local resources could provide neither adequate funding nor the integrated network of facilities necessary to assure maximum efficiency. Federal funds seemed unavailable because President Jackson's veto of the Maysville Road Bill in 1830 precluded expenditure for such projects. It was so obvious that state funding was the only solution that Michigan's first constitution stated that "internal improvements shall be encouraged by the government of this state; and it shall be the duty of the legislature as soon as may be to make provisions by law for ascertaining the proper objects of improvement in relation to roads, canals, and navigable waters." Thus, it was not surprising that in his initial address to the legislature Governor Mason called for an internal improvements program and declared that "the period has arrived when Michigan can no longer, without detriment to her standing and importance as a state, delay the action necessary for the development of her vast resources and wealth."

The legislature agreed with the governor, and the apparent will of the people, and, in 1837, passed a Public Improvement Act which authorized the governor to sell $5 million in bonds, at 5¼ percent interest, to fund building two transpeninsular canals and three transpeninsular railroads. Canals were to connect the Clinton River, near Mt. Clemens, with the mouth of the Kalamazoo River and to link the Saginaw and Grand rivers. Railroad lines were determined by geography: a southern route was to run from near Monroe to New Buffalo in Berrien County; a central route would connect Detroit with St. Joseph; and a northern line would join a site near Port Huron in St. Clair Country to a locale near Grand Rapids in Kent County. These projects were to be overseen by a seven-member Board of Commissioners of Internal Improvements and all profits derived were to be used to repay the $5 million loan.

Undoubtedly the state would have been better served by a less elaborate and expensive proposal. With a population of less than 250,000, the idea of constructing railways and canals into largely unsettled lands held by speculators was financially unwise. It was, however, politically expedient since all sections of the state sought transportation facilities and no politician wanted to risk alienating a constituent by neglecting any locale. The boldness of Michigan's plans seemed even more rash when viewed within the context of the emphasis on railroads. Rail traffic was a very new concept in 1837. Rail lines had been built in England in the 1820s, but it was not until 1830 that the Baltimore and Ohio began operating a thirteen-mile stretch of track in the United States. Furthermore, American civil engineers were few in number and there were not enough Scottish and English engineers with railroad expertise available to satisfy the blossoming demand. Consequently, it was common for untrained and incompetent men to masquerade as engineers. In fact, in 1838 an engineer for the Michigan Southern Railroad was taking a correspondence course in surveying!

Unfortunately, 1837 was not an opportune time for Michigan to seek purchasers for bonds. The Bank of the United States, whose rechartering had been vetoed in 1832 by President Jackson, had been abolished in 1836. Removal of the bank's program for fiscal stability resulted in the creation of "wildcat banks" which issued their own currency—a practice which, in turn, led to spiraling inflation and financial panic. Jackson's "Specie Circular," which demanded that all land purchased from the government be done so in gold or silver, further restricted sales by limiting credit opportunities. Failing to sell its bonds locally, the Michigan legislature in 1838 commissioned the Morris Canal and Banking Company of New Jersey to act as selling agent. In November 1838, the Morris Company purchased 25 percent of the bonds, with the Bank of the United States of Pennsylvania buying the remainder. Payment was arranged at $250,000 per quarter. In 1840 the Morris Company went bankrupt and the following year the Pennsylvania bank collapsed. For Michigan this was a double disaster: first, the state had received only $2.6 million from the sales, and second, it could not recover the bonds for which repayment had not yet been made because the two now defunct purchasers had used them as collateral for other investments. Michigan's hope for a financial windfall had turned into a tragedy; however, another source of potential profit soon came to the fore—mining for precious metals.

The Copper Kingdom

Earliest mining in Michigan was for copper. Ancient Indian legends told of fabulous copper riches, and, during their explorations, Louis Armand de La Honton and Pierre Francois de Charlevoix related to the French government their discovery of an enormous pure copper boulder in the upper peninsula. French officials considered the finding inconsequential and took no action. Nearly one hundred years later, after the British had gained sway over French North America in the Seven Years' War, Charles Townsend, England's chancellor of the exchequer, dispatched Robert Rogers and a small party of men to explore the upper peninsula in hopes of unearthing deposits of gold, silver, and copper. Initial digging brought forth a nugget which was assayed at 75 percent pure silver. Elated, Rogers ordered a thirty-foot shaft dug to uncover more of the precious stones, but none was found. Because mining activities demanded clearing of the forests and construction of roads, fur trappers and traders lodged protests with the British government. Weighing the possibility of wealth obtained from the potential discovery of precious minerals against the certain profit derived from existing fur trade, Crown officials ordered all mining in the Great Lakes region ceased.

American interest in mining was stirred when Cass's North West Scientific Expedition of 1820 visited the site of the fabled copper boulder and confirmed its existence in a report to Secretary of War John C. Calhoun. Immediate exploration and excavation of the region was impossible because the western upper peninsula belonged to the Chippewa and the United States government had neither title to, nor jurisdiction over, it. Furthermore, the remoteness of the region, along with its severe climate, dissuaded most potential prospectors from embarking upon exploratory searches.

In 1841, Douglass Houghton made a report which changed the course of Michigan's economic, political, and social development. Houghton, who had come to Michigan from New York in 1830 at the age of twenty-one to give scientific lectures at the University of Michigan, had visited the Keweenaw Peninsula in 1831 and 1832 with Henry Rowe Schoolcraft and had been appointed state geologist in 1837. During his first two years in office he surveyed the lower peninsula and the Lake Superior and Lake Huron shorelines of the upper peninsula. In 1840 Houghton returned to the upper peninsula for extensive surveying and geological study. The following year his reports confirming the existence of a pure copper boulder along the Ontonagon River and copper deposits throughout the Keweenaw Peninsula were published. Tragically, Houghton's brilliant life was cut short when he drowned in a Lake Superior storm October 14, 1845, but his work had already made him a legendary figure in Michigan history.

Despite Houghton's verification of copper deposits and a rising clamor from fortune seekers eager to mine their way to prosperity, the national government forbade entry into the Keweenaw region until a land settlement with the Indians had been reached. This obstacle was removed October 4, 1842, with the signing of the Treaty of LaPointe. In this pact, chiefs and headmen of the Lake Superior and Mississippi bands of Chippewa sold their holdings between Marquette, Michigan, and Duluth, Minnesota, to the United States in return for more than $800,000 to be paid in twenty-five annual installments and the right to remain temporarily on the ceded territory. Chief government negotiator Robert Stuart, a former aide to John Jacob Astor, later boasted that he had "done in" the Indians by "excluding the usual allowances" of goods and services, educational benefits, and assistance toward ultimate assimilation into white society.

Having acquired clear title to the land, the federal government opened the western upper peninsula to entry in 1843 with the stipulation that every prospector had to obtain a mining permit from the War Department office at Copper Harbor. These permits allowed an individual to explore a specified nine-square-mile area, stake a claim, and receive a lease to the property for three years, with two three-year renewals available upon request. In return, miners had to give the government 6 percent of the value of all minerals mined during the initial three years and 10 percent during the renewal periods. In 1846, after nearly one thousand permits had been distributed, a court decision declared the leasing arrangement illegal. The following year Congress passed a law for the sale of mineral lands in the Lake Superior region, with the minimum bid set at five dollars per acre. Three years later the minimum bid was reduced to $1.25 per acre, the same as had been established for agricultural lands.

Thousands of newcomers, armed with picks, shovels, and explosives, flocked to the western upper peninsula. To assure the safety of the miners, on February 6, 1850, President Zachary Taylor ordered all Indians still on land ceded by the 1842 treaty to prepare for removal west. The Chippewa refused, saying that the treaty's intent was to permit whites to mine the south shore of Lake Superior, not to force Indians from their homeland. A peaceful resolution to the problem was reached in 1854. A new treaty was negotiated which set aside reservations for exclusive occupation by the Chippewa of Lake Superior. Included in the agreement was a ninety-square-mile tract at the head of Keweenaw Bay for the L'Anse and Vieux De Sert bands of Michigan.

It was soon discovered that individuals with hand tools could extract very little copper, and within three years large, well-financed Eastern mining companies had entered the region. Of these, the most successful was the Pittsburgh and Boston Company which owned the rich Cliff Mine along Eagle River. By 1870, when it closed, the Cliff Mine had paid company stockholders more than $2.5 million in dividends.

The three largest copper-producing regions were those at the tip of the Keweenaw Peninsula, along the Ontonagon River, and near Portage Lake. The latter was the richest site, containing the Quincy Mine, which was affectionately dubbed "Old Reliable" because of its continuous production of copper. The Quincy Mine typified the long-term nature of copper mine investment. It opened in 1848 and, despite capital outlays exceeding $900,000 by its owners, by 1860 it still had not returned a profit. In time, patient investors were rewarded, and by 1945, the Quincy had put forth enough ore to permit the company to have paid over $27 million in dividends. Risks and knowledge of a lengthy delay in obtaining profits did not deter investors, and by the outbreak of the Civil War thirty-three firms, financed by more than $4 million from Eastern industrialists and bankers and employing nearly four thousand men, were operating mines in the upper peninsula.

Following the Civil War, copper production in Michigan soared from 25 million pounds in 1872 to a peak of 267 million pounds, valued at $76 million, in 1916. During the period 1847-87, Michigan led the nation in copper output, but discovery of new copper fields in Arizona and New Mexico in 1888 relegated Michigan to third place after that year. Michigan's massive copper production is all the more astounding since the Keweenaw area was mined out by 1867, and within another twenty-three years so was the Ontonagon River range. Only the Portage Lake mines continued to operate into the twentieth century.

Mining companies, investors, and local merchants profited greatly from Michigan's "copper rush." During the years 1885-1918 shareholders in the state's copper mines received dividends of more than $236 million. A share of Calumet Mine stock which sold for one dollar in 1866 was worth one thousand dollars in 1907. Upper peninsula mining firms employed as many as forty thousand men annually. Workers earning high wages were exploited by merchants, doctors, lawyers, and assorted entrepreneurs. As miners began to send for their families, a need arose for schools, churches, teachers, and ministers. With the arrival of these "forerunners of civilization," camps such as Houghton and Hancock were transformed into permanent settlements.

Mining also brought technical and physical advancements to the upper peninsula. Establishment of the Michigan School of Mines, now Michigan Technological University, at Houghton in 1885 was a direct result of copper mining and the desire of engineers to keep abreast of the latest concepts in metallurgy and mining techniques. Railroads were built to meet the needs of the mines, and by 1884, the western upper peninsula was linked to Chicago by rail. New canals, such as the Portage Lake and Lake Superior Ship Canal and that under construction at Sault Ste. Marie, assured upper peninsula residents as early as the 1850s that their region would have water routes connecting it with the rest of the state. To the upper peninsula, copper mining meant much more than revenue—it signaled the region's acceptance as a productive part of the state. Unfortunately, industrial progress took its toll on the upper peninsula's previously unspoiled environment, and by 1895, Torch Lake had become known as "The Red Sea of Michigan" because of copper oxide residue dumped there by nearby stamping mills.

The Ontonagon Boulder

One of the most bizarre incidents in Michigan's history stemmed from the copper fields. In late 1841, Julius Eldred, a Detroit merchant, decided to obtain the fabled copper boulder along the Ontonagon River, take it to Detroit, put it on display, and charge curious spectators twenty-five cents to gaze at "Michigan's natural wonder." Eldred arrived at the site, which was still owned by the Chippewa, and purchased the boulder from Chief Okondokon for $150. Since it weighed more than three tons, Eldred could not move it with the equipment he had brought, so, in the summer of 1842, he returned to Detroit to acquire the men, hoists, ropes, levers, railroad track, and flatcar necessary to dislodge the rock.

When he returned the following year, Eldred discovered that the boulder had been seized by another entrepreneur. Eldred negotiated with his rival and finally convinced him to part with the boulder for $1,365 in cash. The boulder was then hoisted upon the flatcar and pushed along tracks four miles to Lake Superior, where it was loaded onto a ship. Upon reaching Detroit, Eldred encountered another unexpected obstacle when federal agents, acting on a directive from the United States district attorney for Michigan, confiscated the boulder and sent it to Washington, D.C. for display at the Smithsonian Institute. Furious and frustrated, Eldred spent years in court trying to recover his prize possession, but ultimately he was compelled to accept a settlement of $5,664.98 from the government. Even though Eldred did not achieve fame and fortune from his plan, his misadventures drew state and national attention to Michigan's copper country.

Iron Mining

Iron ore was discovered in the upper peninsula in 1844 when William A. Burt, a government surveyor, determined that the cause of his magnetic compass' needle's wild spinning was the presence of iron deposits. Although Burt located several iron ore lodes, especially in the vicinity of Neguanee, reports of his findings were not made public until the following year. Soon after Burt's discoveries were published, three major mining concerns began operation: the Jackson Company, founded by Philo M. Everett of Jackson, Michigan, opened near Neguanee in 1846; the next year the Cleveland Iron Company was established at the same location; and in 1849, the Marquette Iron Company was formed at Ishpeming.

Early excavation for iron ore was relatively easy because the metal was near the earth's surface. Men often uprooted trees, scraped away sod and soil, and used handpicks and sledgehammers to remove the ore. By 1870 deeper mines had been dug and men sent up ore in hand-drawn buckets. Shortly before the turn of the century, steam-driven machinery was introduced to lift ore from the mines, and electric elevators were used to take the miners to and from the depths. As in copper mining, large, well-financed companies bought smaller ones, and then, having acquired a near monopoly, they expended huge sums of money to modernize their operations, construct railroads, and improve harbor facilities. From the mid-1880s, with the opening of the Menominee and Gogebic ranges, until the early 1900s, when large-scale mining began in Minnesota, Michigan reigned as the nation's leading iron-ore producer.

Transportation

A direct consequence of copper and iron-ore mining was the development of lake ore-carriers. During mining's early years, schooners and other sailing ships transported ore, but by 1882 steamships capable of holding 2,100 tons of ore were in operation. In 1886 the first steel ore-carrier was launched, and soon afterwards others reaching a length of four hundred feet and having cargo capacities of three thousand tons were churning through the Great Lakes. Today, ore carriers extend nearly one thousand feet in length and effortlessly store more than twenty thousand tons in their holds.

Improvements in loading and unloading procedure came with increased production demands. Originally ore was loaded onto ships by wheelbarrow and handcart. When the ship reached its destination, men with shovels were dropped into the holds and buckets lowered to them. The filled buckets were lifted from the hold by hoist and their contents heaped along the shore. Because of the difficulty of the labor and the reluctance of mining companies to pay decent wages to stevedores, Indians, who were willing to work for little money, usually were hired to unload ships. As an example, in 1872 the Leland Iron Company paid its Indian employees twenty-five cents per day to unload tons of ore. Finally, in 1899, a steam-powered unloader, which could hoist more tonnage in eight hours than one hundred men could lift in a week, was perfected and put into service.

The Sault Ste. Marie Canal

Perhaps the most significant result of mining enterprises in Michigan was construction of a canal at Sault Ste. Marie. Mine operators realized that if they were to become successful and wealthy, a means of conquering the rapids at the Sault and of allowing easy movement from Lake Superior into Lake Huron, which was approximately twenty-two feet lower, had to be devised. Without a canal, ships laden with ore from Lake Superior mines had to be unloaded, removed from the water, rolled on logs to the lower-water-level lake, and then reloaded. The only alternative to this expensive procedure was the equally unsatisfactory idea of using two ships, one in each lake, and having the ore portaged from one ship to the other. Governor Mason's internal improvement message called for a ship canal at the Sault, but the contractor hired by the state became convinced that the task could not be accomplished for the allotted appropriation and abandoned the enterprise. From 1839 until 1852 Michigan representatives in Congress attempted to obtain a federal land grant to assist in the building of a canal at the Sault. In August 1852, despite objections by opponents that the upper peninsula was as "remote as the moon," Congress authorized Michigan to sell 750,000 acres of public land to raise funds for the desired canal.

The man who became known as the genius behind the project was Charles Harvey. Realizing the importance of such a canal to his employer, the Fairbanks Scale Company, whose owners had invested heavily in Michigan mines, Harvey convinced Eastern investors to form the St. Mary's Falls Ship Company and appoint him to be chief engineer. Harvey had to overcome many obstacles before the canal was completed. The project was beset by cholera epidemics, severe winter weather which stopped construction, and enormous expenses which totaled more than $1 million—twice the original estimate. Despite these overwhelming difficulties, the canal and locks opened on May 31, 1855, less than two years from the beginning of excavation. The canal was operated by the state and was obligated by federal law to charge a four cents per ton toll until such time as the construction costs had been recovered. When the canal was paid for, it was to be turned over to the federal government and all tolls would be removed. This was done in 1881, the same year a second lock was opened in the canal. In subsequent years, three more locks have been added and today, with ocean-going ships entering the Great Lakes from the St. Lawrence Seaway, the Sault canal opens Michigan's upper peninsula not only to American markets, but also to those of the entire globe.

A New Capital

Economic growth was not the only issue concerning the Michigan legislature in the 1840s. The state constitution stipulated that Detroit remain the state capital for ten years, at which time a permanent capital site had to be named. Detroiters wanted to retain the capital designation, but critics argued that the city was dangerously close to Canada in case of another war with England, was not centrally located, and offered a social life which had a corrupt-

The locks at Sault Ste. Marie have undergone great changes since the steamer *St. Paul* was carried through the first lock during the 1870s.

ing influence on lawmakers. Many cities vied for the honor of becoming the capital, and on March 16, 1847, the legislature voted to place the seat of government in Lansing township of Ingham County. Thereafter the question arose of what to name the village which would soon spring up as if by magic. Rejecting such suggestions as El Dorado, Kinderhook, Michigan, and Swedenborg, the legislature decided to name it after the township, Lansing. The choice was well received because many of the settlers there were from Lansing, New York, which was named after John Lansing, chancellor of New York from 1801-10. Once again, Michigan's ties to New York were evident. The capitol constructed in Lansing was replaced by a new structure in 1879 and this architecturally striking, white sandstone building still serves as Michigan's capitol.

The Constitution of 1850

On November 6, 1849, the Michigan electorate approved by a vote of 33,193 to 4,095 the calling of a constitutional convention to revise the existing document. During its deliberations, the convention approved numerous proposals, the most important of which were placing a fifty thousand dollar limit on the state debt and ending all state aid for internal improvements. Other significant measures included allowing unlimited liability for bank officers and stockholders, thereby making unscrupulous financiers legally responsible for their actions, and a statement that all corporations, except those for municipal purposes, had to be formed under general law, which prevented the legislature from granting special favors to individuals.

The new document further stated that state legislators would be elected every two years instead of annually and that legislative sessions would have to be held only once during that period. Furthermore the governor and lieutenant governor were made ineligible for legislative appointment to other offices during their term of service, which was done to prevent them from becoming senatorial aspirants. The judiciary system was revised from a county court system to one based upon eight circuit courts, and all principal state offices, including university regents and members of the State Board of Education, would become elective, rather than appointive, positions.

Although the convention rejected petitions to grant suffrage to blacks and women, it did give the right to vote to aliens who had stated their desire to become citizens and to Indians who had renounced all tribal loyalty. The convention delegates did authorize that the question of black suffrage be placed on a separate ballot, which was done and was soundly defeated 32,026 to 12,840. Obviously many Michiganians agreed with a Detroit delegate who argued that blacks should remain segregated from whites and remain "in their present sphere."

A New Look

The thirteen years since statehood had witnessed tremendous changes in Michigan. Its population had multiplied at a fantastic rate because of improvements in transportation and communication. Beginning statehood during the Panic of 1837 certainly was not an easy task and the financial difficulties incurred by its ambitious internal improvement program had been a near economic catastrophe. Yet, through improved fiscal management and the thrifty policies of Democratic governors and legislatures after 1841, Michigan's economy became so sound that in December 1850 the state treasurer reported a surplus of $36,057.85. Despite such an optimistic harbinger of the future, Michigan was about to undergo the effects of the divisive seeds of conflict which had been sown throughout the nation's history over the question of slavery.

For Further Reading

William G. Shade, *Banks or No Banks: The Money Issue in Western Politics*, 1832-1865 (Detroit: Wayne State University Press, 1972) provides a modern treatment of the financial problems encountered by the states of the old Northwest. The same author's "Banks and Politics in Michigan: A Reconsideration," *Michigan History*, LVII (Spring 1973) and Ronald Seavoy, "Borrowed Laws to Speed Development, 1835-1863," *Michigan History*, LIX (Spring-Summer 1975) offer analyses of financial politics and the origins of fiscal legislation in Michigan.

Robert Hybel, "The Lake Superior Copper Fever, 1841-1847," *Michigan History*, XXXIV (Summer-Fall 1950) gives a solid background of Houghton's activities and the saga of the Ontonagon boulder. Angus Murdoch, *Boom Copper: The Story of the First United States Mining Boom* (New York: Macmillan and Co., 1943) and William B. Gates, *Michigan Copper and Boston Dollars: An Economic History of the Michigan Copper Mining Industry* (Cambridge: Harvard University Press, 1951) are comprehensive studies. Donald Chaput, *The Cliff: America's First Great Copper Mine* (Kalamazoo: Sequoia Press, 1972) is a brief, well written, and well illustrated account of one of Michigan's most important copper mines. A recent study of the mining industry and its impact is Larry Lankton, *Cradle to Grave* (New York, Oxford University Press, 1991).

Concerning politics, Floyd B. Streeter, *Political Parties in Michigan: 1837-1860* (Lansing: Michigan Historical Commission, 1918) is the standard, but dated, analysis. An excellent supplement is Ronald P. Formisano, *The Birth of Mass Political Parties: Michigan, 1827-1861* (Princeton, N. J.: Princeton University Press, 1971) which stresses the ethno-cultural orientation of Michigan politics.

6

Decade of Turmoil

A great reform zeal swept through the United States during the 1840s and 1850s. Religious revivals stressed that man was capable of improving both himself and society. Since these moral crusades for a Utopian America began in western New York, from whence numerous people had emigrated to Michigan, it was to be expected that Michigan would be in the forefront of many reform movements, especially those for temperance and abolition of slavery.

Evils of "Old John Barleycorn"

From its early territorial stage, liquor traffic in Michigan had been restricted. Sale of intoxicating spirits to Indians, minors, servants, soldiers, and prisoners was forbidden, as were all Sunday sales. Liquor vendors were required to be licensed and, in 1845, the state legislature allowed each city, village, and township to vote whether or not it wished to issue licenses. Very few communities chose not to license because fees from sales went directly into the local treasury and were the major source of income for many areas. In 1850 local option ended because the new state constitution forbade issuing of licenses to regulate liquor traffic. Liquor dealers and their attorneys interpreted this to mean that unregulated sale of ardent spirits was legal, and the state supreme court concurred.

Michigan residents opposing the sale and use of "hard liquor" always believed that regulation would be futile, and in 1833 they formed the first of nineteen branches of the Michigan Temperance Society. Initially the organization sought moderation and permitted consumption of an "occasional glass" of wine or beer. However, since whiskey was inexpensive, and permissible substitutes costly, the society was denounced as undemocratic and elitist, and soon temperance advocates were forced into supporting full prohibition.

In 1840 at Baltimore, Maryland, a tailor, carpenter, coach maker, silver plater, and two blacksmiths, all reformed drunkards, formed the Washington Society. They drew up a pledge, signed it, and traveled throughout the country relating their terrible drunken experiences and urging abstinence. The movement reached Michigan in 1841 and, according to one supporter, "spread from town to town, converting everybody by the irresistible power of its advocates."

Meetings were held in nearly every community to warn the citizenry of the evils of demon rum. In Battle Creek in 1841 speakers warned that even one drink could lead to drunkenness, and a local liquor dealer told the cheering crowd that "Washingtonianism had opened his eyes to the evils of liquor selling" and that now every time "he turned the fawcet the gurgling of the liquor sounded to him like cutting men's throats." The final speaker was a Marshall farmer, Robert Hall, who related that when he first arrived his neighbors called him Mr. Robert Hall, then he began to "tipple" and they called him Bob Hall. When "tippling" led to deep drinking, he became "Old Bob Hall," which lasted until he became a drunkard, when his title changed to "Old Hall." Finally, having descended to a gutter drunkard, his neighbors referred to him simply as "Old alco-Hall."

The best known local orator was Augustus Littlejohn of Allegan, who conducted a series of lectures at Climax, Schoolcraft, and Kalamazoo in 1844. He was very professional in his organization and his meetings always followed a pattern: temperance songs, prayer, more songs, a colorful, impassioned speech, signing an abstinence pledge, and closing songs. His power and popularity were further enhanced when liquor dealers attempted to disrupt his meetings.

With passage of prohibition legislation in Maine in 1846 and 1851, models were created which other states could emulate. In 1851 the Michigan legislature drafted a prohibition law, but failed to act upon it. The following year petitions supporting the bill flooded the legislature, and among the petitioners were Governor Robert McClelland, a Democrat, Zachariah Chandler, a Whig, and Isaac P. Christiancy, a Free Soiler. Temperance was an issue that transcended party lines.

On February 12, 1853, the Democratic legislature passed a law "prohibiting the manufacture of intoxicating beverages, and the traffic therein." Under this act liquor could be manufactured for medicinal purposes only, punishments for violators were established, and the legislature was given power to be the sole governing body on the subject of liquor control. Enactment of the law, however, was subject to a popular referendum later that year. If it was rejected by the voters, the law provided for automatic effect in 1870. The election gave overwhelming support for the law, but in 1854 the state supreme court ruled the law invalid on the grounds that the legislature had no authority to pass a bill dependent on a popular vote. In 1855 the Republican-controlled legislature passed the same bill, without the ratification clause, and the court accepted its legality. Clever attorneys soon discovered loopholes in the law and by 1857 Detroit possessed 420 saloons, 56 hotels and tavern bars, 23 breweries, and 6 distilleries.

The war against liquor continued to be waged. In 1874 the Women's Christian Temperance Union was established in Michigan and a Prohibition Party was created. "Red Ribbon Societies" were formed to promote the cause, and organized campaigns to put the question before the voters once again were common. Despite all such pressures, the state legislature not only rescinded the prohibition law in 1875, but also defeated new antiliquor proposals in 1877, 1879, and 1881. Finally, in 1887, a local option law was passed, but ultimately only Van Buren County remained "dry." It was not until 1916 that the state voters again endorsed a state prohibition law.

Bastion of Free Men

Although both the Ordinance of 1787 and a Canadian statute of 1792 forbade slavery in the Northwest Territory and Upper Canada, respectively, involuntary servitude continued in the region for many years. British traders and trappers who roamed the Lakes area after the American Revolution ignored prohibitions on slavery. Even the Jay Treaty, which gave the United States physical possession of the Northwest, circumvented part of the Ordinance of 1787 by stipulating that all settlers and traders could "continue to enjoy, unmolested, all their property of every kind," including slaves. Thus, while no new slaves could be introduced into the region, none could be emancipated either. Nor could slaves look to the Northwest as a safe haven in which to escape, as the Ordinance of 1787 said that all fugitive laborers from other states had to be returned to bondage. Enforcement of this law was strict and as late as 1807 Judge Woodward refused to free two fugitive blacks on the grounds that they would always be slaves by virtue of their past servitude.

As more settlers emigrated to Michigan from abolitionist areas in New England and upstate New York an increased awareness of the immorality and inhumanity of slavery arose. In 1827 the territorial legislature passed a law protecting free blacks from being kidnapped by slave catchers, but the law also clearly defined the black role in society by stating that blacks were neither state citizens nor possessors of any civil rights. Five years later a group of Quakers under the leadership of Elizabeth Margaret Chandler, who wrote poetry and articles for William Lloyd Garrison's abolitionist newspaper *The Liberator*, gathered at Adrian and organized the territory's first antislavery society.

Despite efforts by Quakers, Germans, Jews, and free blacks, Michigan was not immediately won over to the cause of abolition and intense rivalries arose over the issue. In 1833 Detroit residents had to face the slavery question directly when that city underwent what a local newspaper called the "first Negro insurrection." Thornton Blackburn, an escaped slave, had lived with his wife in

Detroit for two years when Kentucky slave catchers arrived to return him to his master. The slavers bribed the sheriff to arrest and jail Blackburn, preparatory for his trip to Kentucky. The day following the arrest, as the prisoner was being taken from the jail, a mob of club- and pistol-wielding whites and blacks attacked the sheriff, killed him and wounded several of his deputies, freed Blackburn and took him to Canada. Terrified Detroit authorities called for a militia to quell the "uprising," and when they arrived the 250-member black community was subjected to indiscriminate beatings and arrests. In response to this violence, Erotius P. Hastings established Detroit's first antislavery society in 1834, and within four years eighteen similar associations were functioning in Michigan.

Antislavery leaders such as Laura Smith Havilland, Erastus Hussey, and Sojourner Truth sought freedom, civil liberty, and suffrage for Michigan's black population. Political leaders of the Whig and Democratic parties, however, were unwilling to go farther than inserting a clause in the state constitution banning slavery. Rebuffed, many abolitionists joined the Liberty Party, led by James Birney of Bay City. While this party was never a major force in Michigan politics, it offered an outlet for Whigs and Democrats to express their displeasure with the positions taken on slavery by the major parties. That dissatisfaction was present, and growing, is evidenced by the fact that in 1840 the Liberty candidate for President received 1 percent of Michigan's popular vote, in 1844 the figure reached 7 percent, and in 1848, under the Free Soil banner, 16 percent; the 1848 figure would have been even greater had not the Democratic candidate been Senator Cass, who received many votes from state loyalty. Ultimately, abolitionist success did not come in politics, but rather through efforts to assist escaped slaves to reach free soil by means of an "Underground Railroad."

The Underground Railroad was so named because it provided secret transportation and used railroad jargon in its messages. Each hiding place was a "station," its owner the "stationmaster," slaves were "fares," and escape routes were "lines." The operation was so secretive that each stationmaster knew only the next station, never the preceding one; thus, if a stationmaster was arrested the chain of stations could not be traced to its usual point of origin in either Kentucky or Missouri. Stations, which could be farmhouses, barns, caves, haystacks, groves of trees, or anything capable of concealing the runaways during the day, were located at ten- to fifteen-mile intervals. At night, slaves would be led on foot or loaded into a wagon bed and covered with hay, and then go to the next station. Occasionally a sympathetic trainman would transport them in a boxcar, making rare instances when the system was truly a railroad.

Stationmasters were alerted to the arrival of runaways by coded messages placed in the personal column of the local newspaper. For example, an advertisement selling "light brown fillys and brown and tan pups," meant that young girls and several mulatto children were arriving.

There were two main routes across the state. The Central Michigan Line

This Union City residence is typical of the many private homes which served as stations for the Underground Railroad.

began at Cassopolis and ran through Schoolcraft, Climax, Battle Creek, Marshall, Albion, Parma, Jackson, Michigan Centre, Dexter, Ann Arbor, Ypsilanti, Plymouth, and Detroit. A Southern Line started at either Hillsdale or Morenci, and went through Adrian, Tecumseh, Ann Arbor, Ypsilanti, Plymouth, and Detroit. In case of discovery, alternate terminals were selected. If Detroit was being watched by slave catchers, either Mount Clemens or Port Huron were used to transport slaves into Canada.

Perhaps the best example of Michigan's antislave fervor in the 1840s is the case of Adam Crosswhite, a mulatto from Kentucky, who, with his family, fled in 1844 via the Underground Railroad and settled in Marshall. In January 1847, their former master sent four slave catchers to bring them back to Kentucky. As they neared the town, an ex-slave known only as "Auction Bell" roused the residents, who met the Kentuckians at the edge of the city. Charles T. Gorham, a prominent businessman, stepped forward and said that Crosswhite was a free man and a struggle would ensue if they tried to seize him. The raiders were arrested, charged with breaking and entering, assault and battery, and illegal possession of firearms, and jailed. In the meantime, Crosswhite and his family were escorted to Canada.

Having lost Crosswhite, the Kentucky master filed suit in federal court seeking damages from Gorham and the other Marshall men who had foiled his attempt to recover his lost property, but the case was dismissed. In mid-1848,

Cass, in an attempt to win Southern support in his bid for the presidency, requested that another trial be held, with a United States Supreme Court Justice presiding. In this trial a carefully selected jury found the Marshall men guilty and ordered them to pay $1,925 restitution. The fine was quickly raised by abolitionists, but Cass's role strengthened the belief that Democrats were the party of slavery and could not be trusted by the foes of that institution.

Another incident which angered Michigan residents also occurred in 1847. Robert Cromwell, who had escaped from his Missouri-owner in 1840 and grown prosperous as a barber in Flint and Detroit, was located by his former master who went to Detroit to reclaim him. The owner bribed the sheriff to bring Cromwell to the courthouse where he would be seized by the owner and his henchmen. Cromwell arrived, was seized and dragged kicking and screaming into the courtroom. District Judge Wilkens, a noted abolitionist, was presiding, however, and he refused to sign a writ allowing Cromwell to be reclaimed. Meanwhile, Cromwell's shouts had attracted the attention of William Lambert and

The famous Underground Railroad had several routes to transport runaway slaves to freedom. On this map, the heavy lines indicate the routes used during the years 1840-60.

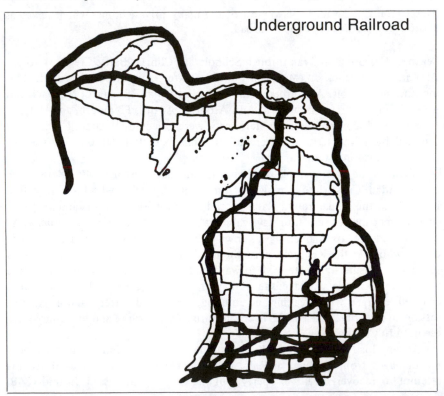

Underground Railroad

STOCKHOLDERS

OF THE UNDERGROUND

R. R. COMPANY

Hold on to Your Stock!!

The market has an upward tendency. By the express train which arrived this morning at 3 o'clock, fifteen thousand dollars worth of human merchandise, consisting of twenty-nine able-bodied men and women, fresh and sound, from the Carolina and Kentucky plantations, have arrived safe at the depot on the other side, where all our sympathising colonization friends may have an opportunity of expressing their sympathy by bringing forward donations of ploughs, &c., farming utensils, pick axes and hoes, and not old clothes; as these emigrants all can till the soil. N. B.—Stockholders don't forget the meeting to-day at 2 o'clock at the ferry on the Canada side. All persons desiring to take stock in this prosperous company, be sure to be on hand. By Order of the

Detroit, April 19, 1853. **BOARD OF DIRECTORS.**

The openness of the Underground Railroad in Detroit by 1853 is seen in this public notice to stationmasters and friends of the operation.

George De Baptiste, two prominent abolitionist leaders, who organized a crowd, freed Cromwell, and took him to Canada. The mob then turned on the Missourian, who was beaten, charged with kidnapping, and jailed. After serving six months while awaiting trial, he was found not guilty. His lengthy pretrial incarceration served as warning to other slave catchers of the treatment they could expect in Michigan.

Other futile raids were made throughout the late 1840s, with Cass County being a special target because of its large black population and proximity to the Indiana state line, which facilitated escape. By 1850, Michigan had become so unsafe for slave agents that Senator Henry Clay, of Kentucky, denounced the state as a "hotbed of radicals and renegades."

In an attempt to stop the Underground Railroad and appease irate Southerners who were threatening civil war, Congress passed the Compromise of 1850 which included a stronger Fugitive Slave Act. By the terms of this law, each state was required by federal statute to return all runaway slaves to their masters. Michigan residents ignored the law and continued the Underground Railroad. One observer noted in 1851 that Underground Railroad traffic increased because the Fugitive Slave Law gave it "more vitality, more activity, more passengers, and more opposition, which invariably accelerates business." In a further show of disregard for federal law, in 1855 the Michigan legislature passed a Personal Liberty Law requiring local prosecutors to defend escaped slaves and forbidding the use of county jails to detain runaways. By 1855 opposition to the Fugitive Slave Act was so widespread that Detroit newspapers carried accounts of "Underground Railroad Operations," which detailed the number of daily arrivals in the city. Michigan had earned the reputation of being a bastion of free men.

As one of the nation's foremost antislavery centers, Michigan attracted many of the country's leading abolitionists. On March 12, 1859, Frederick Douglass, the black abolitionist, spoke to a Detroit audience which included John Brown. After the speech, Brown met with Douglass and local abolitionists to tell them of his planned raid on Harpers Ferry. Douglass urged him to dismiss the idea as too risky. Detroiters disliked the idea also, but only because it did not go far enough. They proposed destroying every church in the South on a given Sunday so that all supporters of slavery could reach Hell at the same time. After Brown's abortive raid and subsequent capture, Michigan abolitionists thought of rescuing him but decided that a dead martyr was more valuable to their cause than a live failure.

The Underground Railroad continued to exist throughout the 1860s, but all of the more than 50,000 slaves who reached Canada, and the thousands more who remained in Michigan to start new lives, had been transported before 1862. On February 7, 1870, a celebration was held in Detroit to mark the official closing of the system. George De Baptiste put the feelings of all into words when he hung a sign on his business door which read: "Notice to all stockholders in the Underground Railway. This office is closed. Hereafter all stockholders will receive dividends according to their merit."

King of the Beaver Islands

During the late 1840s and early 1850s residents of the northern part of the lower peninsula were less concerned with the extension of slavery than with the extension of Mormonism. James Jesse Strang, leader of a band of dissenters opposed to Brigham Young's polygamy policy, took his followers in 1845 from Salt Lake City, Utah, to Racine, Wisconsin, and two years later, in January 1847, to the Beaver Islands in Lake Michigan. Strang's coming enabled Michigan to be the only state ever to have a king ruling over a portion of its territory after its admission to the Union.

Trouble quickly arose between the Mormons and their Gentile, or non-Mormon, neighbors at Mackinac. Fears spread through the Gentile community that hundreds more of the "clannish and ornery Mormon marauders" would follow the initial settlers. Since nearly all of the Gentiles at Mackinac were Catholic, they were furious at the Mormon contention that only Mormons were God's

James Jesse Strang ruled a Mormon settlement on the Beaver Islands and made both himself and the Mormons a political force in Michigan.

chosen people and would inherit the earth, while all nonbelievers would be slain by the Lord. Animosities grew rapidly, and by the summer of 1847, Gentiles were both verbally and physically assailing Mormons. In response, Strang announced that Gentiles were morally bankrupt and survived only by the insidious practice of giving liquor to Indians in return for furs. Concerned that Strang might destroy their profitable business ventures, Mackinac residents bribed ship captains not to bring Mormons to the Beaver Islands and to warn prospective settlers that they would be slain if they tried to join the Mormon colony. Among Gentiles, the cry arose that "the only good Mormon is a dead Mormon!"

Publicly Strang insisted that he was not giving serious attention to Gentile ravings. He claimed that his only interest was to gain complete economic and political control of Mackinac and then to make Mormonism a political force in Michigan. To accomplish this, he expected violence would be required and he was willing to use it. He told his followers that their enemies were God's enemies and that a holy war was necessary to purge the land of its bad blood.

Conditions further deteriorated when Strang announced that on July 8, 1850, he was to be crowned king of the Beaver Islands. Gentiles scoffed, held pageants depicting Strang being crowned with a spittoon, and pledged to throw "King Jimmie" into Lake Michigan. They determined to prevent the coronation by attacking Beaver Island on July 4, and each participant was told to bring his own gun, ammunition, chewing tobacco, and whiskey. Strang learned of the plot and prepared a counterattack. After Mormon cannon fired one shot at the invaders the attack ended and four days later Strang was crowned.

As king, Strang had God-given power to "execute judgment, overthrow the rebellious, punish the wicked, rule the nation, and declare laws." To Strang, anyone who did not pledge him total loyalty was a traitor. This presented political problems, however, as the Beaver Islands were legally part of Mackinac County and subject to state laws. Following a series of arrests for petty violations, Strang realized that state statutes were supreme. He then decided to enter politics, gain power, and have the Beaver Islands made into a separate county under Mormon control.

In 1850 Strang ran a slate of candidates against an anti-Mormon ticket. Even Strang admitted surprise when Mormon bloc voting resulted in the election of his candidates to both the state legislature and county judgeship. Strang finally had his mandate.

As a warning to state authorities and Gentiles, Strang published the following threat, under the guise of a "revelation from God," in his newspaper in February 1851.

Let your fear be upon all men; and the terror of you upon your enemies; for this is the day of vengeance of the Lord, and of your recompense upon your enemies.

Arise and thrash, for I will make thy power iron; the tread of thy foot shall crush; thou shall break in pieces many people, and shall consecrate their spoil unto God, and their dominion to the Lord of the whole earth.

Babylon the Great shall perish before thee. Her cities shall be given to the flames, and the inhabitants to the sword; her government shall be broken to pieces and her dominions taken away.

This was a declaration of war upon Michigan and it made Strang a national figure who was both feared and respected by each major political party. The Whigs and Democrats could not afford to anger Strang and risk losing the Mormon vote in what was expected to be a close election in Michigan in 1852, but neither could they afford to appear so weak that they were appeasing a self-proclaimed king.

In early 1852, President Millard Fillmore, a Whig, decided that his party could gain more votes nationally by being anti-Mormon. Ironically, his decision was based on popular hostility against Brigham Young in Utah, but since Young headed a large, powerful group in the Far West, the President proved his anti-Mormonism against Young's enemy, the weaker and more accessible Strang.

With orders to prosecute all Mormons who defied United States law, the federal district attorney for Michigan set out for the Beaver Islands on the warship *Michigan*, which was laden with cannon, marines, and deputy marshalls. The district attorney seized Strang and thirty-one others and threatened to hang them from the yardarm of the ship if they resisted arrest. Strang assured him that they would go peacefully and stand trial in Detroit. At the trial Strang pleaded that, like Christ, he was being persecuted for his religious beliefs. To the amazement of the district attorney, his carefully selected jury acquitted all the defendants on the grounds that America allowed religious toleration. Triumphantly Strang and the others returned home, and soon afterward the king was elected justice of the peace, township supervisor, chairman of the Board of Health, and member of the state legislature. In the November elections, he delivered the entire Mormon vote to the Democratic Party and, as a reward, the Democratic legislature redistricted the state and made the Beaver Islands a separate county.

Strang believed that he was invincible and he became lax in his control over his followers, concentrating instead on preventing future Gentile invasions. This was an error because many Mormons resented Strang's ever-growing power over their lives. Anti-Strang sentiment gained a leader when a minister, who had been deposed from the church hierarchy for drinking, drew up a plan to join with Gentiles and overthrow the authoritarian ruler. Strang learned of the plot but ignored it, insisting that he was invulnerable to attack.

In June 1856, the warship *Michigan* anchored in the harbor of St. James, but the captain refused to tell Strang why his ship was there. Strang flattered himself by thinking that it had been sent to protect him, as a state legislator, from the rumored assassination plot. Finally, on June 16, an officer invited Strang to come aboard and speak with the captain. When Strang reached the dock, three Mormon plotters shot him, leapt into a longboat manned by a crew from the *Michigan,* and were taken to the ship. The captain then took the assassins to Mackinac where they were greeted by cheering mobs of well-wishers offering them cigars and whiskey.

After Strang's death his followers lost all sense of power and direction. Soon a drunken mob of Gentiles attacked the islands, looted homes and stores, raped women, seized land, livestock, and farm equipment, burned the church and Bibles, and drove all 2,500 Mormons from the islands. Within two weeks of Strang's death, his people were scattered from Green Bay to Chicago, and the kingdom was ended.

Under the Oaks

The 1840s and 1850s saw sweeping political, as well as social, change. During its early years of statehood Michigan was strongly Democratic since most settlers were adherents of the agrarian philosophies of Thomas Jefferson and Andrew Jackson. From 1836 to 1854 Democrats controlled the statehouse for all but two years, and their brief stint out of office in 1840-41 was a result of voter reaction against the depression of 1839 rather than a strengthening of their Whig opposition. During this period the legislature was always dominated by Democrats, and in every presidential election except 1840, that party's candidate easily carried the state. Only a hope that internal factionalism would eventually destroy the Democrats kept the Whig Party functioning.

Whig hopes did have a basis in fact since the Democrats were so badly split that at times it appeared that they attacked each other more vigorously than they did the Whigs. The state party was divided into four major branches: 1) Detroit-based federal patronage appointees who owed their allegiance to incumbent officeholders; 2) fiscal and philosophical conservatives who sought retrenchment in spending and maintenance of the status quo on slavery and other controversial issues; 3) young, liberal abolitionists who were deemed "dangerously radical" by conservatives; and 4) disgruntled westerners who felt the eastern half of the state had too much influence. Despite deep animosities, on election day these warring groups came together and gained victory for the party.

Unfortunately for the Whigs, they too were split, but, unlike the Democrats, they were unable to reconcile their differences for even a day. Conservative merchants and large landholders filled the party treasury but were unwilling to take time from their business ventures to do organizational work or run for office. Party machinery, therefore, fell to young, more liberal men, most of whom were lawyers and abolitionists. Difficulty arose when conservatives refused to support these "radical" candidates, thereby assuring defeat. Conservatives, however, refused to accept responsibility for party losses, choosing instead to blame them on the solidly Democratic Catholic vote.

As the Whig Party swung to the left, many of its conservative members bolted to the American or Know-Nothing Party, which was opposed to Catholics and immigrants. Conservative Democrats, fearing both alien rule of America and civil liberties for blacks, also joined. The Know-Nothings, who received their name by replying "I know nothing about it" to police interrogations concerning destruction of Catholic property, were never a major force in Michigan politics and had disappeared from the state scene by 1856. However, in 1855, at the height of conservative fears, the party did manage to win brief control of local governments in Marshall, Pontiac, Battle Creek, Mt. Clemens, Kalamazoo, and Grand Rapids—all of which had large Protestant and/or ethnic groups with Old World hatred toward Catholics.

To further complicate the political picture, many Whig and Democratic liberals and abolitionists joined the Free Soil Party. By 1850, Michigan, like the rest of the country, was on the threshhold of a major political realignment.

During the 1850s the dominant political issue in Michigan, and the nation, was slavery and its extension into the Western territories. The Compromise of 1850 forestalled the outbreak of a civil war over the question, but displeased nearly everyone. Northerners claimed that maintaining the Fugitive Slave Law was immoral, while Southerners said that the law should be strengthened even more to assure their constitutional right to protection of personal property. The issue broke open again in 1854 with the passage of the Kansas-Nebraska Bill, which repealed that section of the Missouri Compromise of 1820 forbidding slavery in any territory north of a line extending from the southern boundary of Missouri. The new law said that residents of the affected region could vote on whether or not to allow slavery. This plan of "popular sovereignty" had first been proposed by Cass in his 1848 campaign but had been rejected by Northerners who feared expansion of slavery throughout the country and Southerners who believed that since most western settlers were Northerners it was part of a plot to surround and isolate slave states.

Passage of the Kansas-Nebraska Bill caused a popular uproar throughout the North. In Michigan, protest meetings were held at Detroit, Pontiac, Albion, Dexter, Kalamazoo, and numerous other communities. In early 1854, antislavery Democrats and Whigs met with Free Soilers to plan strategy. Joseph Warren,

MASS MEETING!

AT MASON, SEPT. 9th, 1854.

To the People of Ingham County, without distinction of Party:

In view of the recent action of Congress in regard to the organization of Nebraska and Kansas Territories, and the evident designs of the Slave power to attempt still further aggressions upon Freedom, we invite all our Fellow Citizens, without reference to former political associations, who think that the time has arrived for a Union at the North, to protect Liberty from being overthrown and down-trodden, to assemble in

Mass Convention,

On Saturday, the 9th day of September next, at 10 o'clock A. M., at the Court House, in the Village of Mason, for the purpose of putting in nomination suitable persons to fill the County offices, Representative to the State Legislature, delegates to the Congressional and Senatorial Conventions, and to transact such other business as may be deemed expedient.

D. G. McClure, J. W. Holmes, W. Jones, Geo. W. Dart, R. Foster, W. Foster, C. O. Stiles, G. A. Brown, J. W. Soule, A. W. Williams, H A. Ruceght, D. M. Bagley, M. K. North, H. Bisby, J. O. Smith, C. Thomas, H. H. North, Roswell Everitt, O. D. Skinner, Joshua North, H. Lester, F. R. West, J. Paul, M. T Hicks, R Stephens, W M Stephens, H. D. Granger, J. D. Reeves, A. P. Hicks, A. H. Roble, S. S. Gram, C. Reeves, David Hale, R. Howell, K. Johnson, J. N. Bush, H. Baker, H. L. Baker, J R, D. Parker, E. C. Barker, S. Lovell, J. H. Lobdell, J. W. Demerest, W. S. Calking, S L Reed, J. Robson, L. D. Quackinbush, F. N. Grilley, S. A. Tooker, A. Bois, S. Harrington, A Chin, S Sanderson, S Dunn, J W Phelps, John Dunsbach, Jr, Sanford Marsh, Geo Smith, Levi Buck, Geo Ournel, E I, Treat, C White, H Bristol, W H Child, H Convers S R Wilcox, S Cromses, S B Wessels, N Parks, J W Ball, Wm Turner, P C Cook, E F Thompson, N Brace, A Olds, Wm Baldwin, L Merrill, L H Spacer, W F Lindsey, E V Van Epps, E W Cooledge, W B Eldred, T Lester, R W Burdick J T Irish, S Heth, J E North, J North, H Barton, S R Green, Wm Lee, W H Foster, H B Reed, O Webster, S D Newbro, E P Newbro, J H Rowley, A B Bagley, N C Brush, U M Chapple, C C During, John G Flora, W E Root

August 30th, 1854.

After the founding of the Republican Party at Jackson, mass meetings, such as the one called at Mason, were held throughout the state to rally support for the new party.

radical editor of the *Detroit Tribune,* urged a political union "irrespective of old party organizations, for the purpose of agreeing upon some plan of action that shall combine the whole anti-Nebraska, anti-slavery sentiment of the State upon one ticket." Members of all parties seconded this idea and a call went out for a mass meeting to convene at Jackson, July 6. Nearly 1,500 persons assembled on that date and because no building was large enough to accommodate them they gathered in an oak grove. Delegates took the name Republican because they were battling for personal freedom and "against the schemes of aristocracy." A platform calling for repeal of the Kansas-Nebraska Bill and the Fugitive Slave Law was drafted by Jacob Howard, a prominent Detroit attorney and former Whig congressman who was active in the Underground Railroad. Austin Blair, a Free Soiler from Jackson, felt that the platform was too mild and should call for the ending of slavery throughout the nation, but delegates rejected his substitute platform. Finally, candidates for state offices were chosen and a ticket consisting of four Free Soilers, four Whigs, and two Democrats was agreed upon.

To the amazement of most national political observers the new party not only elected Kinsley S. Bingham governor and Jacob Howard attorney general, but also won control of the state legislature. The strength of the party grew and in 1856 it retained all the state offices and control of the legislature, delivered the electoral votes of the state to John C. Frémont, and swept all four congressional seats. With the election of Zachariah Chandler to the Senate in 1857, Republican control of the state was nearly complete. By 1859, when Moses Wisner, of Pontiac, was governor, and Bingham was promoted to the Senate, the Republican Party was firmly in the hands of "radicals" who were willing to destroy slavery and the power of the Democratic Party at any cost—even civil war.

Republican strength in its early years was based on several factors. First, abolitionists were attracted to the party because of its antislavery position; this support was made concrete when the Republican legislature of 1855 passed the Personal Liberty Law. Second, reformers, who were tired of Democratic delays in implementing laws for women's rights and prohibition, turned to the new party, and their support was rewarded by passage of a temperance law and pledges to work for female suffrage. Third, all Protestant churches, except Lutheran, turned to the Republicans, as did the Know-Nothings, as a force to combat the Catholic influence in the Democratic Party. Fourth, farmers, who had been repeatedly denied an agricultural college by the Democratic legislature, voted Republican. Again, Republicans kept faith with their followers, and in 1855 the legislature authorized creation of Michigan Agricultural College outside Lansing. The party was also aided by developing an image of being the friend of both business and labor. Even the new state constitution of 1850, written by a Democratic-controlled convention, seemed to benefit the Republicans. While the document was intended to restrict powers of the governor and legislature, the Republicans used it to set precedents. When their attempts were successful, it strengthened their hold on the government, and when they failed, it was not because of malice but rather a misinterpretation of the wording of the law. Finally, Republicans were fortunate to attract young, vigorous, popular men as candidates, which offset the initial Democratic advantage of having older, well known men such as Lewis Cass, Robert McClelland, Alpheus Felch, and John Barry as their nominees. By 1860 the state Democratic organization was in disarray and Michigan was rapidly gaining a reputation of being one of the most Republican states in the Union.

For Further Reading

While no secondary works exist on early temperance movements in Michigan, several vivid firsthand recollections are available as articles. Among the best are J. Fitzgibbon, "King Alcohol, His Rise, Reign, and Fall in Michigan," *Michigan History*, II (1917); Floyd B. Streeter, "History of Prohibition Legislation in Michigan," *Michigan History*, II (1917); and A.D.P. Van Buren, "Temperance in Pioneer Days," *Michigan Pioneer and Historical Collections*, V (1882) and "Our Temperance Conflict," *Michigan Pioneer and Historical Collections*, XIII (1888). Newspapers, especially the *Ann Arbor Whig* and *Detroit Free Press* also give extensive coverage to the debates over prohibition legislation.

The workings of the Underground Railroad and abolition groups described in detail in Martha Aiken, "The Underground Railroad," *Michigan History*, VI (1922); Charles Barnes, "Battle Creek as a Station on the Underground Railroad," *Michigan Pioneer and Historical Collections*, XXXVIII (1912); William Hobart, "The Crosswhite Case," *Michigan Pioneer and Historical Collections*, XXXVIII (1912); and John C. Patterson, "Marshall Men and Marshall Measures in State and National History," *Michigan Pioneer and Historical Collections*, XXXVIII (1912). An excellent national overview of the development of the abolition movement is Gilbert Barnes, *The Anti-Slavery Impulse, 1830-1844* (New York: Peter Smith, 1933).

Strang and his Mormon colony have been virtually ignored by historians for nearly four decades. The best works on Strang, although hostile to the extreme, are Milo Quaife, *The Kingdom of St. James* (New Haven: Yale University Press, 1930) and O. W. Riegel, *Crown of Glory* (New Haven: Yale University Press, 1935).

Many volumes have been published on the formation of the Republican Party. Standard works are William Stocking, *Under the Oaks* (Detroit: The Detroit Tribune, 1904); Floyd B. Streeter, *Political Parties in Michigan, 1837-1860* (Lansing: Michigan Historical Commission, 1918); and William Livingstone *A History of the Republican Party* (Detroit: W. Livingstone, 1900). A recent volume by Ronald B. Formisano, *The Birth of Mass Political Parties in Michigan, 1827-1861* (Princeton, N. J.: Princeton University Press, 1971) details value conflicts present in society which helped the Republicans. Other useful, though often dated, volumes include Wilmer C. Harris, *Public Life of Zachariah Chandler* (Lansing: Michigan Historical Commission, 1917); Sister Mary Karl George, *Zachariah Chandler: A Political Biography* (East Lansing: Michigan State University Press, 1969); the *Detroit Post and Tribune's* memorial edition, *Zachariah Chandler: An Outline Sketch of His Life and Public Service* (Detroit: Detroit Post and Tribune, 1880); Jean J. L. Fennimore, "Austin Blair: Political Idealist," *Michigan History*, XLVIII (1964); and Henry M. Utley, *Michigan as a Province, Territory, and State*, 4 vol. (New York: The Publishing Society of Michigan, 1906). Election results and all basic information on Michigan politics may be found in the annual *Michigan Manual*.

7

In Defense of the Nation

By 1860 Michigan was solidly Republican and was expected to be instrumental in the election of that party's first President of the United States. Because of his firm antislavery convictions, close personal friendship with Zachariah Chandler, and residency in New York (which, in 1860, was the birthplace of 25 percent of Michigan's population), Senator William H. Seward was the choice of state Republicans for the presidential nomination. In Chicago's Wigwam, which was decked with boughs of Northern Michigan pine, the state's twelve votes were cast on each ballot for Seward. When the nomination went to Abraham Lincoln, the leader of the Michigan delegation, Austin Blair of Jackson, told the convention that Michigan would never lose its affection for Seward but would join with him in support of Lincoln. He then pledged a Republican majority of twenty-five thousand votes in the state for "the gallant son of Illinois."

The campaign was spirited, with Seward visiting the state to speak for the Republican ticket, and Stephen A. Douglas, the Democratic presidential nominee, keynoting Democratic rallies throughout the lower peninsula. The state Republican ticket was headed by Blair, with James Birney of Bay City, son of the famous abolitionist leader, running for lieutenant governor. Democrats countered by nominating for governor John Barry of Constantine, a conservative who had held the position twice previously. In November, Republicans scored an overwhelming triumph, electing Lincoln and Blair by majorities of slightly more than twenty thousand, capturing every state office and congressional seat, and winning all but two seats in the state senate and ten in the state house.

Following Lincoln's election, talk of Southern secession gripped the nation. President James Buchanan did not appear willing to try to save the Union, and took the position that secession was illegal, but so was any attempt by the federal government to prevent it. Buchanan's weakness led Michigan's elder statesman, seventy-eight-year-old Secretary of State Lewis Cass, to resign, saying that he had seen the Constitution born and now he feared that he was seeing it die.

Once South Carolina left the Union in December 1860 events occurred at a rapid pace. Outgoing Governor Moses Wisner addressed the state legislature and urged adoption of a strong resolution in support of the Union and the Constitution. In his emotional message he told the legislators,

This is no time for timid and vacillating councils, when the cry of treason and rebellion is ringing in our ears. . . . Michigan cannot recognize the right of a state to secede from this Union. We believe that the founders of our government designed it to be perpetual, and we cannot consent to have one star obliterated from our flag. . . . I would calmly but firmly declare it to be the fixed determination of Michigan that the federal constitution, the rights of the States, must and shall be preserved.

On January 2, 1861, Blair was sworn in as Michigan's thirteenth governor. In his inaugural address, he warned that the Union had to be maintained at any price, that secession was revolution, and that such treasonous activity had to be punished. Following the lead of the new governor, the legislature emphatically rejected an invitation from Virginia to send delegates to the Washington Peace Conference which was being held in an attempt to devise a nonviolent solution to the nation's problems. In the refusal resolution, the legislature expressed the sentiment of a majority of the state's citizens by stating that "concessions and compromise are not to be entertained or offered to traitors." Senator Chandler, Michigan's most virulent Republican legislator, concurred with this action and wrote Blair that a civil war was desirable because the blood of patriots and tyrants was the "natural manure" of the Tree of Liberty and that "without a little bloodletting" the Union would not be "worth a rush." Michigan would not tolerate compromise on the questions of Union and the extension of slavery into the territories.

On March 15, 1861, the state legislature gave Governor Blair broad powers to furnish men "by draft, voluntary enlistment, or otherwise" to serve in a federal army to put down any rebellion against the central government. This authorization took on added importance when the news of the shelling of Fort Sumter reached Detroit. On April 13, the *Detroit Free Press* ran the headline: "The Blow at Last Fallen. War! War! War! The Confederate Batteries Open on Sumter Yesterday Morning." Three days later Blair met with state officials, businessmen, and civic leaders to raise money to finance equipping one infantry regiment in order to meet the state's quota in Lincoln's call for volunteers. Pledges for $81,020 were received and Michigan's first ninety-day volunteers, the 1st Michigan Infantry, were mustered into the United States Army on May 1. The 1st Michigan Infantry arrived at Washington on May 16, and it is said that Lincoln was so pleased with this tangible demonstration of Western support for the war that he tearfully exclaimed, "Thank God for Michigan!"

The 1st Michigan Infantry presented its colors at Detroit's city hall, May 11, 1861. It was the arrival of these troops at Washington which is supposed to have brought a tearful "Thank God for Michigan" from President Lincoln.

War Politics

On January 2, 1862, Blair addressed a special session of the state legislature which he had assembled to vote on tax measures to finance the war effort. In his message he attacked the Lincoln administration for its conduct of the war and singled out for special criticism the President's refusal to turn the struggle into a crusade to end slavery:

He who is not for the Union, unconditionally, in this mortal struggle, is against it. The highest dictates of patriotism, justice, and humanity combine to demand that the war should be conducted to a speedy close upon principles of the most heroic energy and retributive power. The time for gentle dalliance has long since passed away. We meet an enemy, vindictive, bloodthirsty, and cruel, profoundly in earnest, inspired with an energy and self sacrifice which would honor a good cause, respecting neither laws, constitutions, nor historic memories, fanatically devoted only to his one wicked purpose to destroy the government and establish his slaveholding oligarchy in its stead. To treat this enemy gentle is to incite his derision. To protect his slave property is to help him to butcher our people and burn our houses. No. He must be met with an activity and purpose to equal his own. Hurl the Union forces, which outnumber him two to one, upon his whole line like thunderbolt. . . . If our soldiers must die, do not let it be of the inactivity and diseases of camps, but let them at least have the satisfaction of falling like soldiers, amid the roar of battle, and hearing the shouts of victory. Let us hope that we have not much longer to wait.

In response to this stirring appeal, the legislature passed a resolution stating that "Michigan does not hesitate to say that . . . slavery should be swept from the land, and our country maintained."

Two days later, the Republican legislative caucus selected Jacob M. Howard, of Detroit, to fill the vacancy in the United States Senate caused by the death of Kinsley Bingham. Howard's nomination was opposed by outstate Republicans who supported Blair on the contention that both senators should not reside in Detroit.

War policy dominated the gubernatorial contest in 1862. Blair was easily renominated and ran on a platform calling for the unconditional surrender of the South and support of the Emancipation Proclamation as a necessary war measure. In an attempt to dissociate themselves with "Southern Democratic traitors," Michigan Democrats selected Byron G. Stout, of Pontiac, a former Republican, to head a "Union" ticket. The election reflected declining Northern support in the handling of the war. Blair was reelected, but only by 5,714 votes, and the Union Democrats gained one seat in the congressional delegation, twenty-seven in the state house, and twelve in the state senate.

Following announcement of the Emancipation Proclamation in September 1862, an anti-Radicalism swept Michigan. The powerful and influential *Detroit Free Press* refused to endorse a war to end slavery and called for a negotiated settlement, saying that Lincoln had obviously become a mere puppet of the Radicals. A Monroe County newspaper editorialized that the war had been caused by Northerners and that "Abolitionists in their greed of office" were determined "to prolong the strife as long as possible, destroy the country, and raise hell itself." In Calhoun County, a prominent judge denounced Lincoln as a "damnable Abolitionist" and urged the people "to rise up and hurl him from his chair" before he further sacrificed American soldiers in an "unjust cause."

In early February 1863, heartened by their election successes, Michigan Democrats adopted a state party platform which asserted that the nation was faced with a choice between freedom and despotism. Party leaders contended that Lincoln was a tyrant who was intent on destroying civil liberties through his edicts to suspend the writ of habeas corpus, deny jury trials, limit freedom of speech and the press, and establish martial law in states not in rebellion. In impassioned speeches, delegates attacked the University of Michigan as a hotbed of radicalism and antislavery sentiment, and they reminded the citizens of Michigan that the "United States government was entirely for white men and only white men."

The immediate result of the adoption of this platform was the destruction of the Union Democratic Party. Infuriated by the new direction of their party, prominent "War Democrats," including former governors Lewis Cass and Robert McClelland, announced their allegiance to the Republican Party. To capitalize on this rift in the Democratic ranks, the Republican legislature passed a resolution assuring the people of Michigan that it was

. . . unalterably opposed to any terms of compromise and accommodation with the rebels, while under arms and acting in hostility to the government of the Union, and on this we express but one sentiment—unconditional submission and obedience to the laws and constitution of the Union.

Throughout the war "Peace Democrats" continued to agitate for an end to the struggle by appealing to racial prejudice and war weariness, but to no avail. Calls to restore the Union without the destruction of slavery could not succeed in a state renowned as "the bastion of free men."

In 1864, Michigan delegates to the Republican National Convention supported the renomination of Lincoln, but opposed his choice of Andrew Johnson, a Tennessee "War Democrat," to be his running mate. The delegation stood firm for the Radical incumbent, Hannibal Hamlin, of Maine, and turned to Johnson only to make his nomination unanimous. At the state level, Blair, who had nearly exhausted both his personal fortune and health serving as governor, chose not to run for another term, and the Republicans nominated the wealthy Flint lumber and railroad magnate Henry H. Crapo to succeed him. As in 1862, the conduct of the war was the only issue, but in 1864, this proved beneficial to the Republicans. With the news of General William Tecumseh Sherman's taking of Atlanta thrilling state voters and filling them with hope that the long struggle was nearing an end, they gave the Republican ticket a vote of confidence. Republicans swept every national and state contest, regained the lost congressional seat, and won back seats in the state house and senate. Michigan voters had given a resounding message that they wanted the party that was winning the war to dictate the peace as well.

The Struggle for Freedom

Over 90,000 Michigan men, approximately 23 percent of the state's male population and over half of its military age male population, served in the Union armed forces. Among them were 1,661 blacks, many of whom made up the First Michigan Colored Infantry, which was created in late 1863. Later known as the 102nd Regiment United States Colored Troops, these soldiers were subjected to ridicule by a large segment of the state's residents who believed that blacks were not qualified to fight. The *Detroit Free Press* sneeringly referred to the regiment as the "First Ethiopians," and the Republican *Detroit Adviser and Tribune* regretfully reported high incidents of drunkenness and unruly behavior among black troops. The state's white soldiers wrote songs telling how they were willing to prove their "liberalism" on the race issue by letting "Sambo be murdered in place of myself." Such criticism was unfounded, however, as the 102nd campaigned in South Carolina and Florida during the last months of the war and contributed to the Union victory by destroying miles of Southern railroad.

Another minority which served the country well was the American Indian. During the war more than two hundred of Michigan's Indians, including two chiefs, enlisted in the Union army to, as one put it, "protect the old banner which is the pride of all loyal American people." An Indian company, commanded by Lieutenant Graverat, of Traverse City, was formed in the 1st Michigan Sharpshooters and it compiled an admirable battle record, earning commendation for valor at Spotsylvania.

The "fight for freedom" also drew to its cause thousands of German, Irish, and English immigrants who had not yet received citizenship but wanted to serve their new homeland. In all, Michigan raised thirty regiments of infantry, eleven of cavalry, one of artillery, and one of sharpshooters, while 482 men enlisted in the United States Navy.

Michigan men fought heroically in every theater of the war. They were with McClellan on the Peninsula, Grant in the Wilderness, and Sherman on his "March to the Sea." Individual valor was shown numerous times. At Bull Run General Orlando B. Willcox and his 1st Michigan Infantry suffered heavy losses trying to stem the Rebel advance toward Washington. Major General Israel P. Richardson, of Pontiac, one of the finest officers in the Union army, lost his life leading an assault on an enemy position at Antietam. At Gettysburg the 24th Michigan Infantry, consisting mainly of men from Wayne County and part of the famed "Black Hat" Iron Brigade, proved that its fighting reputation was well deserved. On the first day of the battle they were called upon to hold Seminary Ridge against an overpowering Confederate force. By nightfall the Iron Brigade was forced to retreat with heavy casualties. Of the 496 Michigan soldiers in the fray, 399 lost their lives, but their effort had gained the rest of the Union army enough time to make strategic troop and artillery placements which resulted in the ultimate defeat of Robert E. Lee's army. The 4th and 5th Michigan Infantry fought bravely at Gettysburg as well, helping to secure Big and Little Round Top, while the 7th Michigan Infantry took the brunt of General George Pickett's famous charge on the final day of the battle. Wherever Michigan men served, their commanders always praised their "skill and cool gallantry" under fire.

Of all Michigan's gallant sons who fought in the war perhaps the most famous was George Armstrong Custer, of Monroe, who commanded the Michigan Cavalry Brigade. A West Point graduate who had begun his active service as a lieutenant and aide-de-camp to General George B. McClellan, Custer rose quickly through the ranks. In early June 1862, at the age of twenty-two, he was made captain; later that month he was promoted to brigadier general, the youngest man ever to hold that title; and two years later he became the nation's youngest major general.

As a commander Custer was a striking figure. Major James H. Kidd, of the 6th Michigan Cavalry, recalled,

He was clad in a suit of black velvet elaborately trimmed with gold lace, which ran down the outer seams of his trousers, and almost covered the sleeves of his cavalry jacket. The wide collar of a navy blue shirt was turned down over the collar of his velvet jacket, and a necktie of brilliant crimson was tied in a graceful knot at the throat, the long ends falling carelessly in front. The double rows of buttons on his breast were arranged in groups of twos, indicating the rank of brigadier general. A soft, black hat with wide brim adorned with a gilt cord, and rosette circling a silver star, was worn turned down on one side giving him a rakish air. His golden hair fell in graceful luxuriance nearly or quite to his shoulders, and his upper lip was garnished with a blonde moustache. A sword and belt, gilt spurs and top boots completed his unique outfit.

Custer's attire was a source of pride to himself and his men. Knowing that the most respected infantry unit was identified by their black hats, Custer had his wife make red ties, identical to his own, for each of his soldiers. Soon, to be a "Red Tie" serving with "The Boy General" meant cavalry excellence.

To watch Custer lead a charge was unbelievable and observers said that it was like seeing a "circus rider gone mad." He would be in front of his men, waving either a saber or his hat, and yelling in his high shrill voice, "Come on you Wolverines!" He became so popular that men in other regiments would desert to try to join his force, and once three hundred enlistees petitioned to serve in his command. In return for such devotion, Custer always gave full credit for his victories to his men and blamed only himself for any failure.

Custer's war record was illustrious and earned for him the reputation of being one of the finest cavalry officers in either the Union or Confederate armies. As a reward for his valor, Custer was given the honor of receiving Lee's surrender flag and being present in the McLean house when the Confederate leader surrendered the Army of Northern Virginia to General Ulysses S. Grant. Custer's accomplishments were so appreciated by General Philip Sheridan that he presented the table upon which Lee signed the surrender document to Mrs. Elizabeth Custer, saying that there was "scarcely an individual in our service who has contributed more to bring about this desirable result than your very gallant husband." Grant concurred, adding that Sheridan was the best judge of officers in the army and his confidence in Custer was complete. The Northern people shared in this view and in the postwar victory parades the cheers given Michigan's hero were equal to those afforded Grant.

While Custer was the state's most illustrious soldier, Frank Thompson was its most unusual. Private Thompson enlisted in the Union army in 1861, along with scores of other Flint residents. What made this enlistment different was that in reality Thompson was a male impersonator named Sarah Emma Edmonds. For several years she had masqueraded as a man while selling Bibles to earn a living. In the army she somehow managed to conceal her sex and identity for two years, during which time she served with her comrades in the 2nd Michigan Infantry in the First Bull Run, Peninsula, Antietam, and Fredericksburg campaigns. On several occasions she served as a spy for General McClellan, generally choosing as her disguise that of a woman. In 1863, because of poor health she left the army and returned to civilian life. In 1882 she applied for a pension under her given name. Following a congressional investigation her claim was granted and in 1884 she was awarded full membership in the Veterans Association of the Grand Army of the Republic—the only woman in Michigan to receive such an honor.

Michigan's most unusual occurrence during the war involved the passenger steamer *Philo Parsons*. In 1864 a group of Confederate agents devised a daring scheme to capture the warship U.S.S. *Michigan* on Lake Erie and use it to free several thousand Rebel prisoners held on Johnson's Island near Sandusky, Ohio. The plan called for a Rebel spy to infiltrate the *Michigan's* crew and, on an assigned day, drug the sailors' noon meal, thus disabling them, and making the ship easy prey for a boarding party. On September 19, 1864, at Detroit, a Confederate agent booked passage on the *Philo Parsons* and requested the pilot to stop at both Sandwich and Amherstbergh, Ontario, to pick up some friends who were unable to reach Detroit in time to board. Needing the fares, the pilot agreed. At Amherstbergh a crate was brought aboard which, unbeknownst to the pilot, contained guns and ammunition. Once under way again, the Confederate agent and his men distributed the guns, seized control of the ship, its passengers and crew, and charted a course toward the *Michigan*.

Unfortunately for the Rebels, their plan, which had progressed smoothly, began to fall apart. The governor general of Canada had learned of the plot and, through the British embassy in Washington, warned the American government, which then ordered the arrest of the bogus crewman on the *Michigan*. When the *Parsons* steamed toward the warship, the Rebels were shocked to discover that its guns were manned and ready for an attack. Panic-stricken, the Rebels mutinied and ordered their leader to return the ship to Amherstbergh. Upon reaching that port, the Confederates scuttled the *Parsons* and fled. This abortive raid became more ironic when seven of the Rebels tried to return to the South and were seized and imprisoned on Johnson's Island with the captives they had sought to free.

Having been involved in nearly every aspect of the war effort, it was fitting that Michigan men were involved in one of the final events of the struggle—the capture of Jefferson Davis. When Lee surrendered on April 9, 1865, the 4th

Michigan Cavalry, commanded by Colonel Benjamin D. Pritchard, of Allegan, was campaigning in the Deep South. While in Macon, Georgia, word reached Pritchard that Davis had fled Richmond and was headed toward Macon. On May 7 the 4th Cavalry received orders to search for the Confederate president and prevent him from escaping and reaching the trans-Mississippi region where he might be able to establish a new government and rally the remaining Rebel armies. Three days later, Pritchard's force arrived at the small town of Irwinville and was informed by residents that Davis and his party were camped about a mile and a half away. A predawn raid was made the next day and everyone in the encampment was captured. Pritchard then delivered the most famous prisoner of war to federal authorities at Fortress Monroe in Virginia.

A throng of mourners gathered at the Campus Martius in Detroit on April 16, 1865, to express their grief at news of President Lincoln's death.

As always, the war brought more tragedy than glory. Nearly fifteen thousand of Michigan's military contingent never returned home, while those that did never forgot the horrors of war. These men had not fought and died in vain, however, as their efforts had made certain that freedom and democracy could endure. Governor Crapo echoed the sentiments of all Michigan residents in his proclamation of welcome to the returning soldiers: "Soldiers! You have taught a lesson, not only to the enemies of your country, but to the world, which will never be forgotten."

Life and Labor During the War

During the war the economic growth of the state quickened. Prices and wages rose steadily, demand for manufactured and agricultural goods soared, and as a result industrialists and farmers made fabulous profits.

Because of the shortage of men to work the fields, farmers turned to machinery. Demand for reapers and mowers was so great that suppliers could not meet it. Harrows, cultivators, threshers, and stump lifters became common. Bumper crops of wheat, corn, oats, and rye were sold at record prices to the government as food for the military. Loss of Southern cotton and sugar cane increased the demand for Michigan wool and corn sorghum. While the war raged, Michigan farmers achieved prosperity of which they had never dreamed.

The state's copper-mining industry also boomed during the war, as government orders for brass buttons, copper canteens, and bronze cannons were so numerous that they could not be immediately filled. Even with the incentive of high market prices for every pound of copper produced, severe labor problems resulted in shortages. Mine owners became so desperate that they established a $90,000 fund to finance a Swedish engineer who promised to recruit laborers in Europe. This plan might have worked, as over a hundred Scandinavians arrived at Detroit, but many were lured by army bonuses into the military before they could board the ship which was to take them to the upper peninsula mines. Despite these setbacks, during the war 70 percent of the nation's copper came from Michigan.

Of all the state's industries, lumbering suffered the most, but only by comparison to mining and agriculture. At the start of the war the lumber market was glutted and, even though demand for timber steadily rose, lumbermen did not have sufficient capital to expand their facilities to meet it. By 1865 the price of lumber had doubled its 1861 level but only a fortunate few had been able to use amassed monies to purchase more timber stands. These men made overnight fortunes and most invested their new wealth after the war in the blossoming railroad industry.

In the noneconomic areas of the home front, much was done for the state's military men. In Washington, D.C., a Michigan Soldiers' Relief Association was established to care for emergency needs of Michigan troops in the Army of the Potomac. The association solicited money, clothing, and medical supplies, as well as running a hotel, known as the Michigan Soup House, for Michigan soldiers on leave. In Michigan a local chapter of the relief association collected food, books, clothing, and everything else that friends and relatives thought the men at the front might need. Churches collected and distributed Bibles and religious materials, while women made thousands of bandages to be sent to field hospitals and wrote regularly to loved ones to keep up their morale. Still others contributed to the war effort by purchasing state and federal war bonds. In Michigan, as in the rest of the loyal states, the Civil War was truly one of citizen involvement. Unfortunately, after the battlefield struggle ended, domestic political struggles continued and war hatreds lingered on for years.

For Further Reading

Numerous volumes have been published concerning Michigan's role in the Civil War. Of these, George S. May, *A Bibliography of Printed Sources on Michigan and the Civil War* (Detroit: Wayne State University Press, 1962) and John Robertson, *Michigan in the War* (Lansing: W. S. George & Co., 1882) are invaluable resource tools. The best single volume histories of Michigan's total involvement in the struggle are Frederick Williams, *Michigan Soldiers in the Civil War* (Lansing: Michigan Historical Commission, 1960) and Philip Mason and Paul Pentecost, *From Bull Run to Appomattox* (Detroit: Wayne State University Press, 1961). Frank B. Woodford, *Father Abraham's Children* (Detroit: Wayne State University Press, 1961) is a delightful study of selected persons and events which made Michigan's wartime role unique.

For more specific insight into selected topics, several excellent sources are available. Betty Fladeland, "Alias Franklin Thompson," *Michigan History*, XLII (1958) and "New Light on Sarah Emma Edmonds, Alias Frank Thompson," *Michigan History* XLVII (1963) offer complete details on Michigan's most unusual enlistee. *Michigan Women in the Civil War* (Lansing: Michigan Civil War Centennial Observance Commission, 1963) relates the crucial role played by women in securing the Union victory. Richard Sewell, "Michigan Farmers and the Civil War," *Michigan History*, XLIV (1960) and Herbert Brinks, "The Effect of the Civil War in 1861 on Michigan Lumbering and Mining Industries," *Michigan History*, XLIV (1960) describe the economic impact of the war on Michi-

gan. J. H. Kidd, *Personal Recollections of a Cavalryman* (Ionia: Sentinel Printing Co., 1908) and Washington Gardner, "Civil War Letters," *Michigan History,*
I (1917) put forth the human side of the struggle. Jean Fennimore, "Austin
Blair: Civil War Governor," *Michigan History,* XLIX (1965) offers an excellent
survey of a Michigan wartime leader.

8

Radicals and Reformers

National politics during the thirty-five years following the Civil War traditionally has been depicted as the "Republican Era," a time of one-party rule, scandal, incompetency, and general insensitivity toward the social problems manifesting themselves in a rapidly changing America. Yet, this picture is misleading. Passage of legislation such as the Interstate Commerce Act and the Sherman Anti-Trust Act belie the myth that unregulated business ran the nation. Although politicians were reluctant to discard immediately the Jeffersonian theory of limited government, they did accept the notion of federal responsibility for social and economic reforms, as well as limited regulation of business. It is equally erroneous to characterize the period as one of solid Republican dominance. After 1872 the Democratic Party was always competitive in presidential contests and often controlled the House of Representatives. The United States Senate was continuously in Republican control, but rarely did the victorious party have more than a three-vote margin. Because of the closeness of party strength, both major parties relied on emotional speeches, bands, and parades, rather than issues to bring the faithful to the polls. Avoidance of controversial policy questions was common, as party leaders feared alienating any segment of voters. Consequently, many groups felt left out of the political process and created their own parties in the hope of mustering enough support to convince a major party to adopt their platforms to gain more votes.

Michigan politics were a reflection of the national scene. Ostensibly Michigan was a state which could be relied upon to deliver its electoral votes for the Republican presidential candidate. It was thought to be so safely in the Republican column during this time that no native son was ever seriously considered for a presidential nomination, as that honor went to men living in "swing states" whose electoral votes were in doubt. Every United States senator from 1857 to 1900 was Republican, and Michigan Democrats sent only eleven men to the House of Representatives between 1860 and 1895. Republicans controlled the governorship for all but four years during this time and dominated the state legislature. Yet, Republican dominance was largely illusory. Numerous Republican gubernatorial candidates triumphed only because Democrats and minor parties split the opposition vote. Judicious reapportionment and creation of gerrymandered districts were the only ways Republicans could retain power over the state's congressional delegation and state legislature, which elected United States senators. German and Irish immigrants, who had moved in great numbers into Detroit, were opposed to Republican pledges for prohibitory liquor laws and used their influence to weaken Republican control over Michigan's largest city. Republicans also suffered internal rifts over the issues of paper money, tariff revision, and Detroit's stranglehold of party machinery. Thus, while Republicans represented Michigan's dominant party, their power rested upon an eroding foundation.

Black Suffrage Agitation

Like most Northerners, Michigan residents were ambivalent on the question of black suffrage. Even though Michigan was in the forefront of the antislave movement, in 1850 a proposed amendment to the new state constitution calling for black enfranchisement was defeated by a 7-1 margin. After the war, Senators Jacob M. Howard and Zachariah Chandler strongly backed Radical Reconstruction measures and passage of the Thirteenth, Fourteenth, and Fifteenth Amendments to the United States Constitution, but, at home in Michigan, in 1867 a proposed new state constitution calling for black suffrage was defeated 110,582 to 71,333. Before the election, Democrats and moderate Republicans waged an emotional campaign claiming that blacks were neither mentally competent to cast an intelligent vote nor equals of a white man, and they expressed fears of a mass immigration of blacks to Michigan if the constitution passed. Radical Republicans argued that it was illogical to support black suffrage in the South and oppose it in Michigan, but the soundness of their position was overlooked by the voters.

In 1870 an amendment eliminating racial qualifications for suffrage was narrowly passed by the state's voters. However, residents of the fifteen counties with the largest black population voted against the amendment by sizable majorities. Cynics claimed that the referendum did not mark any change in racial attitudes, but merely a narrow vote of confidence in the newly passed Fifteenth Amendment to the federal constitution, which negated state "white only" clauses to restrict suffrage.

Despite having fought vigorously against black suffrage, Democrats eagerly wooed black voters once they had become eligible for the ballot. Their efforts were stymied, however, as Republican newspapers, such as the *Detroit Tribune*, reminded blacks of the 1863 draft riot in which ". . . a mob of Democrats hunted down and murdered the friends and relatives of the very colored men whose votes they now unblushingly seek." Black delegates were well represented at Republican political conventions and blacks received patronage positions at all government levels. Republicans also supported civil rights legislation and ran black candidates for office. Republicans were, as the Democratic *Detroit Free Press* lamented, the blacks' "best friends."

The Quest for Women's Suffrage

Blacks were not the only group seeking the ballot following the Civil War, as in 1867 delegates to the constitutional convention were deluged with petitions advocating women's suffrage in Michigan. Proponents responded by drafting an amendment granting the franchise to females, but it was defeated 34-31.

Except for giving women the right to vote in school elections, little was done in Michigan during the years 1867-70 to promote women's suffrage. In 1870, the Michigan Suffrage Association and the Northwestern Association were founded, and through their efforts on March 19, 1874, a women's suffrage amendment to the state constitution overwhelmingly passed the legislature. The amendment then was placed on the November ballot to receive the approval of the electorate necessary for it to become law. This referendum was the second of eighteen such votes which would be held in the state between the years 1867 and 1910. Supporters expected that it would succeed because Michigan was a progressive state with a large population, many of whom were descendants of settlers from New England and New York, where women's suffrage had its origins. *Nation* magazine forecast that the "proposal of change" in Michigan would have "greater impact than in any other state in the west." Confident of victory, optimistic suffragists fervently urged passage of the amendment.

The Michigan campaign depended heavily upon appearances by suffrage leaders such as Elizabeth Cady Stanton and Susan B. Anthony. However, "importation of foreigners" who had "grown gray in denouncing the abuse of men, and bemoaning their own unhappy condition" was resented by much of the Michigan press, irrespective of their editorial position on the suffrage issue. Apathy was the major factor, however, working against passage, as most voters did not feel strongly about the question.

In November, the amendment was crushed by a vote of 135,957-40,077. A contributing cause to the defeat was that so-called liquor interests dissuaded Irish and German voters from supporting women's suffrage on the grounds that it would guarantee passage of prohibition legislation. Susan B. Anthony noted bitterly that in Michigan "every whiskey maker, vendor, drinker, gambler, every besotted man was against us."

Following the defeat of 1874, the suffrage movement lapsed into inactivity until 1884 when the Michigan Equal Suffrage Association, with Mary Doe as president and Governor Josiah Begole as vice-president, was founded at Battle

Creek. Shortly thereafter, Michigan's two United States senators, Thomas W. Palmer and Omar D. Conger, made impassioned speeches in Congress advocating national women's suffrage, but to no avail. In 1908, another constitutional convention was convened, but, once again, the resultant new document failed to include a provision for complete female voting privileges, although women taxpayers were allowed to vote on bond issues. Finally, in 1920, after ratification of the Nineteenth Amendment to the federal constitution, an amendment was added to the Michigan constitution giving women equal voting rights.

Senatorial Contests of 1869 and 1871

In 1866, former Governor Blair, who had long aspired election to the United States Senate, mounted a campaign to unseat Chandler. To avert a party split, mutual friends of the two contestants proposed a compromise whereby Blair would withdraw from the race and support the incumbent, who, in turn, would back Blair for the next Senate vacancy in 1871. Blair refused the offer and chose to actively attack Chandler. This proved disastrous since the state legislature was predominantly in favor of Chandler and reelected him by a crushing 75-3 margin.

Two years later, Blair joined William Howard of Grand Rapids and Thomas W. Ferry of Grand Haven in the quest for Jacob Howard's place in the Senate. Blair's cause once again was doomed. In the nominating caucus Republicans from the western side of the state demanded the seat as a reward for furnishing constant Republican majorities. Blair might have weathered the storm of geographic protest, but he could not ride out the turbulence generated by the publication of a private letter he had written in which he slandered both Howard and Ferry and characterized all other senatorial possibilities as "corrupt scoundrels." This personal attack further alienated Blair from party regulars, who gave the nomination to Ferry.

The Liberal Republican Movement

In the 1868 gubernatorial contest, Henry P. Baldwin, of Detroit, easily won election, and two years later was reelected, but only by half of his previous margin. This indication of declining strength concerned state Republican leaders who sought to maintain party power by having the legislature gerrymander congressional districts so that the heavily Democratic counties of Washtenaw, Oakland, and Macomb were split and placed piecemeal with overwhelmingly Republican areas.

During Baldwin's administration, projects initiated by his predecessor, Henry Crapo, were completed. A geological survey of the upper peninsula was made, lock capacity at Sault Ste. Marie was tripled, a ship canal was built from Lake Superior to Portage Lake, and nearly two thousand miles of railroad track were laid in his first two years in office. He supported expansion of the school for the deaf, dumb, and blind at Flint and the asylum for the insane at Kalamazoo, as well as construction of a home for indigent and needy children at Coldwater. In addition, Baldwin recommended to the legislature that a commission be established to study the state's penal, reformatory, and charitable institutions. The study was made and the governor strongly advocated most of the suggested progressive reforms.

Michigan's declining support for the Republican Party was indicative of national sentiments. Revelations of scandal in President Ulysses S. Grant's administration alienated many of the party faithful. Following Grant's renomination in 1872, men such as Charles Francis Adams, Charles Sumner, and Carl Schurz bolted the party and founded the Liberal Republican Party. In Michigan, Liberal Republicans were led by the state's most disgruntled politician, Austin Blair. The former Radical governor echoed the call of the national Liberal organization by urging amnesty for all former Confederates, an end to "bloody shirt" campaigning by Republicans, and elimination of corruption in politics. To further sever his past ties to the regular Republicans, Blair sought, and received, the Liberal Republican nomination for governor to oppose the Republican candidate, John J. Bagley, of Detroit. As might be expected, Blair led the Liberal ticket to a staggering defeat. Only two counties gave either Blair or the Liberal candidate for President, Horace Greeley, a plurality. Blair received only 36 percent of the vote, as angry Republicans denounced their wartime leader as a "traitor" and showed their wrath at the polls. Once again what superficially appeared to be a great show of strength was really more of an indication of opposition weakness.

The Campaign of 1874

Republican fortunes seemed to take another turn for the worse in 1873 when a severe economic depression gripped Michigan and the nation. State farmers, hit hard by the crisis, joined the Patrons of Husbandry, or Grange, in an effort to mobilize their political strength. Within five years Michigan's Grange membership was the ninth highest in the nation. Since most Michigan farmers belonged to the Republican Party, it was faced with mass defections unless it proved responsive to agrarian demands for inflation, prohibition, and regulation of railroads. Unfortunately, Republicans were deeply split on each of these issues.

During the Civil War, the federal government had issued paper currency, called "greenbacks," to expand the amount of money in circulation and finance the war. Following the conflict, a move was begun to redeem all paper funds with gold and silver and to halt printing of "soft money." Michigan's congressional delegation mirrored national and state indecision on this question. Senator Chandler and all but two of the state's nine congressmen supported resumption of specie, or "hard money," payments, while Senator Ferry and the other congressional members opposed it. Ferry argued that the depression had been caused by insufficient currency in circulation, which resulted in lower spending and business closings; to Ferry, further reduction would lead only to more suffering, and, to avoid that, inflation was the only solution. Emotions grew so heated that when Congressman Omar D. Conger warned that unless the economy improved and business increased wages for workers a labor revolt could occur, he was denounced by "hard money" Republicans as being "Communist." Congressional action calling for limited resumption was a compromise which pleased neither side and currency agitation continued for over two decades.

Prohibition was another divisive issue, even though Michigan had had a prohibition statute in effect since 1855. The Republican Party had long been associated with prohibition, primarily as a means of linking Democrats to "whiskey guzzling" Irish Catholics. Prominent Republicans joined "Red Ribbon Clubs," led petition drives for prohibitory legislation, and spoke at antiliquor rallies. However, following the Civil War, Republicans were faced with a dilemma. German-Americans, who had a proclivity to imbibe beer, had supported the Republican Party because of its position on slavery, but now that that question had been resolved they began to demand that their party alter its stand on prohibition. Republican fears increased when state Democrats pledged in 1872 to support temperance rather than prohibition, which drew many Germans from the Republicans. Caught in the midst of this maelstrom, Republican leaders sought the shelter of silence, hoping that by ignoring the liquor question it would fade from public attention. When the issue refused to die by itself, Governor Bagley settled the matter in 1875 by recommending, and receiving from the legislature, repeal of the 1855 statute and the institution of a system of taxation and licensing to regulate liquor traffic.

The question of business regulation, especially control of railroads, was equally damaging to Republicans. Most of the party's prominent members were businessmen who had invested heavily in railroads and who were often lobbyists for special business interests. After the Credit Mobilier scandal, railroad companies were viewed with a critical eye by a reform-minded electorate, and because the scandal had occurred under Grant's administration the Republican Party came under special scrutiny. Once again, Republicans were caught in the midst of an impossible situation: to come out strongly for regulation would alienate the major contributors to the party, but to oppose regulation would imply that Republicans did not care about stopping illegal business practices.

In light of these problems, it is not surprising that the Republicans suffered reverses in 1874. Governor Bagley was reelected by only 3,000 votes, but the party lost 54 seats in the state legislature and three congressional seats.

Zachariah Chandler: Down but Not Out

Democratic resurgence in Michigan in 1874 had an important impact on national, as well as state, politics. Zachariah Chandler's Senate term expired in 1875, and with the Republican majority in the state legislature reduced to ten his reelection was not assured. During his eighteen years in office "Old Zach" had alienated many moderate Republicans by his "coarse behavior," intemperance, unyielding support for black rights, and unending "waving of the bloody shirt" in opposition to any reconstruction policy urging reconciliation with the South. Blatant use of machine politics gave him, and the so-called Detroit Ring of Chandler partisans, complete power over all federal patronage, much to the dismay of younger moderates led by Governor Bagley. Because of his close ties to the Grant administration, Chandler was tainted by the scandals which came to light during the President's second term. These factors combined to make Chandler vulnerable to defeat. When the legislature convened in January 1875, a small number of young Republican lawmakers, mostly from rural southwestern Michigan, joined with Democrats to oust Chandler and replace him with the respected moderate Republican justice of the Michigan Supreme Court, Isaac P. Christiancy.

Chandler bitterly vowed revenge on those "traitors" who had defeated him, and eagerly accepted Grant's offer to serve as secretary of the interior to retain some base of political strength. In 1876 he was made chairman of the Republican National Committee and was instrumental in orchestrating the events which led to the election of Rutherford B. Hayes.

Two years later Chandler was chosen chairman of the Michigan Republican State Committee and brilliantly directed the 1878 campaign. Republicans suffered reverses nationwide, but in Michigan Governor Charles Croswell was reelected to a second term, the entire Republican state ticket was elected, and every congressional district was captured by the Republicans. While this victory was more a result of factionalism among Democrats, Greenbackers, and Prohibitionists than a solid endorsement of Republican policies, nevertheless Chandler was jubilant for once again he was "King of Michigan politics."

In January 1879, amid reports of marital strife and domestic scandal, Senator Christiancy resigned his seat under pressure from President Hayes, who then appointed him minister to Peru. This paved the way for a possible return to the Senate for Chandler. Respected and powerful Radical congressmen Omar D. Conger and Henry Waldron, both of whom aspired promotion to the Senate, threw their support to "the greatest Radical of them all," leaving only ex-Governor Bagley to contest Chandler. The opposition was futile and Chandler won easily. Eyeing the presidential nomination in 1880, Chandler continued his attacks on "Rebel Brigadiers," as Democratic congressmen were derisively dubbed, and warned the nation not to forget past treason committed by Southerners and

Democrats. In November 1879, after delivering one of his famous harangues against Democratic policies, Chandler suffered a fatal stroke. With his passing an era ended in Michigan politics. Radicals and moderates began a grim struggle to claim Chandler's leadership mantle, which further factionalized the already divided Republican Party. The "citadel of Republicanism," as party officials proudly called Michigan, was beginning to crumble.

From Chandler to Pingree

The battle for power first manifested itself in the selection of Chandler's successor. Governor Charles Croswell sought the seat for himself, but did not want to suffer the adverse repercussions which invariably arose from self-appointment to higher office. Thus, he selected Judge Fernando Beaman, of Adrian, who was to serve until the term expired in 1881 and then step aside for Croswell. However, Beaman refused to serve, citing age and ill health, which forced Croswell to nominate another "weak" caretaker. His choice was former Governor Baldwin, a selection which further alienated young moderates in the party, who vowed to oppose Croswell in the future. Two years later, when Baldwin sought reelection, he was opposed by Congressman Conger and ex-Governor Bagley. Conger and Baldwin made an arrangement whereby in case of a stalemate between them the one with the lesser votes in the convention would withdraw and support the other to assure Bagley's defeat. Baldwin did so and Conger was sent to the Senate. The means used to secure his defeat so infuriated Bagley that he moved to California where he lived out the brief remainder of his life. Once again the "Old Guard" had triumphed.

This election was even more significant because it so closely followed the bitter struggle for the gubernatorial nomination in 1880 between wealthy lumberman David Jerome of Saginaw, Thomas W. Palmer of Detroit, and Francis B. Stockbridge of Kalamazoo. After a prolonged contest filled with allegations of bribery, fraud, and slander, Jerome emerged triumphant. In November, the Republican presidential candidate, James A. Garfield, swept to victory in Michigan by a nearly fifty thousand vote margin and carried Jerome into office on his coattails.

Republican newspapers characterized the 1880 election as a "clean sweep" and a "victory by an old time majority," but this enthusiasm proved unfounded. In 1882 Democrats and Greenbackers joined forces to create a Fusion Party. Their gubernatorial standard-bearer was Josiah Begole, a respected, popular former Republican "soft money" congressman from Flint. Governor Jerome came under attack for being aloof, impersonal, intemperate in his drinking, and a tool of vested business interests, and lost his bid for reelection in a close contest. For the first time since the creation of the party in 1854, Republicans had lost control of Michigan's statehouse. More importantly, Republicans discovered that, if their opponents united against them, they were a minority party.

Fusionist control proved short-lived and in 1884 Detroit lumberman Russell Alger recaptured the governor's chair for the Republicans, but only by a mere four thousand votes. Had Begole not been stung by charges of collusion with railroad men in the letting of contracts, his reelection would have been secure.

Public sensitivity to scandal had been heightened by the 1883 contest for the United States Senate seat. Knowledgeable observers were confident that the incumbent, Thomas W. Ferry, would easily be nominated for a third term. However, during the convention, rumors spread that Ferry had been engaged in several questionable financial matters. His denials of any wrongdoing were overshadowed by a charge by Detroit Mayor William Thompson that Ferry had offered him a bribe in return for his support. After nearly two months of struggle and eighty-one ballots, the Republican legislative caucus settled upon Thomas W. Palmer, a wealthy lumberman and former supporter of Zachariah Chandler, for the senatorship. Palmer's election was a milestone of sorts in Michigan politics as it marked the last time a member of the Chandler faction would achieve political prominence.

The years 1886-90 were politically tranquil. To calm out-state fears that the Republican Party had fallen into the grasp of the Detroit based and urban-oriented Michigan Club, the party selected Cyrus G. Luce, a Branch County farmer and former head of the Michigan Grange, to run for governor in 1886. His narrow election over the Fusion candidate, former Democratic congressman George L. Yaple of Mendon, demonstrated the continued stagnation of Republican growth in the state.

The man who ultimately replaced Chandler as Republican kingmaker was James McMillan, a wealthy Detroit businessman. As state Republican chairman, McMillan established a strong political machine. His personal fortune, close ties with railroad and utility magnates, links with the Grand Army of the Republic Veterans Association, and support of the upper peninsula based on his insistence that the region always be represented on the state ticket, formed the nucleus of his political strength.

McMillan's far-reaching influence was shown in the 1887 senatorial race. Senator Conger enjoyed widespread support among the people, but not state legislators, and numerous prominent, wealthy Republicans sought to deny him a second term by using their fortunes to purchase his seat. Moreover, there was pressure from the solidly Republican western side of the state to be represented in the Senate. McMillan, who coveted Palmer's place in 1889 knew that if Conger, who lived in Port Huron, was reelected, the 1889 bid would go to a westerner rather than himself, thus he threw his influence and money behind Francis Stockbridge. With McMillan's aid, Stockbridge narrowly defeated Conger and was sent to Washington as Michigan's second millionaire senator.

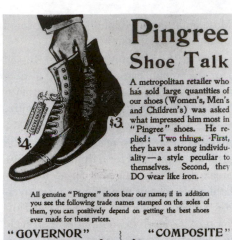

All genuine "Pingree" shoes bear our name; if in addition you see the following trade names stamped on the soles of them, you can positively depend on getting the best shoes ever made for these prices.

"GOVERNOR"   "COMPOSITE"
For Men, $4 $3 For Women

These are special examples of "Pingree" shoemaking. At same prices there are no other shoes so good. They come in all reliable leathers, newest shapes and in various weights, adapted for all occasions, from social functions to street wear.

ASK YOUR DEALER for them and keep asking him until you get them | Write us for Catalog and other information

Hazen Pingree capitalized on his political position by having his company name its best shoe the "Governor." Pingree shoes are said to possess "a strong individuality" and "a style peculiar to themselves"—the same qualities which the governor claimed for himself.

The Pingree Era

The decade of the 1890s opened with continuing reverses for state Republicans. In the 1890 election, Democrats seized control of the statehouse for only the second time in thirty-four years and also gained a majority in the state senate. The only Republican "rising star" was the young, dynamic, progressive mayor of Detroit, Hazen S. Pingree, who had amazed everyone, including his conservative Michigan Club backers, by forging a coalition of businessmen and ethnic groups which carried him to victory in a bastion of Democratic strength.

As mayor, Pingree set the standards which later "progressives" utilized to bring about urban reforms. He constantly battled for the common man against all vested interests, which won him the love of the people and the hatred of his conservative supporters, especially Senator McMillan. When utility companies refused to lower their rates, Pingree called for municipal ownership of gas and light companies; when street railroad firms refused to reduce fares, the mayor threatened to veto their franchise renewal requests and to establish a city-owned transit system; when strikes occurred, Pingree urged arbitration rather than indulging in the common practice of calling in the state militia to act as strikebreakers; and when the Depression of 1893 caused massive hunger, Pingree set aside vacant city lots in which the poor could plant vegetable gardens. To aid those impoverished by the economic collapse, the mayor asked wealthy Detroiters to make financial contributions to a relief fund, but his former backers refused. To shame them, Pingree sold his valuable prize horse at public auction and donated the proceeds to the relief program.

Calls for increased taxes on business, with revenue going to assist the needy, earned Pingree the enmity of nearly every prominent Detroit Republican. Acting from revenge, his former friends attempted to discredit Pingree and ostracize him from the city's elite social circle. They nicknamed the mayor "Potato Patch Pingree" and warned city residents that hordes of potato beetles were headed for Detroit. In addition, his memberships in exclusive clubs were not renewed, banks refused to extend him credit, and his preferred church pew was taken from him. Such petty acts of vindictiveness only increased Pingree's popularity with the masses and he was reelected twice with ever-larger margins.

Pingree soon discovered that many of his proposals for municipal reform were being killed in the conservative Republican state legislature. To be in a position to give more assistance to Detroit, he sought the Republican gubernatorial nomination in 1892 and 1894, but was blocked by Senator McMillan, chairman of the state Republican committee. In 1896, many Republicans realized that their presidential candidate, William McKinley, would have difficulty carrying Michigan on his own, and, in order to assure the success of the national ticket, they urged that Pingree receive the nomination for governor. This was done, and McMillan angrily resigned as state chairman so that he would not have to campaign for a "repugnant" gubernatorial candidate.

During the campaign, Pingree amazed everyone by urging Republicans to split their tickets and vote for him and William Jennings Bryan, the Democratic presidential candidate, whose position on flexible currency was closer to Pingree's own views. The *Detroit News* predicted that a Pingree triumph would be the "greatest personal victory ever achieved by any man in the field of Michigan politics." Pingree campaigned hard and won election by 83,000 votes, which ironically was enough to pull McKinley through as well. Once elected, Pingree again astounded observers by announcing that he was planning to remain as

Republican rally in
Coldwater, 1896.

mayor of Detroit while serving as governor. Told that serving in two offices would constitute conflict of interest, Pingree reluctantly relinquished his mayoral duties.

As governor, Pingree continued to fight for equalized taxation, improved labor standards, and an end to corrupt business practices. Unfortunately, most of Pingree's plans were stopped by a conservative, pro-McMillan bloc in the state senate, whom Pingree derisively called the "Immoral Nineteen." Frustrated, in 1901 Pingree relinquished the governor's chair to his conservative Republican successor, Aaron Bliss, and retired to private life.

Pingree's political legacy was that of social reform. He attempted to revitalize the democratic process and introduce innovative approaches to challenges posed by a new urban society. By skillfully welding a coalition of immigrants and reformers he managed to transcend traditional party lines to defeat the entrenched conservative machine that had dominated Michigan politics for decades. Through Pingree's leadership, Michigan was well prepared to enter an urban-oriented twentieth century.

For Further Reading

While no volume deals exclusively with Michigan politics during the post-Civil War period, insight into the political machinery at work can be gained from William Livingstone, *History of the Republican Party* (Detroit: W. Livingstone, 1900); Harriette M. Dilla, *Politics in Michigan* (New York: Columbia University Press, 1912); and Stephen B. and Vera H. Sarasohn, *Political Party Patterns in Michigan* (Detroit: Wayne State University Press, 1957). Sister Mary Karl George, *Zachariah Chandler: A Political Biography* (East Lansing: Michigan State University Press, 1969) offers an excellent account of the senator's federal career, but neglects his impact on state politics. Melvin Holli, *Reform in Detroit: Hazen S. Pingree and Urban Politics* (New York: Oxford University Press, 1969) is a superior study of the "Father of Urban Progressivism." Radical Republicanism in Michigan is treated in George M. Blackburn, "Radical Motivation: A Case History," *Journal of Negro History* (April 1969) and James C. Mohr (ed.), *Radical Republicans in the North: State Politics During Reconstruction* (Baltimore: Johns Hopkins University Press, 1976). Donald C. Swift and Lawrence E. Ziewacz, "The Election of 1882: A Republican Analysis," *The Journal of the Great Lakes History Conference*, I (1976) discusses the first Republican gubernatorial defeat in the post-Civil War era. Other useful material may be found in Richard M. Doolen, "The National Greenback Party in Michigan Politics," *Michigan History* (June 1963), John Lederle and Rita Feiler Aid, "Michigan State Party Chairmen," *Michigan History* (June 1957), and Lawrence E. Ziewacz, "The Eighty-first Ballot: The Senatorial Struggle of 1883," *Michigan History* (September 1972).

9

Early Ethnic Contributions

In 1860 Michigan's population was 749,113, but by 1890 it had almost tripled, reaching 2,093,889. Detroit, Michigan's largest city, grew at an even more phenomenal pace during that period, increasing from 45,619 to 205,876 or nearly 450 percent. Much of this increase in population was a result of foreign immigration. Between 1860 and 1900 over 700,000 new inhabitants migrated to Michigan, of whom almost 400,000 came from foreign lands. In 1870 Detroit ranked fourteenth among the nation's cities in the size of its foreign-born population, and by 1890, one-fourth of its population was foreign born.

Michigan and Immigration Encouragement

As early as 1845 the state of Michigan actively initiated a policy of attracting new settlers from Europe. Reacting to a joint resolution of the legislature, introduced by State Senator Edwin M. Cust of Livingston County, calling for establishment of an Office of Foreign Emigration in New York, Governor John Barry signed the bill into law March 24, 1845. On April 19, the governor appointed John Almy, of Grand Rapids, as New York agent for landowners seeking to attract settlers to their sparsely populated lands in Ottawa and Kent counties. Almy was paid sixty dollars for two months' work and an additional thirty dollars for the cost of preparing a pamphlet describing Michigan's attractions.

Almy wrote a six-page pamphlet, *State of Michigan—1845—To Emigrants*, which gave general information about the state, praised its resources, and included a map. Over five thousand brochures were printed and distributed to potential immigrants. Although Governor Barry was impressed with Almy's efforts and offered to extend his contract for sixty additional days, Almy declined.

Interest in state-promoted immigration activities did not cease with Almy's retirement. In early 1849 Governor Epaphroditus Ransom sought to encourage

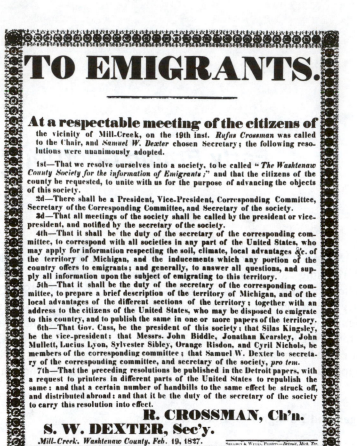

TO EMIGRANTS.

At a respectable meeting of the citizens of

the vicinity of Mill-Creek, on the 19th inst. *Rufus Crossman* was called to the Chair, and *Samuel W. Dexter* chosen Secretary; the following resolutions were unanimously adopted.

1st—That we resolve ourselves into a society, to be called "*The Washtenaw County Society for the information of Emigrants;*" and that the citizens of the county be requested, to unite with us for the purpose of advancing the objects of this society.

2d—There shall be a President, Vice-President, Corresponding Committee, Secretary of the Corresponding Committee, and Secretary of the society.

3d—That all meetings of the society shall be called by the president or vice-president, and notified by the secretary of the society.

4th—That it shall be the duty of the secretary of the corresponding committee, to correspond with all societies in any part of the United States, who may apply for information respecting the soil, climate, local advantages &c. of the territory of Michigan, and the inducements which any portion of the country offers to emigrants; and generally, to answer all questions, and supply all information upon the subject of emigrating to this territory.

5th—That it shall be the duty of the secretary of the corresponding committee, to prepare a brief description of the territory of Michigan, and of the local advantages of the different sections of the territory; together with an address to the citizens of the United States, who may be disposed to emigrate to this country, and to publish the same in one or more papers of the territory.

6th—That Gov. Cass, be the president of this society; that Silas Kingsley, be the vice-president; that Messrs. John Biddle, Jonathan Kearsley, John Mullett, Lucius Lyon, Sylvester Sibley, Orange Risdon, and Cyril Nichols, be members of the corresponding committee; that Samuel W. Dexter be secretary of the corresponding committee, and secretary of the society, *pro tem.*

7th—That the preceding resolutions be published in the Detroit papers, with a request to printers in different parts of the United States to republish the same; and that a certain number of handbills to the same effect be struck off, and distributed abroad; and that it be the duty of the secretary of the society to carry this resolution into effect.

R. CROSSMAN, Ch'n.
S. W. DEXTER, Sec'y.

Mill-Creek, Washtenaw County. Feb. 19, 1827.   Sheldon & Wells, Printers—Detroit, Mich. Ter.

In 1827, Washtenaw County residents formed a society to furnish information on the soil, climate, and desirability of life in Michigan to prospective emigrants.

German and Dutch settlers to emigrate to Michigan. He reinstituted the office of emigrant agent and selected Edward H. Thomson, a former state senator from Flint, to fill the position. By May, Thomson was in New York making contacts with shipping officials. Soon thereafter he prepared a forty-seven-page brochure entitled *The Emigrant's Guide to the State of Michigan*. Printed in English and German, this pamphlet gave a brief description and history of the state, including information about "its rails, climate, markets, agriculture and commercial advantages, imports and exports, the laws relating to education, and many other details of interest and importance to prospective immigrants." During the remainder of 1849, more than fourteen thousand of these glowing advertisements were printed and distributed. An attempt was made in 1850 to continue Thomson's position, but newly reelected Governor Barry refused to act upon a bill which would have provided for funding for the agent and Thomson was recalled.

Nine years later, Thomson, then a member of the state house of representatives, offered a joint resolution for the appropriation of $2,500 to employ an immigration agent. Having passed both houses of the legislature, Governor Moses Wisner signed the proposal into law. Subsequently, two Germans, Rudolph Diepenbeck and George Veenfliet, were appointed to encourage immigration by establishing and manning out-of-state offices in New York and Detroit, respectively. Diepenbeck had five thousand copies of Thomson's booklet reprinted and distributed. By 1861 the agents had been so successful that Governor Wisner reported that in two years more than 1,500 German emigrants, who possessed "a cash capital of $150,000," had been brought to Michigan.

The Civil War halted further extension of the emigration agent program, but in 1869 the legislature appropriated five thousand dollars to hire an emigrant agent to reside in Germany. Max E. Allardt, a lawyer and real estate agent from East Saginaw, was appointed to fill the position. He first made his headquarters in Frankfurt and then moved to Hamburg. Allardt wrote an eight-page booklet, *Der Michigan Wegwiser (The Michigan Guide),* of which approximately thirty different issues were published and distributed primarily in Germany, Bohemia, and Hungary. In 1872, Allardt reported to Governor John J. Bagley that 2,722 Germans had settled in Michigan as a result of his efforts. The governor, however, was not convinced that the results warranted the expense of maintaining a foreign office and in 1874 Allardt was recalled.

Allardt's removal did not end state involvement in active immigrant recruitment. In 1881, Governor David Jerome named Colonel Frederick Morley, a former Detroit newspaper editor, to be commissioner of immigration with his office in Detroit. Like his predecessors, Morley prepared and distributed an advertising brochure. His effort was on a grand scale, as it was 144 pages in length and had a distribution of 42,000 copies. Four years later, Governor Josiah W. Begole, citing that the yearly expense of $11,500 was too high and that Michigan had a surplus of workers, abolished Morley's position. Begole's action, for all practical purposes, ended state involvement in emigration work. Once again, Michigan had been an innovator, as six other states followed its example in active promotion of foreign settlement.

Germans

No group was more eagerly recruited for settlement than the Germans. Staunchly religious, family oriented, industrious, and educated, Germans were viewed as ideal residents for Michigan.

German Lutheran missionaries and settlers arrived in the Ann Arbor area in the 1830s and by 1855 it was estimated that five thousand Germans resided in that region. In 1840 a substantial group of German Catholics founded the settlement of Westphalia in Clinton County, and five years later German Lutherans established Frankenmuth in Saginaw County. Between 1846 and 1855 a combination of poor harvests and the failure of the liberal revolt of 1848 sent more than three million Germans across the Atlantic Ocean. Of that number, many came to Michigan to live with relatives and start new lives. Thus, by 1860, Michigan's German population was nearly thirty-nine thousand.

Germans made many contributions to Michigan's heritage, especially in the area of education. Michigan's basic school laws were derived from the Prussian model, and Bishop Caspar Borgess founded a center for higher education which ultimately became the University of Detroit. Germans were also prominent in lumbering and mining. In the southwestern portion of the state, they pioneered in fruit and berry growing, which became the foundation for the nationally known Benton Harbor Fruit Exchange.

Attempts were made to preserve native cultural traditions through German-language newspapers, schools, churches, fraternal organizations, and organized tours to Germany. With the outbreak of World War I, German-language newspapers were ordered by the federal government to be translated for every post-

Native language appeals, such as this one in German, were made by the state in an effort to attract immigrants.

master before distribution. Speaking and teaching the German language was forbidden, and people with German names were urged by the government either to change them or run the risk of being arrested as traitors. Consequently, World War I resulted not only in the military defeat of Germany, but also in the destruction of much of Michigan's Germanic cultural heritage.

Canadiens and Canadians

Because of its location, Michigan has always been a source of refuge for Canadians. In 1837-38, following an unsuccessful revolt, hundreds of Canadian soldiers fled across the Detroit River to avoid punishment. In the 1840s, British free-trade policies caused a depression in Canadian timber and shipbuilding industries and many workers sought employment in Michigan. During the American Civil War thousands of Canadians came to Michigan to work or join the Union army. Between the years 1870 and 1890, many French Canadiens became disgusted with the failure of the Canadian government to open land for settlement and came to Michigan to work in mining and lumber camps in order to earn enough money to purchase a homestead. The 1890 census reported that there were 63,565 Canadians and 15,436 Canadiens "over ten years of age and engaged in gainful occupations" in Michigan. Of these, nearly 32,000 were farmers, fishermen, or miners, while another 17,000 were engaged in personal or domestic service. Manufacturing occupations attracted approximately 18,000 Canadians and Canadiens, and professional service engaged another 1,200. Most immigrants from across the Detroit River settled in Wayne County, but sizable numbers also migrated to the state's lumber and mining centers in Saginaw and Marquette counties.

English-speaking Canadians melted into the mainstream of American society willingly and easily, but the French-speaking Canadiens were very concerned with preserving their cultural identity. To accomplish this, they established national societies, French newspapers, and Roman Catholic parishes run by Canadien priests. That they ultimately failed in their goal was more a result of scattered settlement patterns than lack of zeal.

The first national society in Michigan was the Lafayette Society, which was founded in 1857. The Association St. Jean-Baptiste was formed in 1864 with the objective of offering a platform for discussion of religious and political questions. The societies grew and in 1869 they invited Mederic Lanctot to speak on the occasion of the centennial of Napoleon's birth. In the course of his address, Lanctot said that Quebec should sever its ties with England and become part of the United States. Members of the French-speaking population were split on this issue, and from that date on dissension over the question of annexation of Quebec destroyed the societies.

With the decline of the national societies, social activity centered around the church, but as years went by only the older French Canadiens persisted in reading native-language newspapers and in making pilgrimages to Quebec. By 1920 a new generation had arisen, seeking assimilation with the rest of Michigan's English-speaking population. Consequently, little remains of Canadien culture in Michigan.

Dutch

One of the more organized immigration efforts undertaken by an ethnic group was that of the Dutch. During the 1840s, a combination of religious dissatisfaction, high taxes, and potato blight convinced many members of the Dutch Reformed Church that they should leave Holland. After rejecting Java and South America as potential settlement sites, the Dutch decided upon the United States. In September 1846, Reverend Albertus Van Raalte, along with his family and fifty-three others, sailed to New York. From there they managed to reach Detroit, where they planned to spend the winter before continuing their trek either to Iowa or Wisconsin. Prominent Detroiters and state legislators persuaded the Dutch to stay in Michigan because it had an established population which was "better educated, more religious, and more enterprising" than that in areas farther west.

Unlike other immigrants, the Dutch went to the extreme western side of the lower peninsula and purchased an area between the Grand and Kalamazoo rivers, where the Black River flows into Macatawa Bay. This location, far from other communities with which to trade, caused financial hardships, and the settlers had to request loans from the Netherlands to sustain them. The Dutch also had problems with their Indian neighbors. In 1847, the Indians, who had sold a portion of their land to the Dutch, planted their crops and then, as was their custom, left to spend the summer hunting and fishing. The Dutch, being unfamiliar with Indian habits, assumed that their neighbors had abandoned the land and they gave it to new settlers. When the Indians returned and found their crops overrun with whites, they demanded that the invaders leave. A temporary settlement was reached, but by 1849 Dutch-Indian relations had deteriorated to such a level that the Indians sold their remaining land in the area to the Dutch and moved north to Traverse Bay. Dutch settlements grew at Grand Haven, Zeeland, Holland, Grand Rapids, and Kalamazoo, and by 1874 over five thousand Dutch called Michigan their home.

Known as excellent farmers, the Dutch earned a reputation for growing celery and made Michigan a leader in its production. Today, the famous windmill in Holland, the annual Tulip Festival, and the Netherlands Museum stand as testimony to the heritage of Michigan's early Dutch settlers.

Cornish and Irish

Originally from Cornwall, a peninsula in England traditionally known for its copper and tin mines, the Cornish represent one of Michigan's most interesting ethnic groups. By the 1850s ores in their native land were becoming depleted and many Cornish found their way first to the lead mines of Wisconsin and then to the copper mines in Michigan's Houghton and Keweenaw counties. Later, they settled in towns such as Ishpeming, Iron Mountain, and Iron River near the Marquette iron range, and in Bessemer, Wakefield, and Ironwood along the Gogebic range.

Cornishmen were strongly independent, staunchly Methodist, and blessed with mining expertise. Because of this latter talent, they generally were hired to serve in a supervisory capacity, either as shift boss or mine captain. Excellent wages, ranging from $65 to $100 a month according to the amount of work each man contracted to do, encouraged workers to write home and urge their relatives to come to Michigan. Legend has it that every time laborers were needed for the mines Cornishmen would quickly recommend a "Cousin Jack" in Cornwall who was eager to come and work.

Some Cornish went into iron mining, but most preferred to mine copper deep in the earth rather than do "bloody ditch digging" for iron. Of the Cornish immigrants who were not miners, nearly all were either Methodist preachers or social workers. By 1900 most of Michigan's Cornish population lived in the Houghton area of the upper peninsula, but large Cornish communities also existed in Grand Rapids and Detroit.

During the years 1846-50, Ireland's great potato famine caused more than 900,000 Irish to emigrate to the United States, and thousands of these new settlers came to Michigan. In Lenawee County so many newcomers arrived that part of the area was named "The Irish Hills." Statewide, the Irish population reached 46,000 by 1900, with strongholds in Wayne, Kent, Houghton, and Marquette counties.

Unlike most other immigrants, the Irish came to Michigan solely to find work. Having few possessions, many Irishmen traveled from county to county mining, digging canals, laying railroad tracks or selling merchandise, especially linen goods. Others, who chose to remain in urban centers, became active in public service employment, particularly in the police and fire departments.

Irish immigrants were devout Roman Catholics who looked to the church for strength and guidance. They preferred to live in isolated Irish communities, such as Detroit's "Corktown," where they could control their own politics, speak openly against Protestants and Englishmen, reminisce about Ireland, read Catholic newspapers, and generally feel free.

The Irish became powerful in the Democratic Party and dominated Detroit politics until the late 1800s. As more non-Irish immigrants arrived in Detroit, the Irish began to feel threatened both economically and politically. Despite their long history of being persecuted and discriminated against in this country, the Irish started a campaign to stop all further immigration to the United States, thereby eliminating new laborers and anti-Irish voters. Failing in this, the Irish steadily lost power in the state and urban governments, and in the twentieth century only Frank Murphy, Frank Fitzgerald, Frank Kelley, and Patrick McNamara have achieved statewide political recognition and influence.

Scandinavians

In 1850 there were only 107 Scandinavians living in Michigan, but by 1890 the number had swollen to over 37,000. Danes, Swedes, Finns, and Norwegians came to Michigan for various reasons. Some were lured by pamphlets which extolled the state's climate and soil; others were recruited by agents for mining, lumbering, or railroad companies; many came to live with relatives and start a new life; still others were drawn to communities such as Grand Rapids which advertised for Scandinavian settlers; and some came simply to avoid military service in their native countries. Regardless of the reasons for their coming, Michigan welcomed Scandinavians as residents because, like the Germans, they were literate, hard-working, religious, and willing to become assimilated.

Swedes constituted the largest number of Scandinavians in Michigan, having strongholds in Kent and Muskegon counties in the lower peninsula and Marquette, Gogebic, Houghton, and Iron counties in the upper peninsula. Bates Township, in Iron County, was regarded as "Little Sweden" because 90 percent of its residents were Swedish. Most Swedes left their native country because of a lack of available farmland, but ironically, once in Michigan, most found jobs in the lumbering and mining industries rather than in agriculture.

Finns, while not as numerous as the Swedes, had as great an impact on the state. Generally Lutheran, Finns believed in strict discipline. They formed numerous temperance associations, workingmen's unions, benefit societies, choirs, and physical culture groups. Dancing, card playing, and theater attendance were forbidden, but all aspects of education were encouraged. In 1896 Suomi College was founded in Hancock, and in 1981, it was the only Finnish institution of higher learning in the United States. Finns were also interested in preserving their cultural heritage and published their own newspapers, calendars, and dual-language dictionaries. Thus, like all other immigrants, Scandinavians helped mold Michigan's society.

The New Immigration

After 1890, most immigrants to the United States came from Southern and Eastern Europe, especially Poland, Hungary, Yugoslavia, and Italy. These immigrants were in striking contrast to their earlier counterparts, as they were usually illiterate, unskilled menial laborers, who chose to live in native-speaking urban ghettos, usually in Detroit, and refused to become assimilated into American society. Despite hostility toward these new immigrants, they did represent the ideal future citizen because they worked hard, were thrifty, craved the status that money would bring, and believed that diligent effort would result in upward social mobility. By 1920 Michigan had 63,000 Poles, 20,000 Hungarians, 56,000 Italians, and 25,000 Yogoslavians as residents.

This influx of new immigrants caused unrest among native Americans and earlier immigrants. Fearing loss of their jobs to these newcomers, they generally agreed with the sentiment expressed in the *Manistee Broadaxe* that it was "time to get out of the asylum business, time to cease to be a dumping ground for the vicious, delinquent product of other nations." The American Protective Association of Michigan, which had been founded in 1890 to save "real Americans" from an influx of Catholics, Mexicans, and Orientals, grew in strength and supported restricted immigration laws. Finally, in 1924, Congress passed the National Origins Act, which restricted the total number of immigrants allowed into the country to 164,000 per year, of whom fewer than 20 percent could come from Southern Europe and none from Asia. Thus, the "Melting Pot" was closed, but the contributions of immigrants to Michigan's economic, cultural, and political development cannot be minimized. Truly, Michigan grew on the muscles of immigrant labor.

Before coming to Michigan, all immigrants first had to register at Ellis Island, New York.

For Further Reading

The two most recent general treatments of immigration and nationality groups are C. Warren Vanderhill, *Settling the Great Lakes Frontier: Immigration in Michigan, 1837-1924* (Lansing: Michigan Historical Commission, 1970) and George P. Graff, *The People of Michigan* (2nd edition, Lansing: Michigan Dept. of Education, Bureau of Library Services, 1974). The role of the emigration agent is covered in two articles from *Michigan History*, William L. Jenks, "Michigan Immigration," XXVIII (1944) and Daniel E. Sutherland, "Michigan Emigrant Agent: Edward H. Thomson" LIX (1975). John Russel, *The Germanic Influence in the Making of Michigan* (Detroit: University of Detroit Press, 1927) covers German contributions. Aleida J. Pieters, *A Dutch Settlement in Michigan* (Grand Rapids: The Reformed Press, Erdmans Co., 1923) is a dated, but useful, story of the Dutch immigration. A. C. Todd, *The Cornish Miner in America* (Glendale: Clark Co., 1967); A. L. Rowse, *The Cousin Jacks: The Cornish in America* (New York: Scribner, 1969); and John Rowe, *The Hard Rock Men: Cornish Immigrants and the North American Mining Frontier* (Liverpool: Liverpool University Press, 1974) are three excellent works on the Cornish. Sister Mary R. Napolska, "The Polish Immigrant in Detroit in 1914" *Annals of the Polish Roman Catholic Union Archives and Museum*, X (1945-46) gives good information on the Poles in Detroit.

There are numerous articles in *Michigan History* concerning ethnic groups in Michigan. Some of the best include: James E. Jopling, "Cornish Miners of the Upper Peninsula," XII (1928); James Fisher, "Michigan's Cornish People," XXIX (1945); Lois Rankin, "Detroit Nationality Groups," XXIII (1939); John Wargelin, "The Finns in Michigan," XXIV (1940); Henry S. Heimonen, "Agricultural Trends in the Upper Peninsula," XLI (1957); and Josias Meulen Dyke, "Dutch Settlements North of Muskegon: 1867-1897," XXXI (1947).

10

Grain, Grangers, and Conservation

Because of Michigan's present status as one of the nation's foremost industrial centers, its long agricultural heritage is often overlooked. As late as 1935, Michigan had more than 18.5 million acres under cultivation and approximately 20 percent of its population listed their occupation as "farmer." By 1970, however, agriculture accounted for a mere 4 percent of the state's production income and only 1.5 percent of the state's residents were farmers. Despite a steady decline in the amount of acres tilled and number of farmers, improved methods of soil usage, high yield seed, and modern equipment have resulted in increased agricultural production. Without question, agriculture is still an important aspect of Michigan's economy, as shown by the 1993 apple harvest of 1.1 billion pounds, valued at $100,000,000, and the more than 130,000,000 pounds of cherries produced annually in Grand Traverse County.

Climate and Soil

Michigan residents are fully aware that the state's climate is unpredictable and can change drastically, within the same area, in a matter of hours. Much of this instability is caused by Michigan's being a peninsula, as the surrounding waters, especially Lake Michigan, greatly affect the state. During the summer months, winds crossing Lake Michigan are cooled, thereby creating a more even climate along western Michigan than anywhere else in the state. Along the Lake Michigan shore the nights are not as cold and the days not as warm as they are farther inland. The western coast also has more sunny days because the land is warmer than the water; thus, westerly winds carrying moisture do not condense and form clouds. In the autumn, Lake Michigan is usually fifteen to twenty degrees warmer than the land and, as a result, the western shore of Michigan has long, mild falls. Autumns, however, are overcast because when the warm, moist lake air comes in contact with the cooler land, it condenses and forms clouds. During the winter, it is this same pattern which causes heavy snowfall in the southwest corner of the state.

Knowledge of climatic conditions is crucial to farmers, who must be aware of the length of the growing season, number of days free from killing frost, and the amount of average rainfall. As might be expected, Michigan has a wide variation in each of these areas. The average number of frost-free days extends from 180 in Berrien County in southwest lower Michigan to 90 in the extreme upper peninsula. Even this is not constant, however, as frost has occurred in the lower peninsula as late as mid-June. Rainfall in the state is nearly perfect for agriculture, with heaviest amounts falling during the growing season of May through July and the least precipitation occurring at harvest time. Average yearly rainfall ranges from twenty-eight inches in drier sections, such as the Thumb, to thirty-six inches along the Indiana border.

Variations are also found in the state's soil composition, and it is not unusual for even small farms to contain several types of soil, each suited to grow only certain crops. All Michigan's soil was originally glacial drift which was carried south by an advancing ice mass. Over long periods of time, the crushed rock weathered and was moved by rivers and streams throughout the state, creating deposits of clay, sand, and swampy muck. Because of the wide range of climate and soil, a great many crops flourish in Michigan.

Effects of the Civil War

The 1860s marked an important transitional period in Michigan's agricultural history. During the early years of statehood, much of Michigan remained in a state of nature. In the early 1850s, a rapid increase in cultivation occurred and the amount of acres put under the plow tripled between the years 1850 and 1860. This massive clearing and tilling is all the more remarkable because it was accomplished almost entirely by hand tools and ox-drawn plows.

Throughout the 1850s new machinery was introduced to the nation's farmers. Michigan agriculturalists were intrigued by Cyrus McCormick's reaper, John Deere's steel plow, Jerome Case's thresher, and a harvester combine invented by their fellow Michiganian Hiram Moore of Climax, but they did not purchase many of them. Two reasons dictated this reluctance to mechanize their farms. First, most Michigan farms were not developed sufficiently for efficient use of machines. Land was still in the process of being cleared, and stump-cluttered fields made machinery impractical. Second, most early farm machinery was horse-powered and, during the pre-Civil War years, Michigan farmers did not own enough horses to operate the new machinery. In the 1830-60 period, settlers used oxen as their primary draft animals. One settler recalled that "in the early days the men who cleared the land used oxen exclusively and the poorer farmers used them for driving about. I don't know how the country could have been cleared if it had not been for oxen. Hauling the forest trees, pulling stumps, and turning over the new soil would have been too heavy work for the strongest draught horses." Although oxen were excellent for clearing and hauling, they moved too slowly to power farm machinery and it was only after the fields had become developed that oxen were replaced by horses.

In the realm of scientific agriculture most frontier farmers were quite backward. They operated under the traditional tenet that a man should work a piece of acreage until it was exhausted and then simply move to another plot. Land seemed limitless and it was deemed foolish to invest money in, and labor upon, depleted soil when fertile virgin territory was readily available. As the state became more settled and land began to grow scarcer, this attitude altered. Farmers realized that productive soil was limited, and they began to practice intensive, rather than extensive, agriculture. Farm journals of the 1850s contained advice on methods to improve land, livestock, and crops. One farmer, angry because his neighbors refused either to experiment with new breeds of livestock or improve their land through proper plowing, wrote the *Michigan Farmer* magazine that he was "sorry to say that a majority of the farmers in this rich town of Grand Blanc . . . do not believe in raising Durham cattle, Spanish sheep, or Suffolk pigs, and some of them think a common two horse plow is just the thing to till corn, and that blind ditches will not pay."

The movement toward commercial farming was accelerated by the opening of Michigan Agricultural College in May 1857 to "improve and teach the science and practice of agriculture." Many state legislators claimed that the school was a waste of money because it was impossible to learn farming from a book. Enough farmers in the state, however, realized that if fertile land was limited, it was essential that soil presently under cultivation be carefully cared for to prolong its productivity. More knowledge concerning fertilizers, crop rotation, cultivation, and pest control was needed, and farmers believed that such information would best be provided by an institution which taught scientific agriculture.

Another reason for farmers' slow acceptance of commercial farming was cost. Most Michigan farmers were closer to poverty than wealth, and farm machinery was expensive. A single-horse thresher adapted to the needs of small grain growers cost $128 in the mid-1850s, and most farmers would have had to borrow money to purchase not only the machine but also the horses necessary to operate it. High equipment costs, coupled with low prices for farm products, reinforced farmers' traditional conservatism and delayed widespread adoption of mechanized farming.

The Civil War had a major impact on Michigan agriculture. When the war began in 1861, a severe manpower shortage hit Michigan farms as large numbers of men enlisted in the Union armed forces. The shortage was alleviated temporarily by women, children, and elderly men working in the fields, but the only permanent solution was mechanization. Farmers began to buy machinery on an unprecedented scale. A Pontiac farmer wrote to *Country Gentleman* maga-

Windmills were a major source of power for farmers. This advertisement extols the virtues of the windmill manufactured by J.G. Gross & Brothers of Saline.

zine that ". . . over two hundred and fifty mowing machines have been sold in this town this season, and the demand was not fully met. Men are of no account now except to vote—steam and horse do the work." The secretary of the Kalamazoo County Agricultural Society noted in 1864:

What a providence, surely, to the American farmer during the present scarcity of labor—the war taking off such a large proportion of the best bone and muscle of the country—that one man, through the aid of improved implements for planting, cultivating, harvesting and threshing, can do the work of ten, at least, under the old-fashioned mode.

Although these statements are exaggerated, it is evident that farm machinery was being used on a wider scale and, for the first time, Michigan had modern farming.

The Civil War also improved the farmers' financial situation and allowed them to make substantial investments both in equipment and land improvements. The federal government spent nearly $6.8 billion during the Civil War for transportation, forage, and subsistence of the army, and much of this amount went to American farmers through price increases on food. For example, in August 1861, red wheat, a major Michigan crop, was listed by the Detroit Board of Trade at 84¢ per bushel. By the end of the war, red wheat was selling for $2.25 per bushel. Soldiers' wages were another source of income for many farm families. The federal government disbursed more than $1.3 billion in wages

The Gale Manufacturing Company of Albion was one of the nation's foremost producers of farm equipment.

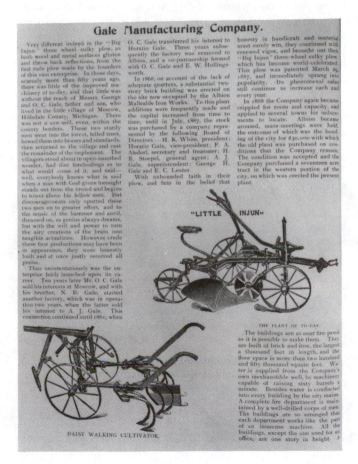

to Union military men, and since many soldiers and sailors were farmers, a portion of this money found its way back to the farm. Massive spending by the federal government created inflation, which helped farmers by enabling them to repay their mortgages with devalued dollars. The war-related financial factors of inflation, increased demands for farm goods, and increased prices combined to give the economic stimulus needed to modernize Michigan's farms. Had it not been for the Civil War, commercial farming would have evolved at a much later date.

Modernization of farming brought with it increased agricultural income and an improved standard of living. During the late 1860s, many farmers moved from log cabins into spacious, white frame houses. To make life more comfortable, farmers bought luxury items such as sewing machines, carpeting, books, furniture, and even bathtubs. A popular luxury item was the screen door, because as a farm woman recalled,

Mosquitoes were one of the torments of early settlers for they had no screen doors or screens for the windows. As dusk came on they would make a smudge by putting damp

The Ralph Josifek family of Antrim County represented a typical Michigan rural household in 1889.

By the turn of the twentieth century, Michigan farmers were using both the traditional horse-drawn wagons and modern machinery in their fields.

chips in a pan and setting fire to them. This pan placed in front of a door would make a smoke screen which kept the pests out. Soon after I was married (1866) we had a screen door which was the first one seen in this neighborhood.

Other items, once manufactured in the home to save money, were now purchased: patent soap substituted for lye soap, kerosene lamps were used instead of candles, and baking powder replaced soda and sour milk. With less household chores and new labor-saving devices in the fields, much of the drudgery inherent in the old style of farming disappeared and life for farmers and their families became more pleasant and prosperous.

One luxury which still eluded most rural Michigan women was professional medical attention. This void often was filled by midwives, known affectionately as "Angels of Mercy." Occasionally these women possessed training, but most relied merely on practical experience. They traveled throughout the farm communities lending their skills, especially in delivering babies, and usually included as many as ten days of postnatal care as part of their service. While there are few written records regarding these women, the role they played in nineteenth- and early twentieth-century Michigan should not be forgotten.

By 1870, modern commercial agriculture, based on mechanization and scientific knowledge of soil, seeds, and livestock, was firmly established in Michigan. This change brought with it a new public evaluation of farmers and their profession. Governor Henry H. Crapo articulated this new rural image in a speech to the state legislature:

Agriculture is no longer what it was once regarded by the majority of other professions of men, and partially admitted by the farmer himself to be—a low, menial employment, a mere drudgery, delving in the soil, a simple round of labors, in which no thought, or mind, or study, was necessary, but it is becoming recognized as a noble science. Formerly, any man who had merely sufficient sense to do just as his father did before him, and to follow his example, and imitate his practice, was regarded as fully competent to become a farmer; and the idea of applying science—of agricultural chemistry—to the business, was sneered at by many of the farmers themselves, denounced as 'book farming,' and resisted as an unwarrantable encroachment upon their own peculiar prerogatives. But at the present time the cultivation of the soil has justly come to be regarded as one of the most noble and dignified callings in which an educated and scientific man can be engaged.

The Patrons of Husbandry

Following the Civil War, several farm organizations emerged, the first of which was the Patrons of Husbandry, or as it was more commonly known, the Grange. Founded in 1867, the Grange was a social, cultural, and educational group intended to bring farm men and women together in a spirit of community cooperation.

The first Michigan Grange chapter was established on June 10, 1872, and by the end of that year six more chapters had been founded. As the effects of the depression of 1873 ravaged the farm community, more Grange chapters sprang up as farmers desperately sought ways to bring about economic salvation. By October 1875, Michigan had the ninth largest Grange membership in the nation with 605 chapters and 33,196 members.

By 1873, the purposes of the Grange had become political and economic. Attacks on railroads, business monopolies, and banks were common. In Michigan, Grangers supported laws to regulate railroads and, in 1874, the state Grange passed a resolution demanding "such legislation as will control and regulate the carrying trade of our country and compel all railroad companies to carry passengers and freight at reasonable and uniform rates."

As part of their program, Grangers established the first large-scale cooperative movement in the nation's history. Stores, grain elevators, warehouses, factories, and insurance companies were created. In Michigan, the cooperatives were very conservative and were operated by county councils and local agencies. A state agent was empowered only to make contracts with manufacturers and dealers. By the late 1870s, firms in Detroit and Chicago were hired to act as agents for filling orders and selling produce, as Grange members realized that they did not possess the experience necessary to make the cooperatives financially successful.

When prosperity returned to the farmers in the late 1870s, Grange membership rapidly declined. A revival was begun in 1881 but the Grange never again

Grange meetings, such as this one held December 1888 at the Ingham County Pomona Hall, were major social events for men, women, and children in Michigan's rural communities.

sought political and economic power. Today, Grange chapters still exist but, once again, they are primarily socially oriented.

Kellogg and Post

Closely linked to Michigan's grain industry was the rise of Battle Creek as the "breakfast food capital of the world." On September 5, 1866, the Seventh Day Adventist Church founded a sanitarium in Battle Creek to promote a regimen of water baths, diet, rest, exercise, fresh air, and health food for its members. Dr. John Harvey Kellogg was named physician-in-chief of the institution, and he was later joined by his brother Will Keith Kellogg. In 1894, the Kellogg brothers, seeking a more digestible substitute for bread, developed the wheat flake. W. K. Kellogg further developed the process, perfected the corn flake, and founded his own company in 1908. Unfortunately, operation of the company created an irrevocable split between the Kellogg brothers. Dr. John Kellogg sold his stock in his brother's company and attempted to establish a competing firm. After a number of lawsuits, in 1920 W. K. Kellogg was granted exclusive rights, except in some minor instances, to use the name "Kellogg" for his cereals.

Meanwhile, in 1891, a young businessman named C. W. Post was hired to work at the Battle Creek santiarium. Impressed by the food served there, in

1894 he began marketing a cereal coffee called "Postum." Four years later he began producing Grape-Nuts cereal and was on his way to becoming a multimillionaire. Kellogg and Post had made Battle Creek the heart of the breakfast food industry.

Twentieth Century Agriculture

Michigan farmers did not share in the economic boom which swept the

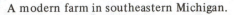

A modern farm in southeastern Michigan.

nation following World War I. Prices for farm products were low and costs for new equipment were rising. In an effort to gain economic security, some farmers turned to other occupations by choice, but countless others were forced to seek new jobs because they lost their farms through delinquent taxes or foreclosure. Consequently, during the 1920s the number of farms in Michigan declined by 13.5 percent, which meant that approximately two million fewer acres were being cultivated.

Many of the remaining farmers turned to specialty crops. Farmers living near urban centers raised poultry, dairy cattle, fruit, and vegetables. Along Lake Michigan, cherries became the staple crop. In the Thumb and Saginaw Valley, beans and sugar beets were major cash crops. Southwestern Michigan farmers grew onions, celery, and mint. In the northern lower peninsula, potatoes, cattle, sheep, and hay were the rule, while the upper peninsula was primarily a dairy region.

The depression drove farmers even deeper into economic ruin. Subsistence farming and sharecropping became common. Ironically, while farm prices sank to new lows, various New Deal programs improved the quality of rural life. Most notable among these were federal road construction projects and the Rural Electrification Act, which brought electricity to four times as many Michigan homes in 1940 than had had access to it ten years earlier.

During the years 1950-79, the number of farms continued to decline, while average farm size rose. Constant improvement of agricultural techniques increased productivity to such a degree that one modern farm worker now produces enough food for twenty people, whereas a century ago a lone laborer produced enough for only four persons.

Another continuing problem affecting Michigan is the high cost of farming. Land prices have soared, wages have risen steadily, and machinery and fuel expenses have become excessive. Conservative estimates show that a person wishing to embark upon a career in agriculture requires a minimum capitalization of $100,000. As costs spiral upward, increasing numbers of farms will fall into the control of major agricultural corporations, who can raise revenue through sales of stock in their "agribusinesses." The era of the family owned and operated farms is rapidly coming to an end.

Waste of Wildlife

While frontier farmers depleted much of Michigan's soil through wasteful agricultural techniques, hunters and fishermen wantonly destroyed much of the state's wildlife. Commercial fishermen strung huge gill and trap nets through spawning beds to catch thousands of fish. Such practices had a built-in weakness, however. The fish were netted as they swam toward the spawning grounds and thus they never had an opportunity to reproduce. Fish living in inland waters fared little better, as fishermen pursued them with hooks, nets, and even dynamite. Perhaps the best example of the scope of waste involved in fishing concerned the grayling, a beautiful game fish which thrived in the Manistee and Au Sable rivers. This fish was not only beautiful, with a dorsal fin having a rainbow of colors, but was also delicious. Over-eager sportsmen sought the grayling avidly, often measuring their skill by the number of bushel barrels they filled. In 1871, a party along the Au Sable caught so many grayling that they left more than two thousand on the shore to rot.

Birds were sought with equal vigor. Quail, grouse, and prairie chickens were killed in such numbers that in many southern Michigan areas they were extinct by 1865. The prairie chicken, for instance, was hunted with every type of gun available. Most popular was the swivel, or punt, gun, which was similar to a small cannon placed on a pole and fired one-half pound of lead balls at a time.

The most tragic example of aviary slaughter involved the passenger pigeon. These beautiful birds arrived in Michigan in early March and remained until early autumn. When they returned to Michigan, residents recalled that the flocks were so large that they blocked out the sun for several hours. Unfortunately, like the grayling, passenger pigeons were delicious as well as beautiful. Because they brought between one and two dollars apiece in the marketplace, professional hunters systematically attacked their nesting places using poles, nets, guns, axes, and fire either to kill or capture the birds. Most slain birds were salted and shipped to markets in Chicago and New York. Many captured birds were distributed to state and national shooting clubs, where during tournaments they would be released one at a time to be fired upon by target shooters—they were live "clay pigeons."

The most devastating slaughter of these birds occurred in Petoskey during March through June 1878. Professional hunters moved in on roosting birds and toppled their low-lying nests, while others set up nets to snare fleeing pigeons. By June, more than one million passenger pigeons had been slain in Petoskey. Massacres such as this continued until by 1914 the species had become extinct.

Similar mass executions were performed by hunters upon deer, especially the Virginia white-tail. Deer were shot, trapped, poisoned, and snared. Hunters shot them as they crossed streams and set out lanterns to cause them to "freeze" at night at the sight of the light, thereby creating an easy target.

While this was occurring, efforts were being made to try to preserve some wildlife. In 1859, the Michigan legislature passed a law forbidding the killing of deer from January 1 to August 1 and the hunting of wild turkey, partridge, and woodcock from February 1 to October 1 annually, so that mating could occur and the species replenish. A five dollar fine was imposed upon violators, but enforcement was lax. By 1863, laws had been passed to protect swans and beavers, and the use of swivel guns was prohibited. In 1871, legislation to protect the grayling and trout was enacted and the use of gill nets was outlawed. Ten years later, Michigan passed the landmark Anti-Market Hunting Act in response to reports that more than one hundred thousand deer had been slain in the state during 1880 by commercial hunters. This law made it illegal to kill any deer or game birds except for consumption within the state. No longer could slain wildlife be shipped to national markets.

Laws are meaningless without strict enforcement and, in many localities, that was difficult to obtain. Thus, in 1887, Michigan became the first state in the nation to hire a full-time game warden. William Alden Smith, the initial game warden, was effective and obtained 220 convictions in his first year in office, compared to a mere 22 the previous year.

In the early 1900s a massive reforestation program was instituted to plant new trees to provide cover for wildlife. Game farms were established to raise birds and animals for transport to areas where they had become extinct or greatly diminished in number. Fish-breeding centers were created and foreign fish, such as the carp, were imported. By 1920, nearly all the conservation principles in practice today had been adopted in Michigan. The Wolverine State has always been in the forefront of the conservation movement, and with Michigan State University's forestry, fishery, and wildlife programs, it remains among the nation's leaders in seeking new ways to protect wildlife and the environment. Michiganians' pride in this endeavor, however, must be tempered by the realization that such programs were made necessary because of the senseless waste of natural resources and wildlife which was practiced by the state's citizens during the early and mid-nineteenth century.

For Further Reading

No works have been published dealing exclusively with Michigan's agricultural growth. County histories and the *Michigan Farmer* magazine offer some insight into rural life, but they are limited in scope. Two articles have been written concerning the effects of the Civil War upon Michigan farmers: Joseph J. Marks (ed.), *Effects of the Civil War on Farming in Michigan* (Lansing: Michigan Civil War Centennial Observance Commission, 1965) and Richard H. Sewell, "Michigan Farmers and the Civil War," *Michigan History,* XLIV (December 1960). The rise of the Grange is recounted in Ford Trump, *The Grange in Michigan* (Grand Rapids: Dean Hicks Co., 1963); Solon J. Buck, *The Granger Movement* (Cambridge: Harvard University Press, 1913); and Kenyon L. Butterfield, "Recent Grange Work in Michigan," *Outlook* (September 17, 1898). Statistical analysis of land usage may be found in Lawrence M. Sommers (ed.), *Atlas of Michigan* (East Lansing: Michigan State University Press, 1977). An excellent account of conservation is Eugene T. Peterson, *Conservation of Michigan's Natural Resources* (Lansing: Michigan Historical Commission, 1960). Pauline Adams and Emma S. Thornton, *A Populist Assault: Sarah E. Van De Wort Emery on American Democracy, 1862-1885* (Bowling Green State University Press, 1989) chronicles the career of a Michigan woman as a political and social activist.

11

Development of Intellectual Maturity

In many ways, Michigan has been a leader in educational development. During British rule, public schools were established for children of soldiers and families living at, or near, military outposts, while private schools were opened for the offspring of officers and wealthy merchants. As settlers trickled into Michigan from the East, they brought with them the Puritan beliefs that education was godly, ignorance the tool of the devil, and a moral society could only result from an educated citizenry. As a result of this background, it was easy for Michigan to uphold the wish of the Ordinance of 1787 that "schools and the means of education shall forever be encouraged" in the Northwest Territory.

School Laws and Financing

In 1809, the territorial council passed a law imposing upon families with school-age children a tax of $2 to $4 per child to support public education. While this levy was rarely collected, it did set the precedent for taxation to maintain schools. Eighteen years later the territorial legislature adopted a primary-school law based on that of Massachusetts. Under this act, every township with fifty or more residents had to hire a teacher "of good morals" to offer instruction, over a six-month period, in reading, writing, arithmetic, English, French, and decent behavior. If a township possessed over two hundred inhabitants, it was required to have a "higher school" which offered advanced training in the basic skills as well as Latin. In 1829 this law was revised, and the provision regarding the types of schools to be maintained according to population was repealed. Under the amended law each township was to elect five commissioners who would divide the township into districts. In each district, three men would then be elected to supply reports to the superintendent of common schools and oversee all educational matters. These early statutes, even though never fully enforced, created the cornerstone for Michigan's program of public education by establishing that schooling was to be nondenominational, state operated, and tax supported. They also made clear that while individual localities could run their own primary schools, the state retained the right to determine curriculum, set the length of the school year, and inspect institutions of learning for adherence to state regulations.

Michigan's public-school system during the early years of statehood is reputedly based on ideas formulated by Reverend John D. Pierce and General Isaac Crary as they sat under an oak tree near their Marshall home. This story has made the tree famous as the state's "educational oak," but it should be noted that the two men had engaged in extensive research before finalizing their plans under the shady oak boughs.

During the winter of 1834-35, Crary, an attorney, and Pierce, a member of the Home Missionary Society of the Congregational Church, studied Victor Cousin's *Report on the Condition of Public Instruction in Germany and Particularly Prussia.* Cousin, a leading French philosopher, educator, and member of the French Council of Public Education, said that in Germany the state supervised a highly efficient centralized program of public education. Impressed by this report, and convinced that such an authoritarian system would not be inconsistent within a democracy, Crary and Pierce, who had been delegated to write the article on education for the proposed Michigan constitution, incorporated several German concepts into their document. Consequently, Article X of the first Michigan state constitution included many liberal, farsighted, and innovative ideas on education. For example, this 1835 constitution authorized the state to hire a superintendent of public instruction who was to watch over "not only the primary schools, but also the university, the academies, and schools of other kinds." While several other states had created a similar position by an act of the legislature, only Michigan had the post made permanent by its constitution. The constitution also stated that libraries should be created as soon as possible in every township and that schools had to be open a minimum of three months every year.

Financing of schools was determined by the new constitution as well. Under the Ordinance of 1785, section sixteen of every township in the Northwest Territory was set aside for educational purposes, with funds raised by the sale of public lands therein having to be spent in support of schools. By this provision, Michigan received approximately one million acres of land. The average sale price proved to be $4.58 per acre, which was less than half of what state officials hoped to receive, but was still $1.00 per acre more than the average in Indiana and Illinois and nearly $3.00 more than that in Wisconsin. The money raised, known as the primary school fund, was either banked or invested, with the interest divided annually among each school district which had been open at least three months during the year. The amount each district received was determined by the number of pupils between the ages of five and seventeen who had attended school. Later, this fund was augmented by tax

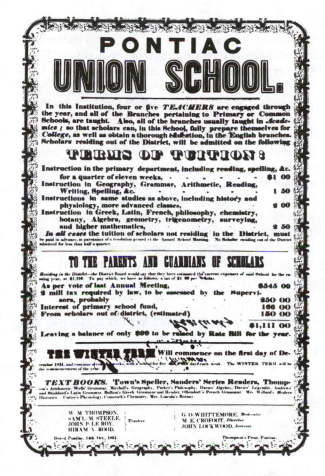

School operating costs, tuition payments, and courses offered in the Pontiac Union School in 1851 are detailed in this announcement to the parents of school-age children in the district.

monies on railroads, telephone and telegraph companies, and a percentage of estate and inheritance taxes. Financing of schools through the primary school fund and primary interest fund continued until 1964 when the state legislature, in accordance with the new state constitution, passed a law that all funding of education should come from the state general fund.

The 1835 constitution also expanded the Ordinance of 1785 to include support of higher education. Under its provisions, "the monies obtained from public land sales granted by the United States for the support of a University, shall be, and remain, a permanent fund for the support of said University with such branches as the public may hereafter demand for the promotion of literature, the arts and sciences, and as may be authorized by the terms of such grant." Moreover, the state persuaded the federal government that funds from land sales should be given to the state, rather than townships, for disbursement.

Despite receiving land grants and other monies, Michigan did not always have free public education. In the early years "rate bills," or tuition statements, were issued by local governments to each family having children in school. Since each child was "rated," or taxed, whenever parents were short of money they simply kept one or more of their children home to reduce their school tax. Moreover, parents were expected to share in the payment of the teacher's salary, provide a portion of his or her housing, and help furnish firewood for the schoolhouse. As a result of these additional demands, many poor families, who felt that they could not contribute their fair share toward the maintenance of the school and were too proud to accept offers for free schooling, refused to send their children to be educated.

John D. Pierce, who became Michigan's first superintendent of public instruction upon the recommendation of his friend Isaac Crary, who had been elected the state's first representative to Congress, urged the necessity of state funding for public schools. He sought to create a comprehensive school system which would be properly staffed and uniformly supervised. In his report to the legislature in 1837, he said that the state should

The first public school district in Michigan was created in 1827 at Monroe. The Bridge School, built in the 1860s, was used until 1955 when it closed following the consolidation of the Monroe School District with that of Dundee.

place the public schools upon high and educated ground, to make them adequate to the wants of the whole community; to place them on such footing as to furnish the best instruction, not only in the more common, but in all the higher branches of elementary knowledge; so that those who send to them may have the satisfaction of knowing that their children are receiving good instruction, as the wealth of the Indies can provide.

Unfortunately, the legislature refused to pass a law for statewide free primary public education until 1869.

In the meantime, Detroit took a bold initiative and, in 1844, established a free public high school. Subsequently several other cities did the same. This was not always a popular step, however. In 1873 a group of Kalamazoo citizens filed a suit against their city for using taxes to support the local high school. The court upheld the city's position, but the decision was appealed to the state supreme court. On July 21, 1874, Justice Thomas M. Cooley spoke for the majority of the court in upholding the lower court verdict. In his ruling he said,

If these facts do not demonstrate clearly and conclusively a general state policy, beginning in 1817 and continuing until after the adoption of the present Constitution in the direction of free schools in which education, and at their option the elements of classical education might be brought within the reach of all the children of the state, then, as it seems to us, nothing can demonstrate it. We might follow the subject further, and show that the subsequent legislation has all concurred with this policy, but it would be a waste of time and labor. We content ourselves with the statement that neither in our state policy, in our Constitution, or in our laws, do we find the primary school districts restricted in the branches of knowledge which their officers may cause to be taught, or the grade of instruction that may be given, if their voters consent in regular form to bear the expense and raise the taxes for the purpose.

Cooley's opinion helped convince state residents of the propriety of state-funded education. Pierce's dream had finally become an accepted reality.

Teachers, Students, and the "Little Red Schoolhouse"

Like all states, Michigan had the famed "little red schoolhouses," so named because they were both little and painted red—a color chosen because it was common, inexpensive, and did not show dirt. Michigan had so many of these schools that a traveler from New York remarked in 1872 that Michigan should be renamed "The School House State."

Before the Civil War nearly all schoolhouses were made of logs, but after 1865 most were of frame, and later brick, construction. Initially, nearly all were one-room structures, usually eighteen-by-twenty feet, and were cold, drafty, and poorly lit. A stove furnished heat in winter, but rarely were lamps available to augment natural light. Schools generally housed twenty to thirty students, ranging in age from five to seventeen years. Long planks served as desks, while planks placed at a lower level formed bench seats. In the front of the room, which was near the warmth of the stove in winter and the open door in the spring and autumn, was the teacher's table on which were kept an inkwell, quill pens, a cherry ruler used both to draw straight lines and crack knuckles, and a birch rod to assure proper classroom behavior. Since it was commonly believed that boys were "totally depraved," discipline was stern and intended to embarrass the offender. Common punishments were having to wear a dunce cap while sitting in a corner, sitting with the girls, and standing on one leg for an hour in front of the class. Usually schools had no blackboards, texts, or paper. During the pre-Civil War years paper was so expensive that students wrote their alphabet and lessons with their fingers in trays of moist sand. Likewise, during that period, reading was often taught from a book the child brought from home, usually the Bible. By the 1870s, however, readers, spellers, arithmetic books, and geography texts were furnished, and many rural school districts were consolidating to form "union districts" in order to furnish a higher quality of education. Nevertheless, one-room schools were still the rule in Michigan until the late 1920s.

Teachers were often ill-trained persons who viewed their occupation as a temporary means of earning a living until something better presented itself. Each school district set its own hiring standards and, in many instances, the only requirements were that the teacher be able to read, write, do arithmetic, and be able to defeat the strongest boy in school in a fistfight. Consequently, women usually were hired to teach only during the summer when the biggest boys were working in the fields and only small children were in school. Low standards were matched by low salaries, and in the late 1880s, even a wealthy community such as Saginaw paid its male teachers a meager $7 a week and females only $4.

Lack of standards brought many totally unqualified persons into the classroom and often physical cruelty was the result. In Clare, for example, a teacher was fired in 1878 for beating a boy about the head so severely that the lad's eardrums burst and bled. After being removed, the man found another teaching position almost immediately in a nearby town that admired his "physical approach" to learning. Other instances of excessive punishment included breaking a student's leg with a rod and giving fifty lashes for throwing snowballs during recess. During the 1870s and 1880s teachers maintained, however, that such force was necessary because students were bringing loaded revolvers, knives, and dynamite caps to school. A popular saying of the time was "I'm going to fill your head with lead," and many students seemed to want to take a literal interpretation of that warning. In any case, savage abuse was common in nearly all schools during the late nineteenth century.

Even though it was common knowledge that many public schoolteachers were incompetent, the state legislature did not pass a law requiring that teachers

The Collins School, east of Reed's Lake, was typical of the many one-room country schools in Michigan shortly after the turn of the twentieth century.

needed at least one year of training until 1925. As late as 1928, anyone with three years' experience could receive a lifetime teaching certificate from the state. Quality of instruction was so poor in the public schools that in some areas of the state parents chose to send their children to federally supported Indian schools which paid teachers higher salaries and demanded much more rigorous qualifications to be hired.

Despite their lack of professional competence, in 1852 Michigan teachers formed a union. The Michigan State Teachers' Association, which became the Michigan Education Association, lobbied for better financing of schools and increased salaries for teachers. Membership grew slowly, however, and it was not until the early 1900s that more than 1 percent of the state's teachers joined the union.

Student attendance was irregular. Parents considered their children as a source of cheap labor, and school was a luxury which could not be afforded during planting and harvesting seasons. To avoid this problem, schools generally opened in mid-October, after the harvest, and closed in late March, before planting. This schedule gave the district enough flexibility to miss a few weeks and still be open the three months necessary to be eligible for state aid. A compulsory attendance law was not passed until 1871, and then it only required children between the ages of eight to fourteen to attend school for at least twelve weeks. In 1883 the length of attendance was increased to sixteen weeks, but the law was rarely enforced. Finally, in 1905, the legislature passed an act requiring all children between the ages of seven and sixteen to attend school for a full nine-month academic year and funds were allocated for districts to hire truant officers to enforce the law.

Higher Education

The first plan for higher education in Michigan came in 1817 when Territorial Judge Augustus Woodward drafted a grandiose scheme for a Catholepistemiad, or University of Michigania. Woodward had previously written a book in which he categorized all human knowledge into thirteen areas and thus he proposed a college with a professorship in each of those subjects. The professors and head of the university were also to "establish colleges, academies, libraries, museums, atheneums, botanic gardens, laboratories, and other useful literary and scientific institutions." Woodward's idea was not merely to create a college but rather to establish an outline for a "complete system of education extending from the lowest grade of primary school to the highest level of college," supported by a 15 percent increase in public taxation, lotteries, and tuition payments. Unfortunately, Governor Lewis Cass was unable to find thirteen qualified men to fill the professorships. Finally, Reverends John Monteith and Gabriel Richard were hired to run the single-building institution, with the former responsible for seven subjects and the latter six.

The university was a disaster. It was too expensive for the struggling territory to support and its name elicited derisive laughter. Even Cass could not pronounce its title and referred to it as the "Cathole-what's-its-name." In 1821 territorial officials repealed the law providing for the Catholepistemiad and then empowered twenty-one trustees to "establish colleges, academies, and to inspect them, to make laws for the government; to appoint all members of the teaching body, fix their salaries, discharge them if thought best; and to control funds." However, no action was taken.

In 1837, Superintendent Pierce urged the state legislature to create a university, with branch campuses throughout the state, which would be controlled by a Board of Regents. In March of that year, the legislature passed a bill establishing the University of Michigan, which was to have three departments: law, medicine, and literature, science, and the arts. As Pierce had suggested, a Board of Regents was appointed and given power to control the university and create nondegree-granting branch universities. The legislature also provided for the eventual founding of departments of agriculture and teacher education, as well as a school for female education whenever sufficient funds were available.

The University of Michigan opened in 1841 with two professors, one in mathematics and the other in language, and six students. Branch campuses were created at Pontiac, Monroe, Kalamazoo, Detroit, Niles, White Pigeon, Tecumseh, and Romeo, but by 1846 financial support had been withdrawn and all were closed.

During its first years in existence, the University of Michigan was beset by problems. The medical school did not open until 1850 and the law school until 1859. Angry citizens complained about fraternities on campus and immorality caused by nonministerial faculty. Churches lobbied for a religiously oriented university and, as a compromise, the Board of Regents, who were badly split on the issue, agreed to choose future faculty both for their academic qualifications and religious affiliations. Dissension continued, and only the passage of a new constitution in 1850, which provided for an elected Board of Regents with complete control over the university and its fiscal policy, saved the institution from ruin.

The appointment of Henry Tappan as president in 1852 gave the University of Michigan a great boost. A Presbyterian minister from New York and a distinguished scholar, Tappan proved to be the leader who set the university on the road to becoming "The Harvard of the West." Like Crary and Pierce, Tappan was an enthusiastic admirer of German universities which stressed scholarship and science. The new president announced that he intended to establish a graduate program and hire faculty solely on their academic credentials. Immediately criticism was leveled at Tappan. Religious groups attacked him for his hiring practices; farmers were incensed at his refusal to start a school of agriculture; and supporters of vocational education claimed that he was an "elitist" because of his emphasis on science and classical subjects. When prohibitionists, abolitionists, and women's rights advocates joined the anti-Tappan forces, the regents removed him in 1863, but his leadership had put the university on solid ground.

Not all Michigan residents favored the University of Michigan's dominance in higher education. Church-supported schools began in Michigan in 1833 with the opening of Kalamazoo College, and within twenty-five years colleges had been established at Adrian, Albion, Olivet, and Hillsdale. Each was hampered, however, by a state law which gave the University of Michigan a monopoly in granting degrees. Furthermore, as long as the Democrats were in power, Tappan, a leader in that party, could convince the legislature that his university would suffer severe enrollment declines if other universities were allowed to grant degrees. When the Republicans gained control in 1855, they fulfilled a campaign pledge and passed a general college bill which established specifications by which colleges could be created and issue diplomas. Following the passage of this law, church-suppported colleges flourished and in 1980 there were over thirty such institutions in Michigan.

Republicans delivered another campaign promise in 1855 by passing a law authorizing the establishment of an agricultural college to be located within ten miles of Lansing. In May 1857, Michigan Agricultural College opened with

From a simple beginning, with a few buildings erected in stump-filled clearings, Michigan Agricultural College emerged to become one of the nation's great centers of higher education—Michigan State University.

eighty-one students, each of whom was required to spend four hours a day working on the college farm in addition to his classroom studies. In 1862, Congress passed the Morrill Act which authorized grants of public land to states for the purpose of supporting the education of farmers and mechanics. Michigan received 240,000 acres under this act and the funds derived from the sale of the land assured the financial stability of the nation's "pioneer land grant college," which is today Michigan State University.

Vocational and technical colleges began in Michigan during the late 1800s. The Michigan School of Mines, now Michigan Technological University, opened in 1885; the Detroit Institute of Technology began in 1909; and General Motors Institute in Flint was created in 1916. The first normal or teacher training school west of the Allegheny Mountains was started atYpsilanti in 1852 and by 1903 normal schools had been opened at Ann Arbor, Mt. Pleasant (Central Michigan University), Kalamazoo (Western Michigan University), and Marquette (Northern Michigan University).

Women's Education

Both public and private schools in Michigan generally were coeducational, although many segregated women into a "female department." Educational leaders urged coeducational schools on all levels, but voters saw little need for it above primary grades since it was believed that females did not require higher education to do "women's work" at home.

Prior to 1855 five private female seminaries had been created in the state.

Hoping to receive funding from the new Republican legislature, new schools for women were opened in Lansing and Marshall. When no financial assistance was given, the Marshall school closed in 1859 and the Lansing seminary shut down in 1871, later selling its buildings to the State School for the Blind. Church schools continued to operate "female colleges" or "female departments," and several even awarded the degree of "Mistress of Arts." After the Civil War, co-educational higher learning finally triumphed and, in 1870, both the University of Michigan and Michigan Agricultural College admitted women.

Special Education

The 1850 state constitution said that "institutions for the benefit of those inhabitants who are deaf, dumb, blind, or insane shall always be fostered and supported." Following the direction of the constitution, in 1854 the legislature provided for the establishment of an institute in Flint for the education of the deaf, dumb, and blind. In 1879 a separate school for the blind was founded at Lansing.

To care for delinquent children, a Boys Vocational School was begun at Lansing in 1855 and a similar school for girls was created in 1879 in Adrian. From 1873 until 1935 a home at Coldwater was operated to support orphans and children of poor parents. In 1936 it was converted into a home for mentally retarded children.

Prior to 1949, relatively few school districts held classes for the mentally handicapped. A partial state reimbursement program for school districts was instituted in 1949, and five years later the legislature passed a law allowing counties to levy special taxes for the implementation of handicapped children's programs. Although not totally solving the problem of educating the mentally handicapped, this marked a huge stride forward.

Recent Educational Advances

At present there are fifteen state-supported colleges and universities, and over 200,000 students attend private and parochial schools in the state. Regional universities, such as the University of Michigan at Flint and Dearborn, are growing in popularity, as are community colleges. Adult education programs are drawing increasing numbers of participants. Without question, Michigan is maintaining its position as a leader in educational progress.

Social and Cultural Enrichment

Even the earliest pioneers agreed that not all intellectual growth was gained in school. Consequently, various aspects of cultural development were fostered.

For example, interest in the theater existed in Detroit as early as 1816 when amateur theatricals were presented by army officers. Although women did not perform in the plays, they painted scenery and made stage properties. In 1830 a barn was converted for theater use. During the Civil War a theater was built, but it burned in 1867; however, in that same year the Detroit Opera House was finished. From 1850 to the turn of the century, German theaters operated in Detroit, presenting plays by such authors as William Shakespeare, Frederich Schiller, and Heinrich Laube. Outstate, many ornate opera-houses were constructed, and as prosperity reached the mining districts of the western upper peninsula, opera-houses, some of which seated over a thousand people, were erected at Calumet, Houghton, Hancock, Lake Linden, and Laurium. During the last decades of the nineteenth century, theaters also housed speakers on the Chautauqua circuit.

In the area of painting, the first "artist of record" in Michigan was James O. Lewis, who did portraits of Father Gabriel Richard and Lewis Cass. Lewis was commercially unsuccessful and had to resort to engraving and die making to support himself. T.W.O.P. (Alphabet) Burnham, of whom little is known, painted the famous picture of the state election of 1837, which was done "in the satirical fashion of Hogarth," and now may be seen in the Detroit Institute of Art. J. M. Stanley and Alvah Bradish were two other noteworthy portrait painters before the Civil War, while in the postwar era Robert Hopkin, William B. Conely, and Geri Melchers gained fame. In 1875, Detroit could boast of the founding of the Detroit Art Association, whose purpose was "to provide exhibitions of works of art and as soon as practicable to establish a permanent Gallery of Paintings and Sculpture in this city and to increase the knowledge and enjoyment by such means as may be deemed expedient." Thirteen years later the Detroit Museum of Art was opened, and, in 1927, a $4 million structure was completed on Woodward Avenue to house the collection which was now known as the Detroit Institute of Art.

Architecture also played a role in the state's cultural development. During the 1830s and 1840s, the Greek Revival style was popular and Marshall became the "architectural capital of Michigan." The best example of Greek Revival found in that city is the Dr. Andrew L. Hays house, but the entire city is rich in architectural interest. Michigan has given the world three great architects: Albert Kahn, the greatest factory architect in history, who designed the General Motors Building in 1920, and who was also responsible for the Clements Library and Hill Auditorium on the campus of the University of Michigan; Eliel Saarinen, a Finnish immigrant, who designed the Cranbrook School and Institute of Science, and the Kingswood School for Girls; and Eero Saarinen, Eliel's son, who designed the Dulles Airport in Washington, D.C., the Columbia Broadcasting System Building in New York, and the John Deere Building at Moline, Illinois.

In the area of literature, a local commentator wrote in 1939 that an "upper case author" was as "rare as a skunk bear" in Michigan, and concluded that

Michiganians were "better at building automobiles that are works of art than we are at fashioning great sonnets, we make better furniture than novels, we concoct better breakfast foods than drama." This alleged lack of great authors may result from problems of definition and categorization. Does birth alone qualify a state to claim an author as its own? If so, Edna Ferber, who was born in Kalamazoo, and Ring Lardner, who lived in Niles as a youth, could be considered "Michigan authors." If authors are claimed by a state simply because they used the state as the location for their works, then Michigan can be proud of James Fenimore Cooper, who set his *Oak Openings* in Kalamazoo; Washington Irving, whose *Astoria* reflected the Michigan fur trade; Henry Wadsworth Longfellow, whose *Hiawatha* immortalized the upper peninsula; and Ernest Hemingway, whose *Torrents of Spring* concerned workers at a Petoskey pump factory. Unfortunately for Michigan, however, fifteen years of residence is generally regarded as the "rule of thumb" for claiming authors as "one's own."

While none of Michigan's native sons or daughters has been recognized as a literary giant, many have done some excellent work. In the nineteenth century some of the best Michigan novels included Caroline Kirkland, *A New Home*, a tale of pioneer life in Livingston County; Major John Richardson, *Wacousta* and *Matilda Montgomery*, which used Pontiac's uprising and the War of 1812, respectively, as historical backdrops; and Constance Fenimore Woolson, *Anne*, a story of Civil War Mackinac.

Lumbering activities have been the theme for several volumes, such as Stewart Edward White, *River Men* and *Blazed Trail*; Eugene Thwing, *The Red Keggers* and *Man from Red Keg*; and Harold Titus, *Timber*. Rural life is realistically depicted in G. D. Eaton, *Backfurrow*, which is considered by some critics to be a "masterpiece among Michigan novels."

Michigan's most prolific writer was James Curwood of Owosso. Several of his novels, most notably *Courage of Captain Plum* and *Green Timber*, are set in Michigan. While critics say that his plots were predictable and the characters stereotyped, his works were commercially successful and were made into several movies.

In more recent times, Michigan's finest authors are Harriette Arnow, who wrote *The Dollmaker*, a poignant tale of a Kentucky family in wartime Detroit; Michigan Supreme Court Justice John Voelker, who, under the pen name Robert Traver, wrote such highly popular novels as *Small Town D.A., Troubled Shooter,* and *Anatomy of a Murder*; and Larry Smith and Jim Harrison, whose *The Original* and *Wolf*, respectively, deal with the changes caused by commercialized exploitation of the wilderness.

Michigan has never been blessed with a poet of the stature of a Carl Sandburg or Robert Frost, but the state can claim at least two famous versifiers. Will Carleton gained fame as "The Poet Laureate of Michigan" for his "Over the Hill to the Poor House." His writings on rural life earned him favorable comparison with Indiana's James Whitcomb Riley. Edgar Guest, whose homely writing earned him the title of "The Poet of Mother, Home, and Heaven," was revered by thousands of readers during the early and mid-twentieth century.

Michigan's residents were also very much interested in music, with nearly every city of any size having a town band. Our heritage of music appreciation is today carried forward by excellent music programs in high schools and colleges and through the efforts of local symphonies. The Interlochen Music Camp, founded in 1927 by Joseph Maddy, has achieved national prominence and has placed Michigan firmly on the world's "musical map."

In education, literature, and the arts, Michigan has always been active. Culture and mental stimulation have always been an integral part of the state's growth and have brought the state respect and admiration throughout the nation.

For Further Reading

The growth of public education is discussed in George L. Jackson, *The Development of State Control of Public Instruction in Michigan* (Lansing: Michigan Historical Commission, 1926) and Martha Bigelow, *Michigan Pioneer in Education* (Ann Arbor: Bulletin No. 7: Michigan Historical Collections, University of Michigan, 1955). A comprehensive treatment is provided by four volumes in the Munson History Fund "History of Education in Michigan," which include Floyd R. Dain, *Education in the Wilderness* (Lansing: Michigan Historical Commission, 1968); Charles R. Starring and James O. Knauss, *The Michigan Search for Educational Standards* (Lansing: Michigan Historical Commission, 1969); Donald W. Disbrow, *Schools for an Urban Society* (Lansing: Michigan Historical Commission, 1968); and Willis F. Dunbar, *The Michigan Record in Higher Education* (Detroit: Wayne State University, 1963).

Cultural and social activities are detailed in the following articles from *Michigan History:* J. B. Deise, "Entertainment in Early Detroit," XXX (1946); Mark O. Kisterl, "The German Theatre in Detroit," XLVII (1963); Melvin H. Miller, "The Chautauqua in Lansing," XL (1956); Clyde H. Burroughs, "Painting and Sculpture in Michigan," XX (1936); and Willis F. Dunbar, "The Opera House as a Social Institution," XXVII (1943).

Useful articles on Michigan literature and architecture include: Arnold Mulder, "Authors and Wolverines," *Saturday Review of Literature* (March 4, 1939); Francis X. Scannell, "The Novelist and Michigan," *Detroit Historical Society Bulletin*, XXI (1964); Douglas Noverr, "New Dimensions in Recent Michigan Fiction," *Midwestern Miscellany No. 2* (1974); and Wayne Andrews, *Architecture in Michigan* (Detroit: Wayne State University Press, 1967).

12

Wood and Rails

During the years 1860-1900, Michigan's commercial development was dominated by the sawing, harvesting, milling, and marketing of timber. Tens of thousands of men were employed in this enterprise, while hundreds more, mostly recent emigrants from New England, used their financial acumen to amass fortunes as "lumber barons." These wealthy men then utilized their money to influence the state's politicians and judges. Because lumbering was so critical to Michigan, its politicians did everything in their power to protect it. When a bill to aide the victims of the great Chicago fire was introduced in the House of Representatives in March 1872, Representative Omar D. Conger, of Port Huron, threatened to defeat it by having it recommitted to his lumber-oriented Committee on Commerce unless a provision allowing Canadian lumber to enter the United States duty free was deleted. The congressman claimed that, as written, the bill would "be injurious to the lumbermen of Michigan and the laboring people of Michigan," and that if Chicago were to be reconstructed, it would be with timber purchased from Michigan and Wisconsin; if not, Conger assured his colleagues that Chicago would "remain in ashes throughout eternity." The offensive section was then removed and the relief bill passed. Seemingly limitless strength rested with lumbermen because of their wealth.

Finding the Timber

Even though southern Michigan was covered with lush stands of sugar maple, beech, ash, oak, and hickory, the region was virtually ignored by lumbermen because hardwood trees had a limited market value. Demand was for the creamy white cork pine and Norway pine found in abundance in central and northern Michigan. Clearing of these pine forests, whose lumber was used primarily for home building and home furnishings, occurred at the rate of 33,000 acres per year during the last four decades of the nineteenth century. By 1882, the Saginaw Valley had contributed over one half of the 8 billion board feet of white pine cut throughout the entire Old Northwest. Unfortunately, indiscriminate cutting, lack of reforestation, and devastating conflagrations caused by careless milling procedures nearly made the stately white pine extinct. Today a small number are preserved in the Hartwick Pines State Park near Gaylord to serve as a reminder of Michigan's natural beauty before the coming of avaricious lumbermen.

To find the location of the best timber, lumbermen hired "pine scouts" or "timber cruisers" to walk the forests and mark on maps the sites of stands of choice trees. Whenever possible, Indians were employed for this task because of their intimate knowledge of the woodlands. Having found the best sites, the scouts then estimated the probable lumber yield in board feet (one board foot equals a board one foot square and one inch thick), and reported on the proximity of the timber stand to waterways by which the cut logs could be floated to mills. Lumbermen paid their scouts with one third of the timber on the property selected, thereby assuring that the men would select the sites which would result in the largest monetary return. After receiving the scouting reports, lumbermen filed claims at the nearest Government Land Office and purchased the land for $1.25 per acre.

Occasionally a timber scout invested his returns in the lumbering business and became a "baron" himself. David Ward, of Port Huron, began his career as a surveyor and "land looker" for lumbermen. In the early 1850s, he started to purchase timber lands in Michigan and Wisconsin, and, by the time of his death in 1900, he was proud to be known as "the richest man in Michigan," with an estate valued at over $10 million.

Competition was fierce and lumbermen went to great lengths to acquire heavily timbered lands, especially in the Saginaw Valley region which possessed both the best white pine and waterways. A major obstacle, however, was that much of the choicest land was held by Indians either as reservations or homesteads. Because until 1870 the federal government refused to permit Indians to sell any timber on their property, lumbermen had to seize the trees illegally. Generally, simple theft was utilized; lumbermen entered reservations, cut trees, and hauled them away. In 1871, Henry W. Sage, one of the state's foremost lumber barons, ordered flagrant cutting of timber on the Isabella Indian Reservation near Mt. Pleasant. After receiving numerous Indian complaints, the government sent an agent to investigate. He discovered that Sage had cleared over ten thousand acres and had been aided in this criminal act by former Congressman John F. Driggs, of Saginaw. No prosecutions were ever made, however, since it would have been impossible to find a judge in Michigan who would rule against a man such as Sage. Practices such as this were so common that during the years 1860-80 over one million board feet of timber, with a minimum value of $36 million, was stolen from Indian reservations.

When Indian land was held as homesteads, capable of being purchased, un-

Michigan Forests

Before large numbers of whites arrived in Michigan, the region was covered by forests. This map shows the location of various types of trees throughout the state.

scrupulous speculators and "timber sharks" used every available means to acquire it. Cheap sewing machines and parlor organs, which missionaries and
teachers had taught Indians to accept as symbols of civilization, were sold with
land mortgages taken as collateral. When Indians failed to meet payment dead-
lines, the goods were repossessed and the land seized as payment. Some speculators induced Indians to borrow fifty or one hundred dollars to improve their
property. Mortgages served as collateral and repayment dates were set for winter
months when Indians were least likely to be able to meet payment. If payment
was made, Indians still lost their land, for whites showed them a clause in the
contract stating that they were obligated to pay a large attorney's fee for handling the arrangements. Another method was to lend drunken Indians money and
demand repayment, with interest, the following day. Creditors threatened imprisonment for Indians refusing to sell their property to cover the debt. Widows
with dependent children were special targets for swindlers. A favorite ploy was
to purchase timber from widows and have them sign what was claimed to be a
receipt but was actually a deed. A similar trick was for agents of lumbermen to
go among starving Indians in winter, claiming to be representatives of charities,
offering them five dollars to purchase food; in return, Indians who were unable
to read, signed receipts which were actually deeds to their land. Occasionally,
physical violence would be used to force recalcitrant Indians to sell their land,
and men were hired to burn Indian houses and bludgeon the owners with clubs
and iron rods.

Two of the major land frauds in the state involved prominent residents of
Saginaw—Arthur Hill and Ezra Rust. In 1872, Hill ordered the burglary of a safe
containing the Michigan Indian Agent's plat maps showing exact locations of
property to be granted as homesteads to Indians. He copied the maps, sent
scouts to examine the timber on each site, and purchased the best from unwitting Indian owners, who had never seen their new land, for a minimum price,
much below its market value. The agent brought suit against Hill for stealing
government documents, but despite testimony against the lumberman by his
hired thieves, Hill was given only a reprimand by a judge who did not wish to
earn the wrath of the powerful lumbering community.

In 1864, Ezra Rust illegally gained control of fifteen thousand acres of
choice Isabella County pine land, which had been reserved for Indian ownership, by bribing two Indians to buy it and then immediately sell it to him.
Indians protested the "Rust Purchase" for six years without success. Then, in
1870, two Saginaw lumbermen, George F. Williams and Timothy Jerome, whose
brother, David, was a state senator and later became a member of the Board of
Indian Commissioners and governor of Michigan, joined Reverend George
Bradley, the missionary at the Isabella Indian Reservation, in a scheme to further defraud these Indians. The lumbermen instructed Bradley to meet with the
Indians and announce that Jerome and Williams would prosecute Rust and restore Indian property, free of cost, if the Indians would sign a contract authoriz-

ing the action. The chiefs asked Bradley to read the contract to them but he refused. They were eager, however, to have their land returned, and knowing that
Bradley was a "minister of God" they did not think that he would do anything
wrong and signed the agreement. Subsequently they discovered that they had
agreed to allow Jerome and Williams to choose land for them on the restored
property, to prohibit all Indian improvements on these selections for ten years,
and to retain exclusive timber privileges during this ten-year period. The Indian
agent notified the government that this contract was made through deception,
and after four years of litigation, it was nullified. Unfortunately, as in so many
cases, nearly all the valuable timber was removed before a court decision was
reached. Michigan was truly a state run by lumbermen for lumbermen.

Cutting and Milling

Once the timber was acquired it had to be cut and milled. To do the cutting,
lumberjacks, or "shanty boys" as they called themselves, were hired. While men

The "Big Wheel," with its strong axle, was used to move logs during periods
of snowless cutting.

of all nationalities were employed, most woodsmen were either Irish, French Canadien, American Indian, or plain Yankee farm boys.

Despite Paul Bunyan tales and movie caricatures, shanty boys were neither happy and carefree nor healthy and robust. Their life was rigorous, dangerous, and tedious. Every morning, except Sunday, they rose at 3:30 and breakfasted on pancakes, steak, potatoes, and coffee. At five o'clock, they began work. At noon, a lunch of meat, potatoes, vegetables, and pie was delivered to them. The meal was taken to the men so that a minimum of working time would be lost. Work continued until sundown, when the men returned to camp for a dinner of roast beef or pork, gravy, potatoes, vegetables, fresh bread, and pie. After a brief period of socializing, bunkhouse lights were out by nine o'clock.

Living conditions were not nearly so good as the food. Usually a camp had a single bunkhouse to hold sixty to one hundred men. Windowless and heated by a stove, the bunkhouse was a gloomy, poorly ventilated, depressing building. Bunks consisted of mattresses of branches and hay sacks for pillows. A common complaint was that every man had bedbugs for his bunkmate. Rules were strict and the use of alcohol was forbidden. Often it seemed that tobacco and fistfighting were the only permissible forms of relaxation. In fact, fighting became a way of life in logging camps, and, as the cutting season grew longer, tempers became shorter and any minor incident could result in a brawl. Moreover, the work of a shanty boy was conducive to illness and injury. For example, in 1884-85, approximately forty thousand men were working in Michigan forests. Of this number, nearly three thousand were hurt in accidents, and a like number were sick for extended periods. Considering the nature of their work, however, perhaps it is amazing that the numbers are so low.

For this privilege of working long hours in a dangerous job, and living in deplorable conditions, a shanty boy received twenty to twenty-eight dollars per month, but wages were not paid until all the logs had been sold the following spring. Lack of ready money was not a hardship, however, as all room and board was furnished for the men, and had they been paid sooner, they merely would have gambled their wages away.

Generally lumbering operations took place during September through March, and the snowier the winter the better it was for logging. Shanty boys designated as "choppers" and "sawyers" used felling axes and, in later years, seven-foot crosscut saws to fell trees and cut them into sixteen-foot lengths; then "trimmers" and "swampers" lopped off all branches. The logs were then dragged by men called "skidders" to a timber trail where "loaders" put them on either a "Big Wheel" cart or horse-drawn sled. To facilitate transporting logs in winter, lumber companies constructed roads to the nearest river and then waited for a heavy snowfall. When snow covered the road, a sled, dubbed "the sprinkler," was put into action. This sled, which carried a huge water tank with plugs on each side, traversed the road dousing it with water to create a thick layer of ice. After several applications of water, the icy path permitted a sled carrying fifty

During the 1887 cutting season this teamster and his horse-drawn sled would transport as much as 100,000 pounds of sixteen-foot logs at one time.

tons of logs to be drawn effortlessly by two horses. If snowfall in the cutting area was not heavy, men were sent to neighboring regions to bring back wagonloads of snow to spread on the roadway. Sand was placed on steep grades to slow the loaded sleds, but often the load shifted forward, crushing both the teamster and horses.

When the logs arrived at the riverbank, they were placed at seven-mile intervals in piles twenty to thirty feet in height and then branded. Marking was critical because every company in the area floated its logs to mills together, and company identification was possible only by branding. Over 3,500 log marks were registered in Michigan, but even branding did not eliminate all problems. Logs were marked on one end with a hot iron; however, "log rustlers" often came to the riverbank and altered brands to aid either themselves or another company. If the brand could not be altered easily, the end of the log was sawed off and a new mark embedded. Finally, companies hired inspectors to patrol the riverbanks and apprehend thieves.

In April, when the frozen rivers thawed, all the logs were rolled into the water, and the log drive began. Thousands of spectators lined the shores to view the annual spectacle of rivers literally jammed from bank to bank with logs. Even after railroads made logging operations practical in all seasons and allowed for mill constructions at sites other than mouths of rivers, many companies continued to use river drives. In fact, this practice was not discontinued until 1911.

Sawmills had been operating in Michigan since 1805 at Detroit and 1822 at Sault Ste. Marie, but these early mills cut timber for home building rather than commercial sale. Once lumbering became a major industry, mills sprang up in nearly every town located at the mouth of a river. Main lumbering centers were Menominee in the upper peninsula and Saginaw, Bay City, Alpena, Ludington, Port Huron, Grand Haven, Traverse City, Muskegon, and Petoskey in the lower peninsula. Large mills were highly mechanized, two-story structures which used a V-trough with a forked chain conveyor belt to lift logs from the river to the second story cutting room. There, logs were sawed into boards sixteen feet in length and one inch thick. Conveyor belts then piled the boards. Nothing was wasted at the mills, as even sawdust was kept and used to fuel machinery. Not all mills were large, however, and for every mill in Michigan which cut more than 10 million board feet annually, there were fifty or sixty cutting less than that number.

This scene of the beginning of a log drive on the Muskegon River in the 1890s shows the magnitude of the winter's cutting, as huge piles of logs line the entire riverbanks.

Fire

Without question, fire was the greatest threat facing lumbermen, and unfortunately it occurred with distressing regularity. Twice, however, major blazes devastated large portions of the state. On October 8, 1871, the same day that Chicago began burning, fires started along the western Michigan shoreline and quickly spread across the state to Lake Huron. In terms of monetary loss and human suffering, Michigan's fires were far more costly than the Chicago conflagration. The town of Holland was destroyed; students at Michigan Agricultural College struggled bravely to save Lansing from being engulfed in flames; and in the Thumb District, 90 percent of the homes were leveled, while twenty-three townships were severely burned and another eighteen suffered partial burning. Lumbermen defensively claimed that gale-force winds had carried sparks from Chicago across Lake Michigan to the Michigan shore, but in truth the fires in Michigan were a result of careless milling and logging which caused sparks to ignite tinder-dry forests.

Ten years later, the Thumb was again ravaged by fire. Huron, Tuscola, Sanilac, and Lapeer counties were swept by flames so intense that potatoes and onions were roasted in the ground and fish boiled in the rivers. One hundred twenty-seven people lost their lives from either the fire or the typhoid epidemic which followed, and the monetary loss caused by destruction of crops and timber exceeded $2 million. Another noteworthy feature of this fire was that the State Relief Committee, organized in Port Huron by Senator Conger, requested the newly formed American Red Cross, headed by Conger's close friend Clara Barton, to aid Michigan's disaster victims. The Red Cross, whose effectiveness had never been tested, immediately responded and proved its worth by furnishing food and clothing to ease the suffering of the needy.

Nature or Money

Despite the effects of these fires, as late as 1900, Michigan was still the nation's leading pine producer. Between the years 1860 and 1900, Michigan gave forth over 200 billion board feet of timber. Put in other terms, this meant that over one billion of the state's trees had been cut. Historians of the lumber industry note that this represented enough lumber to floor the entire state of Michigan with pine boards one inch thick and still have enough remaining to cover Rhode Island or to construct fifty plank roads, sixteen feet wide and one inch thick, from New York to San Francisco. More significant, perhaps, is that, in terms of monetary value, Michigan's "green gold" was worth over $1 billion more than all the "yellow gold" mined in California.

Lumbering had both a negative and positive impact on Michigan. Negative factors centered around the environment. Forests were destroyed, and their

In the late spring of 1892, amid a stump-filled clearing in front of a sawmill, employees of the Wisconsin Land and Timber Company of Hermansville, Michigan, pose to display part of their day's work.

elimination forced animals to leave their native homes. Thousands of other animals were slain by forest fires, while mill pollution fouled the waters and killed countless numbers of fish. Fires scorched the earth so badly that in some areas it could not be farmed for years. The environmental balance clearly was disrupted by the lumber industry. Positive factors, on the other hand, center around economics. The lumber industry induced many new settlers to enter the state, created employment for thousands, offered farmers new markets in which to sell their crops, built dams, roads, and railroads, and fostered such lucrative profits that excess capital could be invested in other developing industries, such as railways. The unanswerable question What is progress and how is it to be measured? certainly is applicable to the state's lumber industry.

Riding the Rails

Closely linked to lumbering as a source of economic growth was the rise of the railroad industry. Michigan's railway system developed in two distinct stages.

Before 1860, rail travel was primitive, dangerous, and uncomfortable. Because of limited rail accessibility to most cities, it was common for passengers either to begin or end their train journey by stagecoach, riverboat, or lake steamer. Following the Civil War, the state's railroads entered into their "Golden Age." Tracks reached nearly every community, and the advent of dining and Pullman cars, air brakes, and standard gauge track made travel both convenient and safe.

Michigan entered the railroad business in 1830 when the territorial council granted what is thought to be the first railway charter in the Old Northwest to the Pontiac and Detroit Railroad Company. This line, however, was never completed. The state's first working rail line, the Erie and Kalamazoo, came about as the result of a struggle between Adrian and Tecumseh over which city should become the Lenawee County seat. Since Tecumseh was larger and had access to the new military road joining Detroit and Chicago, it seemed to be the logical choice. To counteract Tecumseh's advantages, Adrian residents decided to demonstrate their faith in industrial progress by supporting construction of a thirty-three-mile railroad line between their city and Port Lawrence (Toledo), Ohio, through the dismal, previously inaccessible region known as the Black Swamp. This was a bold proposal since the first successful railroad line in the United States—the Baltimore and Ohio—had begun operation only three years

Michigan's first railroad, the Erie & Kalamazoo, had a wood-burning Baldwin engine and a converted stagecoach serving as a passenger car.

earlier in 1830. Advocates of the plan claimed that passengers and freight could go by rail to Port Lawrence and then by ship either east or west. Using horse-drawn cars, the line opened in 1836 and was successful enough to earn Adrian the designation as county seat. The following year the line added the *Adrian*, the third locomotive west of the Allegheny Mountains, and thereby reduced travel time to Chicago by two days. Unfortunately, the Erie and Kalamazoo line went bankrupt in 1840 as a result of the nationwide depression. After being in receivership for nine years, it was leased in perpetuity to the Michigan Southern Railroad Company which later was purchased by the Penn Central Company. Thus, even though the name is changed, the Erie and Kalamazoo line still is in operation.

Businessmen generally favored rail transportation for freight because it offered low cost, speed, and seasonal flexibility; no longer would cargo be unable to be delivered because of frozen rivers in winter or flooded roads in spring. Attempts to entice passengers met widespread resistance, however, because early railways were neither comfortable nor safe. Passenger cars were initially flatbeds with wooden benches attached. Each car was fastened to the next by three-foot lengths of chain. When the engine moved, the chains tightened, one by one, with a sudden force that hurled the riders backward. Once under way, sparks from the engine rained upon the unprotected passengers. To cover themselves, many raised umbrellas which soon caught fire. Since early locomotives could travel only a few miles, at most, without stopping for wood and water, riders were still righting themselves and brushing their smoldering clothing when the train came to a halt. As each chain slackened, the cars crashed into one another pitching the people forward. Fortunately, the trains averaged only ten miles per hour, which spared many of the less hearty riders from serious injury.

The question of rapid mobility was both an asset and a liability to early railroad companies in their attempt to gain passengers. Riders were impressed with the opportunity to fly across the countryside at ten miles per hour for the modest fare of 4½¢ per mile. Likewise, they were supportive of company rules to assure safety by maintaining the ten mile per hour maximum speed and removal of all engineers who exceeded the legal limit. In truth, this limit was not imposed to protect passengers but rather to assist brakemen. Until 1869, with the invention of the Westinghouse air brake, brakemen stopped trains with a manual lever, and any speed over ten miles per hour made their task virtually impossible. In fact, by 1869, the average speed had increased to eighteen miles per hour and rolling stops had become the rule at every station. Ironically, the ten mile per hour speed limit was also a source of concern for passengers. While that speed seemed to be as fast as man should ever travel on earth, it was not sufficiently fast to propel the train up steep hills. Thus, it was common for riders to have to leave the train, push it up the grade, and then leap aboard as it began its descent.

In the early years of railroad travel, passengers and crewmen risked physical danger as well as inconvenience and discomfort. Tracks were poorly constructed, usually with a wooden rail being covered by a thin strip of iron. After a short period of usage, the strip would work loose and shoot through the floor of the cars like a snake striking at a victim. These iron spears, or "snake heads," seriously injured, and occasionally killed, riders. Crewmen had to couple all cars by hand until the advent of the automatic coupler in 1893 and consequently missing fingers were considered the badge of railroad employees. Excitement and danger were the bywords of early rail travel.

Many Michigan residents objected to the spread of railroads for reasons other than danger and inconvenience. Some used moral arguments, claiming that God never intended man to move so quickly propelled by an engine spewing the fire of hell. Religious opposition was so widespread that several companies were compelled to compromise with the moralists and promise never to operate trains on the Sabbath. Strongest opposition came from farmers who said that engines scared their animals and killed livestock that happened to be lying asleep on the tracks. To placate angry agriculturalists, state-owned railways reimbursed farmers for all livestock slain by their trains. This policy led many farmers to carry their old, feeble, and/or dying cattle to the tracks where their death under the wheels of a train would prove profitable. Other farmers, who grew oats, expressed fear that railroads would drive them out of business by making horses obsolete.

The Great Railroad Conspiracy

Farmer hostility to railroads reached a peak during the years 1849-51. In 1846, the state legislature had voted to remove the state from the railroad business. This decision was prompted by purely economic considerations. The state had not yet fully recovered from the effects of the depression and railroad profits were insufficient to meet the costs of operation, maintenance, and interest due on state-issued construction bonds. By 1846, Michigan's indebtedness resulting from railroad ownership had reached $4 million and consequently it eagerly sold its holdings in the Michigan Central and Michigan Southern Railway companies to New England stock corporations for $2 million and $500,000, respectively. Although some citizens feared that private ownership might bring about ruthless price fixing on freight rates, the sale met little resistance either from legislators or the general public.

Once in private control, railroad companies announced that they could not afford to continue the policy of reimbursing farmers for slain livestock. Moreover, the new owners said that the policy had been ill conceived because trains moved so slowly that any "reasonably agile" cow could avoid being struck and that, in any case, it was the obligation of the farmer to keep his animals away from railroad property. Enraged at this new proposal, farmers began what was known as "the great railroad conspiracy."

Throughout the southern tier of counties, farmers sabotaged rail lines. Shots were fired at passing trains, switches were opened to cause derailments, fuel piles were burned, water towers tipped, and large logs and rocks were placed on tracks. The ultimate deviltry, however, was greasing tracks on a hill so that the engine could never reach the crest and would have to return to the previous station in reverse. Miraculously no one was killed by these actions.

The worst violence occurred between Grass Lake and Jackson at the instigation of Abel F. Fitch, of Michigan Centre. Fitch, a wealthy farmer and community leader, ordered all types of violence against railroads, culminating with the burning of the new Michigan Central depot in Detroit on November 18, 1850. Furious over the arson, railroad owners hired a detective to uncover the perpetrators of the crime. As a result of the detective's findings, Fitch and forty-two others were arrested and brought to Detroit for trial in April 1851. Claiming that they were "violent conspirators," the judge set bail so high that it could not be raised. Fitch hired William H. Seward, the noted abolitionist from New York, to defend the accused farmers. The trial lingered on for five months, and Fitch died before its conclusion. His death, along with Seward's brilliant defense, turned public opinion away from the railroad owners and to the farmers. The court verdict freed all but ten of the defendants, but the public sought freedom for them as well. In an effort to stem rising criticism, railroad owners not only requested pardons for the guilty men but also pledged to pay farmers half the value of slain livestock. Farmers accepted this offer, but bitterness between them and the railroads continued for years.

The issues raised by this trial revealed that social and legal institutions had failed to keep pace with technological advances. Perplexing questions arose, such as: Should railroad companies be responsible for fencing their tracks? What were the limits of railroad liability for damages and injuries incurred through rail operations? What was the role of the state in assuring that justice would be meted out to its citizens? Unfortunately, no immediate answers were forthcoming.

Despite these obstacles Michigan's railroads steadily expanded, and, by 1860, three major rail systems—the Michigan Central, Michigan Southern, and Detroit and Milwaukee—spanned the lower peninsula with 799 miles of track. These three lines carried over one million passengers and averaged nearly $3 million in freight traffic annually.

The Golden Age of Railroads

During the last four decades of the nineteenth century nearly every community sought access to a rail line since commerce and settlement seemed to follow the tracks. Occasionally, entire towns would purchase railroad stock in return for a pledge that a "spur line" would be built from the main route to the town. Cities grew where railroads afforded opportunities for economic expansion by merchants and farmers. Many towns existed solely because of the railroads. Durand, for example, survived simply because it was the junction of all the state's rail traffic. By 1900, over 6,900 miles of track crossed the state, and railroads had become not only the major method for freight transportation but also the chief means of mass transit.

Many new railways were extremely small, poorly financed, and intended to serve only local freight traffic. Typical of these limited roads, or "little fellows," as they were affectionately called, was the Mason and Oceana Line, which in 1900 owned twenty-seven miles of track, five locomotives, one passenger car, one baggage car, and two hundred thirty-two freight cars. It employed forty-one men and earned an average of $22,300 per year. Several of these short-line railroads were so lacking in funds that they did not even have a turntable and, as a result, had to make half their trips in reverse. Often fuel and water would be obtained from any available source. Fallen trees and farmers' fences served as fuel, and water would be acquired by dropping a bucket from the moving engine into a nearby stream. The latter earned these lines another nickname— "jerkwater railroads." Many of these lines were ultimately purchased by larger roads and several, especially along Lake Michigan, continued to serve for many years as excursion trains for tourists.

The "golden age" of railroads affected several aspects of life for Michigan residents. Large cities, with their accompanying sprawl and filthy tenements, developed around railroads. Urban life became increasingly difficult for the lower and middle classes, as the wealthy sought refuge from the dirt and noise of the city by moving to homes farther away. As the phenomena of suburban life expanded, people who remained in the undesirable inner-city neighborhoods were said to live "on the wrong side of the tracks," which really meant "near the tracks." Even architecture was affected by the growth of rail systems. Businessmen desired to be near rail depots, and, in order to accommodate as many as possible, multilevel "skyscraper" office buildings were erected. In addition,

Durand, with its architecturally striking Union Station, has been the center of Michigan's railroad activity for more than a century.

depots were, in many instances, architectural masterworks which reflected a town's self-esteem. Like European cathedrals in the Middle Ages, in nineteenth century America, the depot was the symbol of community pride and prosperity. While time and disuse have taken their toll on many of the magnificent Victorian columned, towered, and marbled structures, a few remain. Durand, the rail capital of Michigan, is at present remodeling its classic station and once again rail passengers will be able to thrill to its beauty.

Railroads also provided status for travelers, as often only the wealthy and socially prominent rode trains. Railroad companies prided themselves on their service, especially in the dining cars. Every table was graced with Irish linen cloths, polished silver utensils, and fresh flowers. Six-course meals, which usually included a choice of lobster, pheasant, oysters, filet mignon, and fresh fruit for dessert, were available for less than a dollar. Dignity and proper behavior were expected from all passengers, and conductors had the authority to remove from the train anyone who was unruly or profane.

Between the years 1880 and 1910, laws were passed by the state legislature to regulate fares and to assure publication of schedules. The most significant change, however, was instituted by the railroad companies themselves. As late as 1883, Michigan had at least twenty-seven different time zones, which made scheduled arrival of freight nearly impossible to determine. To facilitate business transactions, the railroad lines agreed in 1884 to synchronize all their clocks by a telegraphic signal each morning at exactly nine o'clock. By thus creating a standard time zone, merchants could be promised with reasonable certainty when their merchandise would arrive. This led to businessmen likewise drawing up their hours according to the train schedules, and, as a result, Michigan had a single time zone.

A significant advance in railroad technology came from a Michigan African-American engineer, Elijah McCoy. Born in Canada and educated in Scotland, McCoy arrived in Michigan after the Civil War. He invented a steam engine system which replaced manual lubrication with an applicator mechanism housed in the locomotive cab. Thus, the engineer could precisely allocate lubricating oil distribution both with speed and safety. McCoy founded the Detroit Lubricator Company and ultimately patented seventy-eight inventions. When other lubricating devices came on the market, discerning engineers rejected them and demanded "the real McCoy."

Another advance in rail travel occurred in 1886 when the first electric train in Michigan, and only the third in the United States, began operation in Port Huron. Such trains, known as interurbans, went between cities and initially were an extension of electric streetcar lines. The advantages of interurban travel were speed and convenience. By adding a third rail, interurbans were able to negotiate curves more smoothly and accelerate more quickly than ordinary trains. Express runs, known as "limiteds," reached speeds of sixty miles per hour. By 1918, Michigan had nearly one thousand miles of interurban and streetcar track,

The Port Huron Electric Railway Company operated the first interurban system in the nation.

which carried nearly 380 million passengers a year for fares averaging slightly over six cents.

As the number of automobiles, buses, and trucks increased in the 1920s, use of interurbans declined, and, by 1935, all had gone out of business. As Willis Dunbar, the foremost authority on Michigan railroads, noted, interurbans reflected "a passing phase in the history of Michigan transportation." A response to urbanization and the need for immediate rapid mass transit, interurbans filled the gap between the passing of horsedrawn trolleys and the coming of internal combustion vehicles.

Upper Peninsula Railroads

Most of Michigan's rail lines were built in the lower peninsula, but a few small lines, nearly all financed by mining and lumber companies, were constructed in the upper peninsula. These lines, typified by the Lake Superior and Ishpeming Railroad which was only two miles in length, ran from lumber camps and mines to the nearest harbor. By 1915, the upper peninsula had nineteen rail lines, carrying $8 million of annual freight traffic, which represented 16 percent of the state's total freight revenue.

The major difficulty which beset upper peninsula railroads was that their only land link to the nation's markets was through Wisconsin. This, coupled with the lack of sufficient population to provide profitable passenger service, precluded sizable funding by Michigan investors. A partial solution to this problem was offered in 1883 when two wooden railroad car ferries began transporting freight cars across the Straits of Mackinac. These ferries were less than successful in their initial efforts as they ran aground three times and severely damaged both themselves and their cargo. It was soon discovered that the ferries also were not structurally sound and had a tendency to break apart in storms and rough harbor water. To try to avoid losing the ships in port, one company ordered oil to be poured into its harbor in an effort to calm the churning sea. It was not until 1896 that the first steel rail-car ferry, the *Pere Marquette*, was put into service. While it was an immediate success and was followed by the addition of four more ferries, the ships sailed between Ludington and Manitowoc, Wisconsin, and

thus were of no benefit to the upper peninsula. As the lumber and mining industries declined and regular steamship service reached the upper peninsula, rail
traffic became nearly extinct.

Decline of the Railroads

Railroads began to suffer a rapid loss of popularity as both businesses and
passengers turned to automobiles, trucks, buses, and airplanes for rapid transit.
Many small lines were either abandoned or merged into larger ones, but even
major roads were nearly all forced into receivership by the Great Depression.
During the decade of the 1930s, freight revenue dipped 10 percent and passenger ticket sales plummeted 60 percent. Railroads enjoyed a brief revival
during World War II because of gas rationing, tire shortages, and the unavailability of automobiles for purchase, but following the war, another decline
took place and by the 1960s nearly all passenger trains in Michigan had been
discontinued. As fuel costs rise and a demand for mass transit is again raised,
perhaps Michigan's railroad industry will once again grow, but it will never
reach its former heights of the turn of the twentieth century.

For Further Reading

Michigan's lumber industry is vividly portrayed in Rolland H. Maybee, *Michigan's White Pine Era,* 1840-1900 (Lansing: Michigan Historical Commission,
1964) and Lewis C. Reiman, *When Pine Was King* (Ann Arbor: University of
Michigan Press, 1952). Timber frauds against the Indians are fully described in
Anita S. Goodstein, *Biography of a Businessman: Henry W. Sage, 1814-1897*
(Ithaca: Cornell University Press, 1962) and Bruce A. Rubenstein, "Justice
Denied: Indian Land Frauds in Michigan, 1855-1900," *The Old Northwest,*
II (June 1976). Other informative articles, all in *Michigan History,* are: Leo
Alilunas, "Michigan's Cut-over Canaan," XXVI (1942); Herbert Brinks, "The
Effect of the Civil War in 1861 on Michigan's Lumber and Mining Industries,"
XLIV (1960); and William G. Rector, "Railroad Logging in the Lake States;"
XXXVI (1952).
    The standard work on Michigan's railroads is Willis Dunbar, *All Aboard:
A History of Railroads in Michigan* (Grand Rapids: William B. Eerdmans Pub.
Co., 1969). A briefer, but equally interesting, work is Frank Elliott, *When the
Railroad Was King* (Lansing: Michigan Historical Commission, 1966). The farm
revolt against railroads is superbly told in Charles Hirschfeld, "The Great Railroad Conspiracy," *Michigan History,* XXXVI (1952). Interurban development
is recounted in Junius E. Beal, "The Beginnings of Interurbans," *Michigan
Pioneer and Historical Collections,* XXXV (1907).

13

The World of Wheels

Gasoline-powered internal combustion motorcars, or "road wagons," had been developed in Belgium and Germany as early as 1860, but they were thought of primarily as mere toys and not as possible replacements for horse-drawn carriages. Americans shared this view and even after Charles and Frank Duryea, of Massachusetts, established the nation's first automobile company in 1893 the general public remained unconvinced that "horseless buggies" were more than dangerous, expensive playthings for the idle rich. This belief was put in verse on an anti-automobile postcard near the turn of the twentieth century:

He owned a handsome touring car, to ride in it was Heaven
He ran across a piece of glass . . . the bill, $14.97.
He started on a little tour, the finest sort of fun,
He stopped too quick and stripped the gears . . . the bill, $99.41.
He took his wife down to shop, to save the horses was great,
He crashed into a grocery store . . . the bill, $444.88.
He spent his pile of cash, and then in anguish cried,
I'll put a mortgage on the house, and have just one more ride.

It was not until Ransom E. Olds, of Lansing, entered the scene that automobiles became popular in the mass market.

Olds' " 'Mobile"

In 1886, at the age of twenty-two, Olds developed a steam-powered auto-mobile, but he quickly turned his attention to perfecting a gasoline power-source because he believed that the inevitable boiler problems would prevent "steam-ers" from becoming popular. His goal was to construct a small, lightweight vehicle which would cost approximately the same as a good buggy and team of horses. By 1896 he had made his first car, but it fell short of his expectations as it was heavy, weighing one thousand pounds, and large, having two seats and a five-horsepower engine. Following a successful test run of his invention, Olds, with financial backing from Lansing businessmen, founded the Olds Motor Vehicle Company. Even though the company manufactured only six cars in 1897, Olds wanted to expand his operation and unsuccessfully sought funds from New York bankers. However, a wealthy Detroit lumber baron, Samuel L. Smith, pledged $350,000 to Olds if he would relocate his body plant to Detroit. Olds agreed and in 1899 mass production of his cars, which sold for $1,200, began. Sales were disappointing and Olds decided to redesign his product.

In 1900 Olds marketed his "dream car," an open, single seat, curved-dash sportster, which weighed 700 pounds, cost $300 to manufacture, and sold for $650. This car intrigued the public and 425 new "Oldsmobiles" were sold. Unfortunately, despite Olds' claim that his automobile was "built to run and it does!" mechanical failures plagued owners. Breakdowns were so common that cynics responded to Olds' slogan that his car was so well made that drivers had "nothing to watch but the road" by saying "yes, but you can get damned tired of watching the same piece of road all the time." To silence critics, in 1901 Olds hired Roy D. Chapin to drive an Oldsmobile from Detroit to an automobile show in New York City to prove his car's durability. Chapin made the 820-mile journey in 7½ days; his vehicle reached an average speed of 30-35 miles per hour, while consuming 30 gallons of gasoline and an unexpectedly high 80 gallons of water. After the successful completion of Chapin's trip, which the *Detroit Times* enthusiastically likened to the journey of Paul Revere, Oldsmobile sales steadily rose, reaching four thousand in 1903.

To promote sales further, Olds turned to mass marketing. His product was regularly advertised in national magazines, including the *Ladies' Home Journal.* Olds sought to curry favor with women drivers by suggesting that his car would be convenient for shopping, visiting, or merely touring the countryside. Safety was also emphasized as Olds noted that his car, controlled by a single dependable lever, was a much superior vehicle for a woman than a buggy directed by the reins of a potentially unruly team of horses. In fact, superiority over horses was a major element of early automobile sales promotions. Typical of this technique is this pro-horseless carriage poem:

> It doesn't shy at papers as they blow along the street;
> It cuts no silly capers on the dashboard with its feet;
> It doesn't paw the sod up all around the hitching post;
> It doesn't scare at shadows as a man would at a ghost;
> It doesn't gnaw the manger and it doesn't waste the hat,
> Nor put you into danger when the brass bands play.

Even Olds, on his eightieth birthday, joked that he began working on the automobile because he "didn't like the smell of horses on the farm." Olds also sent agents to Europe to create a market, and shortly before her death in 1901 Queen Victoria purchased an Oldsmobile. Moreover, Oldsmobile was the first car to be immortalized in song as one of the nation's best known melodies became "In My Merry Oldsmobile."

Oldsmobile was also the first company to issue sales manuals to dealers and instruction booklets to buyers. Included in Oldsmobile's famous "don't list" to owners were:

> Don't take anybody's word for it that your tanks have
> plenty of gasoline and water and your oil cup
> plenty of oil. They may be guessing.
>
> Don't do anything to your motor without a good reason
> or without knowing just what you are doing.
>
> Don't imagine that your motor runs well on equal parts
> of water and gasoline. It's a mistake.
>
> Don't make "improvements" without writing the factory.
> We know all about many of those improvements and
> can advise you.
>
> Don't drive your Oldsmobile 100 miles the first day.
> You wouldn't drive a green horse 10 miles till
> you were acquainted with him. Do you know more
> about a gasoline motor than you do about a horse?
>
> Don't delude yourself into thinking we are building
> these motors like a barber's razor—"just to sell."
> We couldn't have sold one in a thousand years, and
> much less 5,000 in one year, if it hadn't been
> demonstrated to be a practical success.
>
> Don't confess you are less intelligent than thousands
> of people who are driving Oldsmobiles. We make
> the only motor that "motes."

In this fashion Olds initiated the concept of "factory authorized service" as the best means to protect the purchaser's investment.

In 1902, following the destruction of his Detroit plant by fire, Olds returned his operation to Lansing. Two years later, as a result of a feud with the Smith family over management policies, Olds sold his stock in the company and founded the Reo Motor Car Company. In 1905 he produced a car which he believed was so perfect that he did not think that it could be improved upon in the future. This car, REO the Fifth, had thirty-five horsepower, could reach forty-five miles per hour, seated five comfortably, and cost only $1,055. REO sales quickly surpassed those of Oldsmobile, but by 1908 the latter had regained sales supremacy primarily because Olds lost his enthusiasm for running his new

Single-lane roads filled with ruts and rocks proved a challenge to early automobiles such as this 1911 Oldsmobile.

company. Olds continued as chairman of the board at Reo until 1936, but he never was the driving force in the industry that he had been before he became an extremely wealthy investor and philanthropist who did not have enough time to devote to his work. However, Olds' place in history was assured by his popularization of the automobile.

Henry and His "Lizzie"

As a result of Olds' success, thousands of individuals seeking quick profits entered the automobile industry and by 1907 there were 270 car-manufacturing companies in Michigan. Few survived, but those which did made fortunes for their owners and stockholders. One of these men who profited from Olds' efforts was Henry Ford, the Dearborn inventor whose feats in the automotive industry became legendary.

With financial support from James Couzens, Horace Rackham, and John and Horace Dodge, among others, in June 1903, the Ford Motor Car Company was created. Ford sought to "democratize the car, so that everyone could afford one." He intended to build an automobile more powerful than the Oldsmobile and which would also be light enough to travel muddy roads without getting stuck, large enough to hold an entire family, easy to operate, simple to repair, and inexpensive.

Despite his hopes, the 1903 "Fordmobile," which was quickly renamed the Model A, was not a serious threat to Oldsmobile. While the Model A was the most powerful car built in 1903, it was also four hundred pounds heavier than the Oldsmobile and cost nearly two hundred dollars more. Having sold only 658 units, the following year Ford introduced three new automobiles: the Model C, a lightweight runabout costing either eight or nine hundred dollars depending on engine size; the Model F, a small touring car which cost one thousand dollars; and the Model B, a five passenger, four-cylinder touring car which sold for an unbelievable two thousand dollars. During the next three years Ford continued his journey through the alphabet and produced Models K, R, S, and N. Of these, only the last was successful. The Model N, even though heavier than both the Oldsmobile and newly popular Buick, was powerful enough to reach forty-five miles per hour, fuel efficient at twenty miles per gallon, and cost only six hundred dollars. Ford had finally developed a competitive car.

In 1908 Ford unveiled the automobile which made him famous—the Model T. The "Tin Lizzie," as it was affectionately dubbed, was an instant success, with 25,000 sold the first year. Its popularity was ironic, however, since at 1,200 pounds and $850 dollars, it was neither light nor inexpensive.

Early automobiles often fell victim to the state's poor roads which became muddy quagmires after every heavy rainfall.

Ford promoted the Model T as the "farmers' car" and ran advertisements stating that "your harvest is incomplete without a Ford." Sales soared as contented owners told their friends about their functional, dependable, durable, and versatile car. One elated farmer wrote Ford that his Model T could do everything except "rock the baby to sleep and make love to the hired girl." This success led to a slogan warning farmers: "Don't Experiment, Just Buy a Ford."

Ford constantly stressed dependability and durability rather than luxury in his cars. Not until 1926 was the Model T marketed in any color except black because Ford claimed that offering a selection of colors would delay production and increase costs—both things which Ford refused to do. By perfecting Olds' assembly-line technique Ford managed to increase production while reducing costs. To stimulate sales, he passed on savings to the consumer by cutting the price of his cars. In 1912 the Model T sold for $600; in 1916 only $360; and in 1924 the price was down to an amazing $290. Moreover, despite price reductions, increased sales volume resulted in even higher profits. From 1917 to 1924 Ford controlled over half of the automobile sales market and in 1923 sold 1,817,891 cars. The *Detroit News* informed its readers that in 1923 Ford not only had become a billionaire but also that his daily income was $264,026.41. Sales continued to grow and, at its peak in 1924, Ford sold cars at a rate of 250 per hour every 24 hours for 300 days.

The Model T became so popular that, like the Oldsmobile, it was glorified in songs such as "Henry Made a Lady Out of Lizzie" and "The Little Ford Rambled Right Along." The latter is worth noting because it contained a not-so-subtle attack on the quality of products made by Ford's competitors:

> Now Henry Jones and a pretty little queen
> Took a ride one day in his big limousine,
> The car kicked up and the engine wouldn't crank
> There wasn't any gas in the gasoline tank.
> About that time along came Nord
> And he rattled right along in his little old Ford
> And he stole that queen as his engine sang a song
> And his little Ford rambled right along.

Ironically, the success of the Model T helped bring about its demise. It was so durable that it never wore out, thus eliminating a market for return customers. As roads improved, the Model T's sturdy construction was less important and purchasers began to look for luxury and style rather than quality. In 1925 sales declined, and two years later, Edsel Ford, who had become president of the company in 1918, convinced his father, who retained the ultimate power in the firm, to discontinue production of the Model T. That May, following the production of the 15,000,000th "Tin Lizzie," the company began to manufacture a new Model A. When the new car was introduced in New York City, a mob of over one million people crushed into showrooms to view it. The Model T was gone, but the Ford Motor Company was destined to maintain a prominent place in the production of automobiles.

Ford and Society

A major reason for the success of the Ford Motor Company was public adoration of its founder. Always the champion of farmers, Ford became the "workingman's friend" in 1914 when he raised the salaries of his employees from $2.30 to $5.00 a day, saying that he did so because it seemed unfair that the only people in America who could not afford to buy a car were the men who made them. In 1914 workers throughout the nation praised Ford as the only automobile manufacturer with a heart, and they became fiercely loyal to his product. Ford became the working-class car and Henry became a national figure.

Unlike other wealthy industrialists, Ford was never seen by the public as a "robber baron." Despite his fortune, which exceeded $700 million at the time of his death in 1947, Ford retained his love of simple things and his middle-class values. The creation of Greenfield Village was intended as a monument to middle America. As Will Rogers said: "Ford is rich but he understands our problems. He is one of us."

Even Ford's well-known anti-Semitism was popular with many Americans. In 1920 his newspaper, the *Dearborn Independent,* instituted a series of ninety-one articles on "The International Jew: The World's Problem." Jews were blamed for controlling gambling casinos, operating houses of prostitution, running Wall Street, and undermining American morals by monopolizing the Hollywood motion picture industry and producing explicit films. Public reaction to Ford's stand was overwhelmingly favorable. Ford's anti-Semitism grew so intense that he not only ran articles in his newspaper claiming that Jews were nonwhite and Jesus was not a Jew, but also he financed a New York detective agency whose sole duty was to uncover scandalous behavior on the part of Jewish businessmen. In 1939 the well-known anti-Semite, Adolf Hitler, praised Ford as "the one great man in America" because of his attacks on Jewish influence.

Strict rules placed on his employees further strengthened Ford's hold on middle America. His policy of firing workers who smoked or chewed tobacco, drank alcoholic beverages, used profanity, or expressed approval of dancing and jazz music was welcomed by people fearful that America's morality was disintegrating during the "Roaring Twenties."

Ford continued to run the company, through Edsel, until his son's death in 1943. Although nearly eighty and somewhat senile, Ford then assumed active control of the firm. As sales declined and Ford demonstrated his failing mind by asking to see employees who had not been with the company for twenty years,

Edsel's wife threatened to sell her stock in the business to the public unless her son Henry was elevated to the presidency. The elder Ford reluctantly agreed.

Under Henry Ford II the company expanded and remained an industry leader. Using his grandfather's credo that cars should be easy to repair and inexpensive, Ford introduced the popular Maverick, Mustang, and Pinto models. Today, continuing to try to live up to its motto, "Ford has a better idea," the Escort and Mustang convertible have kept Ford competitive in the world market.

Growth of an Industrial Giant

Olds' chief competitor at the turn of the century was not Henry Ford, however, but David D. Buick, a Scottish immigrant who had settled in Detroit and entered the plumbing business. As a plumber, Buick invented the lawn sprinkler and a process for bonding porcelain to metal bathtubs, both of which would have made him a millionaire had he decided to manufacture them. Buick's dream, however, was not to become a famous plumber, but rather to perfect an internal combustion engine for automobiles. While working toward his goal, he developed a small, lightweight gasoline engine suitable for propelling farm implements and rowboats. Like his other inventions, this engine could have made a fortune for Buick, but he discarded it in favor of a larger power source for horseless carriages.

In 1901, he founded the Buick Auto-Vim and Power Company, but it was beset by financial problems, and in 1903, was sold to James H. Whiting, manager of the Flint Wagon Works, who moved the plant from Detroit to Flint. The following year the Buick Motor Company, as it was renamed, manufactured 37 cars and the next year only 750. Production and sales were minimal primarily because people were not convinced that the Buick was worth its $850 price. To stimulate sales, Buick and other company officials drove their automobile through Flint and nearby cities to prove its dependability. These test drives did not have their intended results as the cars malfunctioned so often that critics said: "Buicks will get you wherever you want to go but they won't get you back." Because the firm continued to lose money, Whiting removed Buick as company head in 1904 and replaced him with William Crapo Durant. Buick remained with the company long enough to repay his many debtors in Detroit and Flint, but he died a pauper in 1929. Buick's life was a tragic reminder that not all brilliant inventors were fated to succeed in the automobile industry.

"Billy" Durant, grandson of former Governor Henry H. Crapo, was forty-two years old when he took control of Buick. A successful wagon and carriage maker with a deserved reputation as a "planning wizard" and "marketing genius," Durant reversed the company's downward slide. He wanted Buick to be "the people's car" and accordingly he visited farmers to determine what they sought in an automobile; he convinced blacksmiths that they should engage in automobile repairs so that rural residents could have mechanical work done conveniently; and he pressured his Flint friends into purchasing large blocks of Buick stock. To demonstrate their durability, speed, and handling, Durant entered Buicks in road races and by 1908 they were constant victors. Hill-climbing events became Buick specialties and consequently Michigan residents referred to steep inclines as "Buick hills." By 1906 production had soared to 750 units, and in 1910 Buick had become so popular that one of every six cars sold in the United States was a Buick.

Having made Buick a financial success, Durant turned his attention to increased production of his cars. To accomplish this, he lured Albert Champion, Charles Stewart Mott, and the Fisher Brothers into moving their ignition, axle, and body plants from Boston, Utica, New York, and Detroit to Flint. As Buick grew so did Flint; its population rose from 13,000 in 1900 to 91,000 in 1920 making "The Vehicle City" one of the wealthiest and fastest growing communities in the country.

Durant's major dream, however, was to merge several automobile companies into a corporation which would compete for sales but have a single financial base. It would not be a monopoly because it would encourage competition and have separate management for each division. Large investors would be attracted to such a corporation because of the low risk involved, for Durant believed that if the corporation was large enough to manufacture several styles and models it could meet every public demand. Thus, in 1908, Durant set out to gain control of "every car in sight." Throughout the year he purchased over thirty automobile companies, including Oldsmobile, Oakland (Pontiac), and Cadillac. On September 16, 1908, General Motors was created. Its incorporation was not met with fanfare, however, as only *The Flint Journal* considered the story newsworthy enough to print.

In 1908 Durant tried unsuccessfully to purchase the Reo and Ford Motor Companies. Both Olds and Ford were willing to sell, but the deal collapsed when Ford demanded $8 million in cash, which was excessive even for Durant. Later in 1910 a slump in car sales drove General Motors revenue down and Durant was forced to borrow $12,500,000 to avoid bankruptcy. Conservative Eastern bankers, who had financed Durant's expansion program, demanded as a condition of the loan that he resign as president lest he further deplete company resources by more consolidations.

After losing General Motors to the bankers, Durant decided to build a small, inexpensive car to compete with the Model T. He entered into partnership with Louis Chevrolet, his former racing driver, and began manufacturing automobiles bearing the famous driver's name. Subsequently he bought out his partner, instituted his legendary marketing techniques, and made enough money so that by 1915, with backing from the DuPont family, he owned the majority of General Motors stock. To the amazement of the business community, not only had Durant regained control of General Motors, but his new company actually owned it.

As president of General Motors, Durant again set upon expanding the corporation. His energy was boundless and one of his plant managers recalled that

When Mr. Durant visited one of his plants it was like the visitation of a cyclone. He would lead his staff in, take off his coat, begin issuing orders, dictating letters, and calling the ends of the continent on the telephone, talking in his rapid easy way to New York, Chicago, San Francisco. . . . Only the most phenomenal memory could keep his deals straight; he worked so fast that the records were always behind.

His major addition to the corporation was the Frigerator Company, which later manufactured "Frigidaire" appliances. When the nation plunged into a postwar recession in 1920, Durant attempted to prop up General Motors stock by purchasing it himself. Having exhausted his personal resources and a $23 million loan, Durant was once again forced to relinquish his control of the corporation by nervous banking concerns. On November 30, 1920, Durant, having agreed to leave office in return for payment of all his debts, was succeeded by Pierre S. DuPont. Durant took his removal philosophically, saying: "Well, they took it away from me, but they cannot take away the credit for having done it."

In 1923 Alfred M. Sloan became president of General Motors and immediately embarked upon a reorganization program. In the future, General Motors divisions would compete for sales with other companies rather than against themselves. Furthermore, a "status ladder" was created by which consumers could demonstrate their increasing affluence through the purchase of General Motors products. Beginning with the inexpensive Chevrolet, purchasers worked their way through Pontiac, Oldsmobile, and Buick before reaching the luxurious Cadillac. Sloan's idea of appealing to the buyers' superficial desires and ego, rather than emphasing the quality of the car, gave General Motors a wide lead over Ford in sales. Ford angrily charged that the only reason Chevrolet outsold the Model T in 1926 was that it came out in a new style every year. This allegation was undoubtedly correct as the Model T was superior in design and construction, but quality was not important to the status-conscious nouveau riche of the 1920s. General Motors had become the giant of the automotive industry—a position it has steadfastly retained ever since.

Chrysler and American Motors

Another leader in the automobile industry was Walter P. Chrysler. In 1922 Chrysler resigned his position as vice-president of General Motors to assume the presidency of the nearly bankrupt Maxwell-Briscoe Motor Company. Three years later, after restoring a sound fiscal structure to the firm, it was reorganized as the Chrysler Corporation. Two new models, the Plymouth and DeSoto, were introduced to compete with Ford and General Motors in the low- and middle-price market. In 1928 Chrysler purchased the Dodge Motor Company. Chrysler stressed speed, engineering excellence, and luxury in his cars and some of his models sold for over five thousand dollars. When the Great Depression set in, Ford and General Motors, which catered primarily to the middle and laboring classes, lost much of their market, but Chrysler's sales of expensive models remained stable. Thus, the depression helped make Chrysler a serious competitor with the "Big Two" of the automobile industry.

American Motors Corporation, the youngest of the major automobile manufacturers, developed from the mergers of several old, established firms. The Hudson Motor Company, founded in 1909 by Detroit merchant Joseph L. Hudson, Roy D. Chapin, and several former Oldsmobile employees, produced the popular Essex, the nation's first fully enclosed car. Charles W. Nash, a former president of General Motors, founded the Nash Motor Company in 1916 at Kenosha, Wisconsin. In 1954 Nash and Hudson merged to become American Motors. Later the corporation purchased the Kaiser-Willys-Overland-Jeep Company and agreed to buy engines from the financially troubled Studebaker-Packard Company. American Motors struggled for several years until its new president, George W. Romney, introduced the Nash Rambler, the first modern compact car, which brought fiscal stability to the company.

Effect on Society

Michigan developed as the center of the automobile industry because of its abundance of available capital to invest in new enterprises, its leadership in the carriage manufacturing business, and the extraordinary number of skilled craftsmen and inventors who resided in the state. Not only did the automobile alter the economic growth of Michigan and the nation, but also it revolutionized American society.

No other invention affected every aspect of American life to the extent of the automobile. According to some social historians, the coming of the car marked the beginning of widespread decline in respect for law and order, as speed limits were exceeded, illegal turns made, and parking rules flaunted. Smoking habits changed as men began to utilize cigarettes and cigars more than a pipe because the latter was difficult to relight while driving. Morals were dramatically affected as young lovers left the front porch and mother's watchful eye to whisper sweet nothings to each other in the back seats of cars. Houses became smaller, with fewer bedrooms, because guests no longer had to remain overnight. Women's skirts rose so that they would not become enmeshed with the accelerator, brake, and clutch pedals. Tourism thrived and in 1915 automobile dealers promoted the initial "See America First" campaign. In 1920 over 10 million people were housed at auto courts, and five years later, the first motor hotel, or motel, was built. As mobility increased and people visited new areas of the country, job transfers became common. Family ties were weakened as cars made it easier for young adults to leave home. Also, automobile companies helped to create factory towns, replete with substandard housing, tent cities, and poor sanitation. Michigan put the nation on wheels and it was never the same again.

For Further Reading

As might be expected, numerous accounts of Michigan's role in the automobile industry exist. The most recent, and by far the most complete, general history is George S. May, *A Most Unique Machine* (Grand Rapids: William B. Eerdmans Pub. Co., 1975). Richard Crabb, *Birth of a Giant* (Philadelphia: Chilton Book Club, 1969) is interesting but not as readable as May.

Stories of General Motors abound. Arthur Pound, *The Turning Wheel* (New York: Doubleday, 1934) is a company-authorized history of General Motors' first twenty-five years and offers a wealth of information on that company's founders. George S. May, *R. E. Olds* (Grand Rapids: William B. Eerdmans Publishing Co., 1978) is a recent, thorough treatment of the Lansing inventor based on Olds' papers. Another excellent account based on primary source material is Lawrence Gustin, *Billy Durant: Creator of General Motors* (Grand Rapids: William B. Eerdmans Pub. Co., 1973). Durant's life is also recounted in John B. Rae, "The Fabulous Billy Durant," *Business History Review* (Autumn, 1958). Alfred Sloan's term as president is detailed by him in *My Years with General Motors* (Garden City, N.Y.: Doubleday, 1964). The growth of Buick and Chevrolet are described in George Dammann, *Seventy Years of Buick and Sixty Years of Chevrolet* (Glen Ellyn, Ill.: Crestline Pub., 1973 and 1972). DuPont's role at General Motors is recorded in Alfred Chandler and Stephen Salsbury, *Pierre Dupont and the Making of the Modern Corporation* (New York: Harper & Rowe, 1972). Chandler also gives a vivid account of early automobile development in *Ford, General Motors, and the Automobile Industry* (New York: Harcourt, Brace and World, 1964).

Ford's impact on industry and society is portrayed in countless volumes, the best of which are: Reynold Wik, *Henry Ford and Grassroots America* (Ann Arbor: University of Michigan Press, 1972); Booton Herndon, *Ford* (New York: Weybright and Talley, 1969); Keith Sward, *The Legend of Henry Ford* (New York: Russell and Russell, 1948); and Allan Nevins and Frank Hill, *Ford: Expansion and Challenge* and *Ford: Decline and Rebirth* (New York: Scribner, 1957 and 1962).

No works deal exclusively with Chrysler or American Motors, although the latter is treated briefly in Clark Mollenhoff, *George Romney: Mormon in Politics* (New York: Meredith Press, 1968).

14

From Bull Moose to Bull Market

Near the turn of the twentieth century the great reform movement known as progressivism took root. This movement was unusual in that it originated during a period of economic prosperity, whereas most other American reform impulses began during economic distress. Progressivism was never an organized, monolithic movement but was rather a spontaneous, sporadic response by various groups to what they perceived to be threats to both their way of life and the nation's traditional values. Three major factors were responsible for the rise of progressivism: industrialization, immigration, and urbanization.

Industrialization had brought rapid change, especially in the development of large corporations which seemed to be able to manipulate economic and political power to the detriment of the general public. As a result of this corporate growth, a maldistribution of wealth became evident. An average laborer was fortunate to earn one thousand dollars per year, while the president of Standard Oil, John D. Rockefeller, received an annual income of over $50 million. To many, this was paradoxical and contradictory in a nation that stressed egalitarianism and equal opportunity.

Growth of cities caused new societal problems as well. Decreasing agricultural prices coupled with a declining rural population meant that the Jeffersonian ideal of the yeoman farmer being the cornerstone of the Republic was rapidly becoming a fading memory. In the cities, unprecedented demands, caused by thousands of persons crowded into areas which had not expanded as quickly as the population, forced municipal officials to try to provide mass transit, sanitation, police and fire protection, and urban renewal caused by the urban explosion. Even the simplest tasks seemed overwhelming. In urban areas, for example, the question of availability of public rest rooms raised the enormous economic and political issue of who was to pay for sewage disposal and operate the sanitation department.

Hordes of immigrants, particularly from southeastern Europe, who often possessed what appeared to be strange cultural and religious customs, thronged to large industrial centers. These "huddled masses" lived in ghettoes, retained their native language and culture, and generally were despised by native-born Americans and earlier immigrants who claimed that the newcomers took jobs from them, served as unwitting tools for corrupt urban political bosses and their machines, and spread "un-American" ideas such as socialism.

Amid this atmosphere of social and economic upheaval Ida Tarbell, Lincoln Steffens, and other writers known as "muckrakers" were hired by magazines such as *McClure's* and *Cosmopolitan* to report on problems facing American society. In a series of exposés they revealed the extent of corporate malpractice in the oil and meat-packing industries, as well as corruption in large city governments. As a result of these articles, many people began to call for increased regulation of business, better protection for workers, and popular control over all phases of government. It was a last attempt at preserving individualism in an increasingly impersonal society.

Early Michigan Progressives

Progressivism operated on the local, state, and national levels. At the state level, the most completely progressive program was in Wisconsin where, under the auspices of Governor Robert "Fighting Bob" LaFollette, policies of clean government and responsibility to the electorate were promoted. The "Wisconsin Idea," as it became known, soon spread to various states, including Michigan.

Many scholars have debated the nature and support for the progressive movement. Recent studies indicate that it was so varied, diverse, and dependent upon local issues, geography, and other factors that responsibility for its development cannot be ascribed to any particular social group or class. Examples of this diversity can be seen by comparing reform efforts in two of Michigan's major cities, Grand Rapids and Detroit.

In Grand Rapids, George E. Ellis, mayor from 1906 to 1916, represented both progressive reform and old-fashioned bossism. He relied on a political coalition of ethnic voters, traditional Republicans, and blue-collar workers to keep him in office. He was not averse to visiting saloons, especially in German sectors of the city, and assuring his constituents that on the crucial liquor question he stood for regulation, not prohibition. Under his administration, flood control, creation of parks, extension of water service, and hospital construction were promoted. Ellis also spearheaded a successful drive for improved city government by the use of initiative, referendum, recall, nonpartisan elections, and a merit system for city employees. Under Ellis, Grand Rapids steadily transformed into a progressive urban center.

In Detroit, progressive reform reflected the more traditional upper-class leadership. The banner of reform was first raised by the Detroit Municipal League, which emphasized such programs as municipal ownership of utilities.

In 1912, the league dissolved following a bitter dispute between its president, Joseph L. Hudson, and its secretary, Anthony Pratt. The vacuum left by its collapse was soon filled by the creation of the Detroit Citizens League, headed by Henry Leland, president of the Cadillac Motor Company. This organization stressed morality and the "responsibility of the better classes" to "free Detroit from the tyranny of corrupt politicians and evil saloon keepers." It was closely associated with Protestantism, and, unlike Mayor Ellis of Grand Rapids, actively supported prohibition and opposed labor unions—positions which prevented the league from obtaining wide ethnic minority membership. Leland and the league perceived immigrants as "a potentially dangerous political and social force" which had to be controlled. Thus, Grand Rapids and Detroit represented reform movement organizations of distinctly different types, yet both had the similar goal of urban improvement.

One incident of reform in Detroit deserves special attention because of its rather bizarre nature and because it resulted in the Detroit Citizens League succeeding in its campaign for adoption of a new city charter. In 1912, reform Democratic Mayor William B. Thompson, who advocated municipal ownership of utilities, suspected corruption in the city council and hired the Burns Detective Agency to have one of its men pose as an officer of the Wabash Railroad Company. The agent was to contact city councilmen concerning a petition to close a street in order to construct a railway terminal. The council subsequently passed the petition, and shortly thereafter nine councilmen were arrested and charged with accepting bribes of up to one thousand dollars to support the company request. Only one was brought to trial, but conflicting testimony of witnesses resulted in his acquittal. The trial and resulting publicity did, however, prove advantageous to the league and other reform groups urging the elimination of corruption in city government. In 1918, a new charter, providing for nonpartisan city elections and creation of a nine-member council to be elected at large, was approved by the voters of Detroit. Reformers rejoiced that the "vote buyers" and "vote swappers" would lose much of their influence, but, in practice, interest groups continued to play a major role in the city government.

Chase S. Osborn—"Mr. Progressive"

Although George Ellis and Henry Leland reflected progressive ideals, it was Chase S. Osborn who deserves the title of Michigan's "Mr. Progressive." Originally a journalist, Osborn owned the *Sault Evening News* in the upper peninsula and developed it into a thriving and influential enterprise. A lover of the wilderness, on one of his journeys he discovered Moose Mountain, a rich iron range in Ontario, Canada. With his economic security thereby assured, he turned to travel and politics as outlets for his energies. After having published a two-volume work on his trek through South America, he served his state as game and fish warden, railroad commissioner, and regent of the University of Michigan. In 1900 he waged an unsuccessful campaign for the Republican gubernatorial nomination and then retired from politics until 1910, when he once again sought the nomination for governor.

Osborn pledged that if nominated and elected he would fight for stricter child and female labor laws, conservation, increased state regulation of business, honest and efficient state government, primary election laws, and workmen's compensation. A vocal critic of the conservative policies of both President William Howard Taft and Governor Fred Warner, Osborn waged an active, vigorous campaign. Using an automobile extensively, he traversed the state and gave over seven hundred speeches. His zeal was rewarded as he captured the Republican nomination and then defeated the Democratic nominee, even though his opponent was supported by conservative Republicans.

Under Osborn's leadership the legislature passed a number of reform measures, including regulation of railroads, express companies, and saloons; expansion of state authority over business; revision of the state tax structure; ratification of the Sixteenth Amendment to the United States Constitution; enactment of a state primary law; and reorganization of the National Guard. The governor's most outstanding achievement, however, was passage of the state's first workmen's compensation law. Osborn had become acquainted with this idea in 1898 when, during his European travels, he met Professor Paul Hensel of Heidelberg University, who provided him with extensive details on Germany's system of workmen's compensation. He also battled unsuccessfully for such traditional progressive reforms as initiative, referendum, and recall, but his efforts undoubtedly paved the way for their eventual passage.

The Campaign of 1912

The political campaign of 1912 was confusing on both the state and national level. Initially, Governor Osborn, despite his liberalism, declared his support for the incumbent, conservative President, Taft. When it appeared that Robert LaFollette might receive the Republican nomination, Osborn attacked the Wisconsin Progressive in a speech which received national coverage. Along with six other Republican governors, he then called for Theodore Roosevelt to enter the race. The former President agreed, but, following a bitter contest filled with personal slanders, he was defeated by Taft. When Roosevelt later ran under the Progressive, or "Bull Moose," banner, Osborn chose not to desert the Republicans and follow him. Instead, he shocked political experts by urging progressives to vote for the Democratic nominee, Woodrow Wilson. Before the campaign ended, however, the quixotic Osborn was touring the Midwest speaking

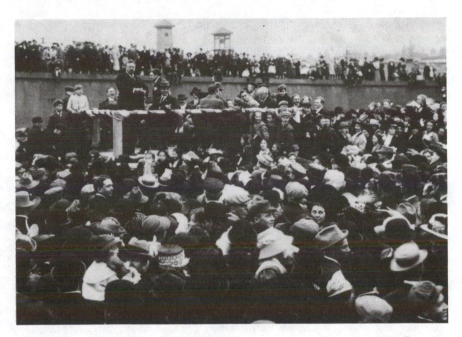

During his 1912 campaign for the presidency, Theodore Roosevelt, the Progressive Party candidate, made a tour of the upper peninsula and spoke at several rallies, including this one at Marquette.

for Roosevelt—but he avoided making any campaign speeches in Michigan which certainly aided Democratic candidates.

The split between Taft and Roosevelt forces caused severe rifts in the Michigan Republican Party. At conventions in Wayne and Calhoun counties, fistfights erupted over selection of delegates to the state convention in Bay City. Ultimately, two separate delegations of Taft and Roosevelt backers were elected and each attempted to have their credentials declared valid.

At the state convention the major concern of both factions was to capture the six at-large delegate seats to the national convention. Frank Knox, a Roosevelt supporter, was chairman of the Republican State Central Committee, and Truman H. Newberry, another Roosevelt backer, was the convention chairman, but the remainder of the convention committee was for Taft. On the eve of the convention a meeting of the State Central Committee was called by its secretary, but Knox refused to attend, claiming that it was illegal. At this meeting permanent and temporary chairmen were selected as was a sergeant-at-arms who was instructed to admit only Taft delegates. The sergeant-at-arms, along with fifty men, attempted to seize the convention hall in the evening but was stopped by National Guardsmen who had been sent by Governor Osborn to maintain order. In the morning the sergeant was permitted to take charge, which infuriated Roosevelt's followers. During the session, some Roosevelt men, who had managed to enter the hall by either sneaking through the basement or climbing through transoms, tried to make their way to the speaker's platform. Fistfights broke out and Senator Albert Beveridge of Indiana, the featured speaker, had to be ushered out a side door without giving his speech.

Eventually troops quelled the disorder and, as in the county conventions, two slates of delegates were selected. At the national convention, however, only Taft delegates were recognized, which drove many Roosevelt delegates to follow their defeated hero into the Progressive Party. The uncivilized behavior of the Republican delegates at Bay City caused the *Detroit News* to make the solemn commentary that "the Republican party of Michigan cannot but feel ashamed of its action at the state convention" and that such activity dispelled any doubt as to the need for a state presidential primary.

In November, Roosevelt carried Michigan's electoral votes for President, while the Democratic candidate for governor, Woodbridge N. Ferris, founder of Ferris Institute, also triumphed. Under Ferris more progressive legislation was passed, including the addition of initiative, referendum, and recall to the state constitution.

In 1914, former Governor Osborn won the Republican nomination for governor but was defeated by Ferris largely because conservative Republicans, remembering the 1912 contest, backed the Democratic incumbent in an effort to repay Osborn for his defection from Taft. Two years later, Republicans united to elect Albert Sleeper, a staunch conservative, and progressivism in Michigan came to a temporary halt.

Crisis in Calumet

The upper peninsula continued to attract attention even after its favorite son, Governor Osborn, left office. In July 1913, copper miners in the Keweenaw Peninsula went on strike seeking an eight-hour workday, a minimum three dollars daily wage, and recognition of the Western Federation of Miners as their bargaining agent. Mining company officials refused to recognize the union and stated that no striking workers associated with the union would be rehired. The company position was strengthened because Cornish miners refused to join the walkout and, as a result, production continued, although at a lower level.

As the strike progressed, both sides became more inflexible. Clarence Darrow, the noted criminal lawyer, went to the area and agreed to present the miners' position to Governor Ferris. The governor, however, refused to intervene, saying that the problem was local and not subject to interference from Lansing. By the end of July, new workers and strikebreakers had been imported by the companies. In response, strikers organized marches and parades, while miners throughout the nation sent money and supplies to sustain their brethren. On August 14, violence erupted as strikebreakers attacked a group of unarmed miners. Before the recently dispatched state militia reached the scene, two miners had been killed.

President Wilson sent an investigator to Calumet to report on the crisis. The agent recommended compulsory arbitration, which was acceptable to the miners but not the companies. Because Governor Ferris refused to force mediation on private business, no early settlement was possible.

By September, stratification among striking miners was evident. All English-speaking workers, except the Irish, were talking about resuming their jobs, but the foreign miners and Irish were growing increasingly militant. Hostility heightened in late November when Charles Vernetti, head of the Italian miners, told the strikers: "We will stand together till we plant the flag of liberty at all the mines, not the dirty Stars and Stripes, but the red flag of our redemption."

On December 8, a new crisis arose when three native-born, procompany workers were murdered in their sleep. Antiforeign sentiment soared and vigilante groups were formed to drive away "un-American agitators." To ease tension and reopen the mines, company officials agreed to accept all worker demands except Federation recognition. This pleased most workers and it appeared that the strike was nearly over.

This expectation was dashed, however, when, at a Christmas Eve party for strikers' families at the Italian Hall in Calumet, someone yelled "Fire!" At least seventy-two men, women, and children were killed in the ensuing panic. When rumors spread that the culprit was a strikebreaker and that other strikebreakers had barred the doors of the hall to prevent escape, hatred reached new heights.

In the early spring of 1914, the strike finally ended. Many disgusted miners had left the region and gone to Detroit and Flint to seek jobs in the rapidly expanding automobile industry. On April 13, the remaining miners voted by a 2-1 margin to return to work. Reform in the mines, like so many other social and political dreams, never reached fruition.

The End of "Demon Rum"

One of the key reforms sought during the progressive era was temperance. While popular in the pre-Civil War period, the call for limitation of liquor had not gained support during the late nineteenth and early twentieth centuries primarily because saloons were popular, especially among the new immigrants from southeastern Europe, and neither major political party dared to alienate such a large segment of potential voters. In addition, saloons not only provided refreshment after long days of toil, but also furnished newspapers, magazines, meeting rooms, billiards, free lunches, and public rest-rooms. For many Americans the saloon was the social center of their town.

Temperance received new impetus with the founding of the Anti-Saloon League in 1905. Under its leadership, prohibition forces began to muster a campaign which would ultimately achieve its goal of statewide prohibition. Beginning in 1907, local option elections by county began and within three years thirty-six Michigan counties had voted to become dry.

The campaign for prohibition reached its peak in 1916 when the famous evangelist Billy Sunday, sponsored by 120 Detroit area churches, swept through the city. Sunday, an enthusiastic, stirring preacher, told his audience that smoking, dancing, and drinking were cardinal sins. His impact on his listeners was so great that one described him as "the Democratic convention, the circus, the World Series, Chautauqua, and a declaration of war all rolled into one." Girls pledged that "lips that touch liquor shall never touch mine," and Henry Ford was so moved that he declared that if Michigan went dry, he would turn every brewery into a refinery to produce fuel for automobiles. Sunday's campaign, along with that of other earnest prohibitionists, had an effect on Michigan, and in 1916, state voters approved a prohibition amendment by over eighty thousand votes. Once again Michigan set the pace for the rest of the nation as its act went into effect a year before the Eighteenth Amendment to the Constitution made prohibition a national law.

Women's Suffrage

Even though Michigan women did not have total suffrage by 1919, many pieces of legislation had been passed to aid the lot of the working woman. State laws provided for a ten-hour work day, no Sunday labor, and prohibition of women under twenty-one years of age from working in jobs which endangered their life, health, or morals. In 1911 the legislature removed the power of a husband to retain his wife's earnings, and two years later a commission was established to set minimum wage laws for women.

In regard to voting rights, an attempt to grant suffrage was defeated in the 1908 Constitutional Convention. In 1912 Governor Osborn, an avowed backer of women's suffrage, promoted a suffrage amendment, but it was defeated by a margin of less than 800 votes in a statewide referendum. The following year, the same proposal lost by nearly 100,000 votes as some opponents of the measure claimed that the government would be in danger from votes of a "certain class of women" and the "unstable proletariat vote." Opponents also argued that suffrage might create a "new strain" on family relations if husband and wife were of differing political sentiment. It was not until the adoption of the Nineteenth Amendment to the United States Constitution in 1920 that Michigan was forced to amend its state constitution and provide women the right to vote.

World War I

Although most Michiganians, like the majority of Americans, did not really believe that the war in Europe would directly affect them, one prominent Michigan resident had been studying the military events and expressed grave concern. Henry Ford, the Dearborn industrialist and pacifist, opposed putting the United States on a war footing. He said that preparedness made the country like a "man carrying a gun" looking for trouble. He even was reported as saying that every soldier and sailor ought to have the word "murderer" embroidered on his breast. Convinced that "men sitting around a table, not men dying in a trench" would settle the dispute, Ford decided to send a "Peace Ship" to try to bring the warring factions to their senses. He chartered a Scandinavian liner, the *Oscar II*, and set sail with a group of peace advocates on December 4, 1915. The assemblage was not representative, as it contained many reporters and teachers, but no businessmen, farmers, scientists, labor officials, or industrial leaders, except Ford. One cynic remarked that it was "the strangest assortment of living creatures since the voyage of Noah's Ark."

Because of ill health, Ford left the ship when it landed at Norway, but the voyage continued to Sweden, Denmark, and Holland, where the pilgrimage ended and most of the travelers returned home. As a result of the voyage, a peace conference was arranged. Kaiser Wilhelm even presented an offer of negotiation, but his attitude was so hostile and belligerent that it failed to elicit any positive response from the Allies. With intensified German submarine warfare, the conference ceased operations. Although Ford's efforts failed, he was sincere in his desire for peace and to bring about an end to the killing in Europe.

On April 6, 1917, Congress declared war on Germany and the nation began mobilization. Michigan, however, had begun its preparations three days prior to the actual declaration as Governor Sleeper and Attorney General Alex Groesbeck developed legislation to put Michigan in a state of readiness. The legislature immediately acted upon the recommendations which included creation of a War Preparedness Board whose members would consist of the governor, attorney general, state treasurer, secretary of state, and superintendent of public instruction. This board was endowed with broad authority and was empowered to disburse monies from a $5 million fund which had been established by the legislature for preparedness purposes.

The war preparedness fund was used for a variety of programs. Soldiers were given equipment that the federal government was unable to supply adequately. The fund also made four hundred dollar loans to enable officers to purchase their own uniforms.

Army training facilities were developed at Camp Custer near Battle Creek and an air force base, Selfridge Field, was built near Mt. Clemens. To facilitate transportation near the military bases and to improve supply distribution between Detroit and Toledo, money was allocated from the war preparedness fund to improve roads. Money was also provided so that the State Board of Health could set up offices to detect and contain venereal diseases at military camps.

Because food production was a very important part of the war effort, Michigan created a Food Preparedness Committee. Once again the war preparedness fund was tapped to provide over a thousand tractors and plows for resale to state farmers and to purchase scarce seed. Thirty-six additional county agricultural agents were hired to help farmers improve production. Over 29,000 war gardens were started under the direction of students from Michigan Agricultural College and over 30,000 boys and girls were recruited to do farm work and help with harvests. Michigan's agricultural war effort was so effective that farm acreage increased by 30 percent in two years.

State security was also deemed very important. An American Protective League was established to make sure that there were no "war slackers." Unfortunately, this often led to abuses against innocent people whose only "crime" was having a Germanic name or not raising a war garden. Sometimes abuse was verbal, but at other times homes were covered by yellow paint and physical violence occurred. As fear seized Michigan residents, anything even remotely connected with Germany was considered evil. German proper names were Americanized, German foods such as sauerkraut and frankfurters were renamed "liberty cabbage" and "hot dogs," dachshunds became "liberty-pups" and Berlin, Michigan, changed its name to Marne.

To provide further for the safety of the state, a "Home Guard," consisting of six thousand men and boys, was raised to replace the federalized National Guard. A second unit, the three-hundred-man Michigan State Constabulary, the forerunner of the state police, was created to patrol railroad tunnels, docks, defense installations, and munitions plants. The constabulary also put an end to the International Workers of the World strikes in the iron mines of the upper peninsula. The commander of the unit later reported that he was convinced that the strikes had been formulated by "paid organizers" who had been furnished with "a supply of German money." No solid evidence to prove this allegation was offered, but it did further convince Michiganians that the enemy was close at hand.

Units from Michigan served gallantly in combat. Guardsmen from Michigan and Wisconsin were joined to form the 32nd, or "Red Arrow," Division, so designated because of its distinctive shoulder patches. The 32nd participated in a number of major engagements, including the Oise-Arsnie, in which it bore the brunt of the German attack, and the Meuse Argonne offensive. Over 800 of its officers received decorations, but its heroism came at a high price as its losses were 2,898 killed and 10,986 wounded. One unit of the National Guard, the First Ambulance Company, distinguished itself with the famed 42nd, or "Rainbow," Division, so named because it was comprised of Guard units from twenty-six states. The 85th Division, consisting mostly of Michigan soldiers, was in France as an occupation force in 1918. Later elements of this division were assigned to Archangel, Russia, to assist the anti-Communist forces there. Known as the "Polar Bears," they served in Russia until July 1919.

As might be expected, Michigan industries played a significant role in the war effort. Ford factories manufactured submarine chasers, and both the Lincoln and Packard Motor Companies produced aircraft engines. Although the automobile industry was not requested to abandon completely its normal production, by the end of the war most output was militarily oriented.

Michigan furnished 133,485 men, or 3.6 percent of the personnel who served in the American armed forces during the war. Of these, 45,917 were volunteers. Nearly 5,000 Michiganians died during the conflict and another 15,000 were wounded. The state did not forget its returning heroes who had fought to "make the world safe for democracy." When the war concluded, Michigan established a board in New York to meet the returning soldiers and assist them in any way possible. Like every other state, Michigan was proud of its contribution to what President Wilson pledged was "a war to end all wars."

The Newberry-Ford Senatorial Struggle

In 1918 the Sleeper Republican regime was routinely returned to office, but "political fireworks" occurred in the senatorial campaign. In the Republican primary were Truman H. Newberry, former assistant secretary of the Navy under Theodore Roosevelt and long a power in state Republican politics, former Governor Chase Osborn, and industrialist Henry Ford. The latter had the distinction of also running for the Democratic nomination at the personal urging of President Wilson, who wanted another supporter for the League of Nations in the Senate. Newberry ran a lavish campaign, spending over $176,000, which was considerably in excess of the federal campaign limit of $10,000. Ford made little effort at campaigning and uttered only two statements before the election, one in support of women's suffrage and the other in defense of his son Edsel's draft deferment. Newberry carried the Republican primary easily, and Ford won the Democratic nomination.

In the general election Ford ran a surprisingly strong race, losing by slightly less than eight thousand votes. His strength came from the working class, especially in Wayne County where he captured 65 percent of the vote. Embittered by his defeat, Ford petitioned the Senate to examine Newberry's campaign expenditures. As a consequence of the inquiry, Newberry, along with sixteen co-defendants, was prosecuted by the Justice Department for violating the Federal Corrupt Practices Act. He was found guilty, fined ten thousand dollars, and sentenced to two years in prison. The senator appealed his sentence to the Supreme Court, which overruled his conviction by a 5-4 vote.

The United States Senate also debated whether or not to expel Newberry, and despite eloquent pleas for removal by progressives Robert LaFollette and

George Norris, the Michigan senator was allowed to retain his seat. On November 19, 1922, Senator Newberry resigned, still claiming innocence of any wrongdoing. His replacement was James Couzens, a close friend of Henry Ford and a liberal former mayor of Detroit. Soon the rift in the state's political scene was healed.

The Red Scare of 1919-20

One of the most distressing results of the war was the "Red Scare" of 1919-20. Americans viewed the 1917 Bolshevik Revolution in Russia with horror. Stories spread that the new Communist regime was breaking families, crushing labor unions, destroying churches, and confiscating private property. To many, the potential dissemination of Communist ideas to our shores represented a threat to the cornerstones of American society. Fears heightened in 1919 when a rash of strikes against major industries occurred, which were followed by a series of mysterious mail-bombs being sent to prominent opponents of the strikes. A. Mitchell Palmer, attorney general of the United States and himself a target of a bombing, asserted that subversive foreign elements trying to destroy America were responsible for the acts of terrorism. To prevent further unrest, Palmer ordered J. Edgar Hoover, a young detective in the Justice Department, to put an end to the "Red threat." Under Hoover's vigorous leadership thousands of suspected "bomb factories" were raided without warrants. Their occupants were held without bail and found guilty of committing felonies without benefit of a trial.

On January 2, 1920, local, state, and federal authorities conducted a nationwide "Red raid," which resulted in the arrest of 5,483 aliens, nearly all of whom were innocent of any crime except that of being a "foreigner." Several Michigan cities were involved in this event. In Detroit, the Communist Party headquarters, the House of Masses, was stripped bare and over eight hundred persons were arrested. Thirty-six persons were taken into custody in Grand Rapids and another fifty-six in Flint. Federal authorities lavishly praised Michigan law enforcement agencies for their cooperation in ending the Red menace in the state.

In planning this raid, federal authorities neglected to prepare suitable accommodations for those arrested. Many were held in county jails, but in major metropolitan areas, where seizures were numerous, temporary detention centers had to be created. In Detroit, conditions were deplorable. The *Nation* magazine reported that

. . . eight hundred men were imprisoned for from three to six days in a dark, windowless, narrow corridor running around the big central areaway of the city's antiquated Federal building; they slept on the bare stone floor at night, in the heavy heat that welled sickeningly up to the low roof, just over their heads;

they were shoved and jostled by heavy-handed policemen; they were forbidden even the chance to perform even a makeshift shave; they were compelled to stand in long lines for access to the solitary drinking fountain and one toilet; they were denied all food for twenty hours, and after that they were fed on what their families brought in; and they were refused all communications with relatives or attorneys.

The Detroit raid was even more tragic because nearly all those arrested were innocent. Included among those taken at the House of Masses were a seventeen-year-old boy who was looking for a job, several men at the first floor cafe who had stopped for a glass of "near-beer," and a curious visitor who wanted to view the hall. The raid also netted twenty-two men in the nearby Workingmen's Sick Benefit and Educational Society hall, which had been incorrectly identified as the International Workers of the World headquarters. Nor were those arrested the only ones to suffer. Families went without food as husbands being held incommunicado could not sign orders allowing their wives to withdraw funds from their bank accounts.

Officials of the Justice Department finally admitted that they had arrested innocent citizens, but asked reporters not to mention it in their stories. These illegally detained, dirty, unshaven men, who had not even had a change of clothes for six days, looked the part of "Bolshevik terrorists" when they were paraded through the streets of Detroit on their way to another jail. Eager newsmen fanned the flames of the "Red menace" by placing guns near a pile of books and pictures of Marx and Lenin taken from the House of Masses.

Mayor Couzens finally demanded that the prisoners receive humane treatment and that the Detroit police should no longer cooperate with federal authorities. The general public, however, praised Palmer and urged him on in his crusade to save America.

Hooch, Hoodlums, and Hoods

The 1920s have been popularly depicted as a time when prosperity reigned and Americans yearned for the prewar stability which President Warren Harding called "normalcy." However, the 1920s could not be "normal" in terms of earlier decades because the country had been revolutionized by another of Michigan's contributions—the automobile. In 1900 barely 4,000 automobiles were produced, but by 1929 the number had risen to 5,620,000, and the industry employed over 370,000 persons. Job opportunities provided by automobile factories lured thousands of immigrants to Michigan, especially Detroit. The state's population soared from 3,668,412 in 1920 to 4,842,325 in 1930, and Detroit's total residency passed 1,500,000 making it the nation's fourth largest city.

Much of this population increase was a result of foreign immigration, as by 1930 Michigan claimed 849,297 foreign-born residents. Black migration from Southern states also increased the population. In 1920 there were only 60,082 blacks in Michigan, but a mere ten years later the total neared 170,000.

Detroit rapidly became the focal point of American industrialism and foreign visitors flocked to the automobile capital of the world to pay homage to the "Great Industrial Prophet." One British traveler related that "as in Rome one goes to the Vatican and endeavors to get an audience with the Pope, so in Detroit one goes to the Ford works and endeavors to see Henry Ford." Another European visitor recalled that when he first saw Detroit he felt like a "seventeenth century traveler must have felt when he approached Versailles." So powerful was Ford's impact on the popular mind that college students selected him as the third greatest figure in the history of mankind, and, in 1928, over five hundred thousand people ordered a new Model A even though Ford had announced neither its style nor price.

Some critics expressed the opinion that the emphasis on obtaining a better life through material benefits developed by science and industry was excessive and misplaced. In particular these critics were disturbed by the Detroit automotive leadership in promoting this materialistic spirit. Arthur H. Vandenberg, conservative editor of the *Grand Rapids Herald,* declared: "Save us Babbit at his best, interested in his own home—living with his own wife—striving to educate his own children—helping along his church—still believing in a just God—loving his country and his flag—preserving a few ideals—a good citizen and Samaritan." Unfortunately, few observers found this ideal in Detroit. A writer for the *New Republic* stated that "Detroit was the sum of the age," a city that was "prosperous, brittle, effective, hard, and the slave of the mechanistic monster." He added that it was "the market of personality embodied in the god production," and that it "must go on, it cannot stand still and cannot go to bed." Detroit typified America's frenzied style of living. A writer for the *Nation* bemoaned what he called the "Fordizing of a pleasant peninsula," and complained that Michigan's pastoral image was being replaced by "factories and help-wanted billboards"; it had become a state where the term "sublime" meant a Ford factory and where people "would do anything for a sale."

Critics also were disturbed at the flaunting of prohibition laws in Detroit. Liquor from Canada, particularly from a large distillery in Walkerville, Ontario, flowed freely across the Detroit River, making Detroit "a flagrant example of a wide open booze town." As many as 25,000 illicit saloons, or "blind pigs," operated in Detroit and did a $215 million business. The *New York Times* accurately proclaimed that Detroit was the "Rum Capital of the Nation" and that liquor trafficking was Michigan's second leading industry.

There was scarcely a place along the St. Clair and Detroit rivers where smuggling did not occur, and it is estimated that as many as five hundred thousand cases of illegal liquor entered the state every month. The amount of ardent

The Michigan Constabulary, which was the forerunner of the state police, display cars and whiskey captured from the noted Billingsly gang who bootlegged liquor from Canada into Michigan during prohibition.

spirits entering Michigan increased dramatically with the completion of the Ambassador Bridge in 1929 and the Detroit-Windsor Tunnel the following year. Quantities of liquor smuggled into the country by way of the tunnel were so great that it became jokingly referred to as the Detroit-Windsor Funnel. By 1931 Detroit had earned the dubious distinction of being cited by the federal government as leading the nation in prohibition violations.

Much of the illicit liquor business was controlled by criminals. In Detroit, the notorious Purple Gang vied with the Licavoli family for underworld supremacy. Accounts of murders among gangsters were regular items in Detroit newspapers, but fortunately it was rare for any nonmobster to be victimized. In addition to bootlegging, criminal activity included kidnapping, bombing, bookmaking, drugs, and prostitution. The latter vice was so widespread that during the first six months of 1926, 3,213 women were brought before Detroit Recorders Court on charges of prostitution, and over 700 brothels operated in downtown Detroit.

In 1932 Michigan repealed its prohibition statutes and the following year it became the first state to ratify the Twenty-first Amendment to the United States Constitution, which repealed national prohibition. A State Liquor Commission was created and on April 7, 1933, consumption of alcoholic beverages once again became legal.

Lawlessness was fostered further by the growth of the Ku Klux Klan. Preaching that foreigners, blacks, Jews, and Catholics were undermining Protestant morality and taking jobs from "white, real Americans," the Klan made sizable inroads in Michigan's urban centers. Flint, Saginaw, Bay City, Lansing, Kalamazoo, Muskegon, and the conservative Dutch communities along Lake Michigan were fertile recruiting grounds for the Klan, but Detroit was its main target. In 1920 that city's population was 25 percent foreign-born and it had the fastest rate of black immigration in the nation. By the mid 1920s, Michigan's Klan claimed eighty thousand members, half of whom resided in the Detroit area.

Politically the Klan was quite strong, electing mayors in Flint in 1924 and Detroit in 1929, as well as many state legislators. In Detroit one of the reasons for the success of Klan candidates was that Jewish voters stayed home rather than choose between a Klan candidate or one backed by Henry Ford, one of the country's leading anti-Semites. Ford openly blamed Jews for making obscene movies, bootlegging, and spreading immorality through their music, especially songs written by Irving Berlin.

Michigan's Klan was so well organized that it published its own newspaper, *The Fiery Cross*, held Christmas ceremonies led by a masked, hooded Santa Claus, and founded its own music business, The Cross Music and Record Company of Detroit. Even passage of the Burns Anti-Mask Law of 1923, which was intended to drive prominent men out of the Klan by forcing them to show their faces during public gatherings, did not diminish Klan strength in Michigan because many law enforcement officials were Klan members and refused to enforce the law. Thus, throughout the decade of the 1920s Michigan's Klan burned crosses with regularity.

The Politics of Normalcy

Alex J. Groesbeck, Michigan's attorney general under Sleeper, was elected governor in 1920 and reelected in 1922 and 1924. Groesbeck was a highly effective administrator and innovative executive, who reorganized Michigan's government so that the unwieldy bureaucracy became more accountable and efficient. Under his guidance the legislature passed a bill creating a State Administrative Board, composed of all elected executive officers except the lieutenant governor, which was given broad powers, with the governor retaining a veto over all its decisions. Also, five departments—agriculture, conservation, labor, public safety, and welfare—were formed, consolidating the duties of over thirty separate bureaus. To bring Michigan out of debt, Groesbeck convinced the legislature to pass a corporate franchise tax, which proved so successful that there was a substantial budget surplus by the time he left office.

The governor was interested in the state's educational and penal institutions as well. Both the University of Michigan and Michigan Agricultural College were given funds for campus improvements and building construction. Renovations were made at the Boys Vocational School at Lansing and the Girls Training

School at Adrian. In December 1924, the first concrete was poured for new prison buildings at Jackson, which ultimately would become the largest walled prison in the nation.

Groesbeck's greatest contribution as governor was his support for a modern highway program which, he proudly claimed, took "Michigan out of the mud." Although thousands of miles of roads had been built prior to Groesbeck's taking office, most of them were gravel and dirt that became virtually impassable during spring rains. A Highway Loan Board was established to market a $50 million bond issue, the proceeds of which were to be used solely for road construction. The state was aided further by a $31 million allocation from the federal government under a 1916 act which granted road-building funds to states on a matching dollar basis. When the money from the bond sale was depleted, the legislature passed a two-cent gasoline tax to finance highway improvements. By the end of Groesbeck's three terms as governor, over 6,500 miles of state roads had been improved and over 2,000 miles of concrete highway had been laid.

Despite his admirable record, Groesbeck was opposed for renomination in 1926 by conservatives, led by Vandenberg, who believed that the governor was too liberal and Detroit oriented. Conservatives united behind Fred Green, long-time mayor of Ionia, and he handily defeated both Groesbeck in the primary and his Democratic opponent in November. Green's administration enjoyed the final years of the decade of prosperity. Reelected in 1928, Green was the first of many governors who would be forced to deal with the awesome impact of the Great Depression.

For Further Reading

No single volume exists which adequately covers the Progressive era and the 1920s in Michigan. Frank B. Woodford's *Alex J. Groesbeck: Portrait of a Public Man* (Detroit: Wayne State Press, 1926) is the best secondary source for the period. *Frank Murphy: The Detroit Years* (Ann Arbor: University of Michigan Press, 1975); Harry Barnard, *Independent Man: The Life of Senator James Couzens* (New York: Scribner, 1958); C. David Tompkins, *Senator Arthur H. Vandenberg: The Evolution of a Modern Republican, 1884-1945* (East Lansing: Michigan State University Press, 1970); and Robert M. Warner, *Chase Salmon Osborn, 1860-1949* (Ann Arbor: University of Michigan Press, 1960) deal with the lives of important political figures of the period. Allen Nevins and Frank E. Hill, *Ford: Expansion and Challenge, 1915-1933* (New York: Scribner, 1957) offers coverage of Ford's political ventures. Robert Murray, *The Red Scare* (Minneapolis: University of Minnesota Press, 1955) is the standard work on the wave of anticommunism which swept the country. David Chalmers, *Hooded*

Americanism (Garden City, N.Y.: Doubleday, 1965) details Ku Klux Klan activities in every state. Useful also are the following articles from *Michigan History:* Larry D. Engelman, "Dry Renaissance: The Local Option Years," (Spring 1971); "Billy Sunday: 'God, You've Got a Job on Your Hands in Detroit," (Spring 1971); "Old Saloon Days in Michigan," (Summer 1977); Jack Elenbaas, "The Excesses of Reform: The Day the Detroit Mayor Arrested the City Council," (Spring 1970) and "The Boss of the Better Class: Henry Leland and the Detroit Citizens League, 1912-1924," (Summer 1974); and Anthony R. Travis, "Mayor George Ellis: Grand Rapids Political Boss and Progressive Reformer," (Summer 1974). The Calumet Copper Strike of 1913 is detailed in William Beck, "Someone Yelled 'Fire,'" *Detroit Magazine*, April 8, 1979.

15

Depression Life in an Industrial State

Because Michigan's leading industry was production of automobiles, which in the 1920s were still considered by many people to be luxury items rather than necessities, the state was quickly ravaged by the depression. In 1929, 5,337,087 vehicles were manufactured, but two years later the figure had plummeted to 1,331,860. The nonmanufacturing sector was affected as well and farm prices drastically declined. By 1933, farmers were so desperate that they threatened to use violence to prevent judges and sheriffs from seizing their land and homes as payment for delinquent taxes or unpaid mortgages. Fearing a riot, the legislature in 1933 postponed repayment of delinquent taxes and land tax sales for a minimum of five years. Unfortunately, faced with an immediate, dire crisis, much of Michigan's political leadership acted to compound, rather than alleviate the suffering of their constituents.

The Stigma of Poverty

To understand why both the Republican and Democratic parties shared the belief that the people had a duty to support their government but the government had no obligation to support its people, it is necessary to examine the traditional American view of unemployment and poverty. In America, the poor have always been scorned because most people consider poverty an unnecessary disgrace in this "land of plenty." This belief is rooted in the English Poor Law of 1601 which stated that people were poor because of laziness. To give the impoverished any assistance would merely reward and perpetuate their laziness, and therefore relief should be meted out only to prevent starvation. This concept became Americanized in the "work ethic," which professed that happiness and self-fulfillment could be realized only from a life of diligent labor.

When the depression struck, workers raised by this code believed that their unemployment was a result of a personal, rather than societal or economic, flaw, and they were humiliated by their plight. Men would accept any form of work before seeking public assistance. Only when their families grew hungry would they, with tears of shame in their eyes, stand in breadlines. The greatest tragedy, however, was that state and local governments fostered this unwarranted shame by keeping alive the myth that unemployment was caused by men too lazy to earn a living. During the depression, fourteen states forbade relief recipients from voting, nearly all required "relievers" to sign paupers' oaths, and, in Michigan, the Genesee County Board of Supervisors went so far as to propose that all second-generation relief recipients be sterilized.

The New Boy Governor

Michigan's governor during the years 1931-33 was Wilber M. Brucker, thirty-six-year-old conservative supporter of President Hoover's policies of "rugged individualism" and combating the depression through local and private relief agencies. When he took office in January 1931, Michigan's unemployment level was 18 percent; in 1932 it rose to 43 percent; and the following year it reached 46 percent, compared with the national level of 24 percent. The governor's response was to state repeatedly that employment opportunities existed for everyone willing to work. This, however, was not true. In late 1930 an advertisement in a Detroit newspaper called for five hundred men willing to do heavy construction to apply for jobs the following morning. Over twenty thousand applicants came, only to be informed that the advertisement had been unauthorized and no hiring was to be done. On another occasion, in 1931, over one thousand men responded to a call for sixty cement carrier positions. Despite the governor's proclamations, the unemployed of Michigan wanted jobs, but none existed.

Local relief programs soon could no longer meet the soaring needs of the unemployed. Charitable organizations were on the verge of collapse by 1932, mainly because large contributors of previous years either had lost everything in the stock-market crash or were hoarding their money. In 1931 the Detroit Community Chest fell over $500 thousand short of its goal. In an effort to raise funds, Michigan's liberal Republican Senator James Couzens pledged a personal donation of $1 million to relief agencies if other wealthy Detroiters would pledge another $9 million. For suggesting that the rich should sacrifice to assist the less fortunate, Couzens' friends not only criticized him, but also ostracized him from their social groups. Consequently, by 1932 Michigan's relief agencies, which had spent over $55 million the previous year, were nearly bankrupt.

Governor Brucker, however, was unmoved and in late 1931 refused an offer of federal assistance, wiring President Hoover that "the people of Michigan will take care of their own problem." He established a State Unemployment Commission, consisting of 105 prominent citizens, to study the problems of unemployment and make suggestions on how to remedy the situation. The governor also made speaking tours to other states urging them to purchase more goods from Michigan, which seemed to ignore that Michigan was not alone in its financial woes. In 1931 the governor announced his opposition to a proposed old-age pension law because it was financed by a property, rather than a head, tax. He further threatened to veto any unemployment compensation bills passed by the legislature, saying that the industrial instability which caused unemployment was a national, not state, problem, and if Michigan passed an unemployment compensation bill it would draw attention to the state's problems and over-emphasize them in people's minds. Moreover, he argued that such a bill would force industry out of Michigan and into states which did not compel an employer to pay laid-off workers. "Rugged individualism" was alive, but not doing well, in Michigan.

The Plight of Detroit

Of all Michigan cities, Detroit was hardest hit by the depression. Much of Detroit's problem was that while most automobile workers lived in the city, many of the largest automobile companies, especially Ford, were located outside the city limits and therefore were exempt from city taxes. Because of the unemployed automobile workers, Detroit quickly claimed the largest relief program in the state, and conservative critics began to complain that drifters were coming to the city merely to get a "hand-out." While it is true that many people arrived in Detroit in the early 1930s, few, if any, came for a "hand-out." Most were lured to the city by Governor Brucker who announced in early 1931 that he knew that automobile production was to increase and hiring would begin, and by Henry Ford, who, having slashed his payroll by 75 percent in August 1931, was promising in February 1932 that his new V-8 engine plant would hire thousands of workers. When these promises failed to become reality, the poor could not afford to leave and try to find work elsewhere.

In 1931, Frank Murphy, a liberal Democrat with strong ties to organized labor, was elected mayor of Detroit and pledged to wage war on unemployment. First, he tried to register the city's 48,000 families on relief to determine the exact magnitude of the problem. Next, he established job referral services to assist the unemployed in finding work. Third, following the example of Pingree, he encouraged people to plant "thrift gardens" and offered vacant city lots to be used as farms. Finally, he induced owners of abandoned factories to lease them to the city for the purpose of being converted into temporary housing for the unemployed. To Murphy, the first duty of his administration was to feed, clothe, and house the needy.

This approach greatly disturbed conservatives throughout the state, and many of them, especially bankers, threatened not to purchase any more City of

Detroit bonds unless Murphy reduced the welfare rolls by at least fifteen thousand. Murphy refused, but the Common Council overruled him. Opposition to Murphy's relief program intensified when it was discovered that one of the mayor's aides had embezzled $200,000 in welfare funds. The fact that he was caught and all but $20,000 was returned did little to curtail criticisms that the relief organization was mismanaged. This belief was further strengthened when Henry Ford attacked all welfare recipients as "freeloaders" and Murphy as a "Santa Claus" wasting Detroit's money.

Brucker echoed these sentiments, saying that Detroit "suffered mostly through its own generosity in establishing the dole" and that "one of the chief factors contributing to local inability to meet the present needs" was "the hopelessly inefficient and wasteful organization of relief work" in that city. He said that the city had been on a spending orgy and that the state should not have to assist it out of debt. Ultimately he authorized a $1.8 million loan to Detroit, but even that was not enough to meet the city's needs.

Riot at the Rouge

Conservative reluctance to support massive relief programs was partly rooted in a fear that liberals and unemployed workers were in league with Communists plotting the overthrow of the existing economic and political structures. This fear seemed to be substantiated on March 7, 1932, when three thousand Communist-inspired demonstrators gathered in Detroit preparatory to going to Dearborn to present Henry Ford with demands for union recognition, improved working conditions, and relief for laid-off company employees.

At the Dearborn city limits the protestors, carrying banners saying "Tax the Rich and Feed the Poor" and "We Want Bread, Not Crumbs," were met by forty Dearborn policemen, who refused them entry because they had failed to obtain a parade permit. Angry marchers pushed the police aside, which resulted in the police hurling tear gas into the throng. A riot ensued and marchers flung rocks and pieces of concrete at the retreating police. The Dearborn Fire Department arrived, but by the time they connected their hoses to force streams of icy water on the mob the fighting had reached the gates of the Rouge Assembly Plant. Police, assisted by Ford's security forces, fired into the crowd, killing four and seriously wounding nineteen others. After two hours the marchers withdrew and the battle was over.

Four days later an estimated fifteen thousand mourners, many of whom belonged to Detroit's two thousand member Communist Party, attended the funeral of the slain marchers. Speeches were made before the coffins, which rested under a huge red banner bearing a picture of Lenin. Mayor Murphy, despite a popular outcry, permitted this overt propaganda to occur, saying that the Constitution granted the rights of free assembly and free speech even to radicals. Ironically, the Communists repaid the mayor by unsuccessfully attempting to link him with Ford as a "tool of Wall Street" and enemy of the people.

Although this so-called hunger march was undeniably planned and led by Communists, nearly all the participants were not party members, but rather former Ford workers who sought aid or a promise of possible future rehiring from the company. After refusing comment for several days, Ford issued a statement denouncing all the marchers as Communists who intended to destroy his plant to symbolize the overthrow of capitalism. Public opinion did not support Ford's position and his popularity reached a new low. Latent worker hostility, which had been fueled for years by Ford's policies of increased employee productivity, decreased wages, arbitrary firings, and uncertainty of hours, now burst into the open, and the stage was set for further unrest among automotive workers.

Closing the Banks

The Democratic landslide of 1932 swept Republicans from power in Michigan. The new governor, William A. Comstock, was faced with an immediate crisis upon taking office in January 1933. From December 1929 to December 1932, nearly two hundred banks in the state had closed, leaving depositors in financial ruin. In Detroit, where the situation was most critical, only six banks were still functioning in 1933. Of these, four were independent and relatively solvent, but the two largest, the Guardian Union Company and the Detroit Bankers' Company, were extremely unstable, and since they controlled other smaller banks throughout the state their survival was imperative.

These major banks had a large percentage of their assets in mortgages and bonds which had become virtually worthless as the depression worsened. Of the two Detroit banks, the Guardian group was in a greater danger of collapse, and in 1932 it had had to borrow $15 million from the federal Reconstruction Finance Corporation. Desperate for more operating capital, the following January it requested an additional $50 million. Federal examiners, finding insufficient collateral to guarantee the entire loan, promised to provide part of the funding if large depositors, such as General Motors, Chrysler, and Ford, would supply the balance. General Motors and Chrysler agreed, realizing that if the large Detroit banks failed many smaller ones throughout the state would follow suit, but Henry Ford, a lifelong critic of banks, refused. Even a personal plea from President Hoover could not budge Ford from his belief that a private citizen should not have to help underwrite the United States Government and the Reconstruction Finance Corporation, which had been created to manage situations such as that in Detroit.

On February 12, 1933, bankers from New York and Chicago met in Detroit with government officials, local bankers, and leading industrialists. The following

In 1932, an enthusiastic Franklin D. Roosevelt campaigned for the presidency in Detroit, the nation's most depression-wracked city.

evening, having failed to find a solution to the Guardian crisis, they agreed that the bank should not reopen for business. Governor Comstock, in order to prevent panic withdrawals from other banks when the news of Guardian's closing became public, on February 14 ordered that all banks in the state be closed until February 23.

Comstock's action threw citizens into a frenzy. People with money in checking and savings accounts suddenly were temporarily destitute, and businesses were paralyzed. On February 21, Comstock extended the "Bank Holiday," but allowed banks to make limited withdrawals to depositors and to accept funds for safekeeping. Other states followed Michigan's lead and on March 6, only two days after his inaugural, President Franklin D. Roosevelt declared a national "Bank Holiday."

On March 21, the Michigan legislature passed a bill enabling solvent banks to reopen under strict supervision. The two large Detroit institutions, however, were liquidated. In an uncommon act of generosity, big depositors waived all claims to funds in order that depositors with amounts under one thousand dollars in the Guardian group and three hundred dollars in the Detroit Bankers' Company could be repaid in full. By the summer of 1933 the crisis had passed, and the creation of the Federal Deposit Insurance Corporation to insure savings up to five thousand dollars did much to restore popular confidence in banks.

Governor Comstock received widespread criticism for "illegally" closing the banks, but his quick action not only preserved Michigan's financial integrity but also served as a model for the rest of the nation.

The governor was also attacked for supporting a three cents on a dollar sales tax. Rumors spread that the money collected was to be used to build the governor a mansion, and these stories were not quelled until Comstock offered a reward to anyone who could prove their truth. Even his support of a workmen's compensation law could not alter negative opinion of Comstock, and in 1934, Republicans were restored to power and Frank Fitzgerald was elected governor.

The Voice from the Pulpit

In the midst of the bank crisis many voices stirred the masses, but none had the impact of Father Charles E. Coughlin, a Catholic priest who had a weekly radio broadcast from the Shrine of the Little Flower in Royal Oak. An ardent Roosevelt advocate in 1932, Coughlin blamed the depression on big business and bankers, who, he claimed, existed only by robbing the poor and helpless. He warned that "banking was a crap game played by the unscrupulous expert with other people's money," and spread the false story that directors of major Detroit banks had urged their wealthy friends to withdraw their funds shortly before the "Bank Holiday." His attacks on banks and investment companies temporarily diminished after Roosevelt's election, creation of the Federal Deposit Insurance Corporation and Securities and Exchange Commission, and publication of a *New York Times* expose' on how he had lost nearly fourteen thousand dollars of his "contributions for charity" in a bad stock-market investment and was heavily in debt to several Detroit banks.

In December 1934, Coughlin established the National Union for Social Justice, with its stated goals being "to uphold and defend the right of private ownership of property and to promote the welfare of all Americans, regardless of race, creed, or social situation." He urged his followers to support passage of a minimum wage law, profit-sharing plans, and increased unionization of labor.

In 1936, Coughlin's career began to decline. Calling Roosevelt a "liar" and "double crosser" because of the administration's farm and economic policies, Coughlin urged the election of William Lemke as President. He went so far as to denounce Roosevelt as "the dumbest man ever to sit in the White House" and accused him of being both sympathetic to communism and a tool of an "international conspiracy of Jewish bankers" who wished to rule the world economy. By 1937 his broadcasts were little more than anti-Semitic, anti-Roosevelt diatribes, and he was ordered by the church hierarchy to cancel his radio program. In 1942, the government had to ban mailing of his magazine, *Social Justice,* because of its opposition to America's making war against anti-Communist, anti-Jewish Nazis. Father Coughlin's days of glory were over, but his legacy of extremism continued.

Black Legion

While Father Coughlin's sermons offended many people's sensibilities, a far greater threat to civil liberties arose when the United Brotherhood of America, or the Black Legion, came to Michigan. Founded in Ohio in 1931 as an outgrowth of the Ku Klux Klan, the legion reached Michigan that same year and found eager acceptance among former southerners living in Detroit, Flint, Lansing, Saginaw, and other industrial centers. Like the Klan, the legion was a secret, ritualistic society which was opposed to Jews, blacks, Catholics, and everything and everybody perceived as a threat to "white, native-born Protestant, 100% Americanism."

In Michigan the legion was headed by Arthur Lupp, a state milk-inspector, who was appalled that "real Americans" were unemployed while "Communists" had jobs. His followers were mostly poor ex-southerners in their early thirties, who had little or no education and worked as unskilled laborers. By contrast, Lupp and the legion hierarchy were well-educated and native-born Michiganians, who, in many instances, held state or municipal government positions and were able to hire scores of their untrained members and put them on the public payroll. At its height, the legion claimed 200,000 Michigan members, but its power centered around a cadre of vicious thugs who were responsible for at least fifty-seven killings in Detroit alone during the years 1931-36.

Prospective members underwent an elaborate initiation ceremony during which they swore, at the point of a pistol, to "exert every possible means" to bring about the "extermination of the anarchists, Communists, and the Roman hierarchy and their abettors." After the oathtaking, each new legionnaire received a membership card stating that the brotherhood was strictly for Protestants, with its goal the protection of Protestant social and economic interests, and a bullet, which was accompanied by a warning that its mate would kill him if the secret oath was ever violated. Members were then assigned to one of several legal front organizations, many of which had such highly suspicious names as the Bullet Club, Night Riders, or Black Knights, and told to await instructions from their leaders.

Often the leadership issued orders simply to satisfy a personal lust for cruelty or vengeance. As Frank Woodford, a leading historian of Detroit aptly stated, "anyone . . . who incurred displeasure was liable to a midnight ride to a secluded spot where he might be shot, horsewhipped or otherwise abused by a pack of vicious self-righteous imbeciles who had convinced themselves they were only meting out justice."

Typical of such senseless brutality was the May 1935 murder of Silas

A Black Legionnaire in ceremonial garb presented both a ludicrous and terrifying image.

Coleman, a black Detroit concrete worker. Five of his white coworkers, all legion members, visited Coleman at his home and told him that they had been instructed by their foreman to bring Coleman to him for payment of eighteen dollars in back wages. Before going to the plant, the six men stopped at a tavern to celebrate Coleman's good fortune. The legionnaires then drove Coleman to a field and shot over thirty rounds of pistol fire into him. When the assassins were arrested and questioned, they professed a friendship for their victim and confessed that they had shot him simply because they "wanted to see what it was like to kill a Negro."

The Michigan Legion's power came to an abrupt end after its members killed a twenty-two-year-old Detroit WPA worker who had allegedly beaten his pregnant Protestant wife. On May 22, 1936, the victim was kidnapped, shot ten times, and his body left lying on a road. Police quickly gathered evidence, made arrests, and induced one of the suspects to confess. His testimony implicated not only his coassassins, but also his immediate legion superiors. Arrests of these lower echelon leaders started a chain reaction of confessions which ultimately led to Lupp. By the end of 1936, public indignation over revelations of legion terrorist activities had caused the remaining members of the group to disband, never to plague the state again.

Sit-Down Strikes

The elections of 1936 saw a slight Democratic resurgence in Michigan. Roosevelt, supported by Senator Couzens, who had been defeated for renomination by ex-Governor Brucker, carried the state by 500,000 votes. His coattails were long enough to cause narrow victories for Prentiss M. Brown for the United States Senate and Frank Murphy for governor.

Murphy's immediate problem as governor was how to deal with workers going on "sit-down strikes." The "sit-down" was a new device, first used in 1936 by rubber workers in Akron, Ohio, to force management to bargain collectively. In Michigan, automotive workers found the technique especially suited to their purposes for several reasons. First, because they were unskilled, a regular strike was useless. Management merely called in strikebreakers, often members of the Black Legion, to drive off the "Communist" strikers and then hired new men to replace them. Second, because of their unskilled condition, the American Federation of Labor, a craft union, refused to accept automobile workers as members. This meant that the only union available for automobile workers was that run by the company. In 1935 this was partly remedied by creation of the Committee for Industrial Organization, which included the United Automotive Workers. Management, however, still refused to bargain with this new, weak union. Third, by locking themselves in the plants, workers believed that management would be reluctant to take any action which might result in destruction of machinery and thus would be forced to negotiate peacefully. On December 30, 1936, the question was put to the test as workers at the General Motors Chevrolet and Fisher Body plants in Flint instituted a "sit-down."

Flint, in 1936, was a natural setting for worker unrest. The mayor, city manager, police chief, judges, school-board members, welfare officials, and the

On November 15, 1935, the local membership of the Automotive Industrial Workers Association called a strike against the Motor Products Company of Detroit.

President Franklin D.
Roosevelt and
Democratic Guber-
natorial candidate
Frank Murphy, 1936.

local newspaper were all controlled by General Motors. Over 80 percent of the
city's 150,000 residents depended, either directly or indirectly, on General Motors
for their livelihood. In a year when the average factory worker earned a maximum of $900, General Motors reported record net earnings of $238,500,000
and its 1,678 salaried employees, including officers and directors, received
$10,408,000. In 1936 a General Motors worker could be fired at the whim of
his foreman, would endure unpaid lay-offs between model changes which lasted
for three to five months, would have no unemployment insurance or control
over the amount of hours to be worked, and would be subjected to "speed-ups"
in production caused by firings of other workers. More than any other factor,
the "speed-up" demands brought about the strike. Forced to work at an incredible pace, with the fear of lay-offs always in their minds and an army of unemployed outside, and company spies inside to harass them, Flint auto workers
seethed with discontent.

Once in control of the plants, workers issued a list of grievances which
included demands for reinstatement of men fired for union activities, company
agreement to recognize the UAW as the sole bargaining agent for the workers,
minimum wages and maximum hours, and an ending of "speed-up" production.
Corporation officials, however, refused to negotiate until the workers vacated
the plants, and they called upon Governor Murphy to dispatch troops immediately to evict the strikers. On January 5, 1937, Murphy announced that his policy
was to remain "absolutely neutral" in the dispute. The company then organized
a letter-writing campaign to attack the governor for failing to protect the right
of private ownership of property even if so doing meant the death of a few
"labor dictators" and "Communists." The Flint Alliance, made up of General
Motors employees and local businessmen, was formed allegedly to speak for

the majority of workers by denouncing the strike and expressing a desire to return to their jobs. A court injunction against the strike was sought, but it proved useless when it was discovered that the judge who had issued it owned 3,665 shares of General Motors stock. In desperation, on January 11, General Motors ordered the Flint police to storm Fisher Body Plant Number 2. Before Murphy could send in the National Guard to restore order, the police had been driven back by a barrage of icy water and bolts. The "Battle of the Running Bulls," as it became known, resulted in fourteen workers and twelve policemen suffering wounds. Flint was in a state of civil war.

On January 13, Murphy met with General Motors officials and persuaded them to agree to negotiate once the workers left the plants, but the workers refused to leave and even ignored another court injunction. Informal negotiations did occur, however, and by February 4, the only worker demand was that the UAW be recognized as sole bargaining agent. For the next week Flint was like an armed camp as four thousand National Guardsmen, one thousand deputized vigilantes, and the Flint police surrounded the five thousand sit-downers, who had been without heat and lights for several weeks because General Motors shut off all power in the plants. Despite pleas from the mayor that the police attack, on February 11, General Motors gave in and the strike was over.

To avoid a similar occurrence, Chrysler accepted UAW representation of its workers, but Henry Ford steadfastly refused to recognize the UAW or any other union and he turned his Rouge plant into an armed fortress to repel the anticipated onslaught. Public opinion initially was with Ford because UAW militancy and willingness to work with Communists was viewed by many people as a threat to property rights. On the other hand, the UAW had to organize Ford workers or risk losing everything it had gained at General Motors and Chrysler.

On May 26, 1937, several UAW officers, including Walter Reuther, director of the union's General Motors Division, went to the Rouge plant to distribute leaflets. They were met at an overpass by members of Ford's security police and were brutally beaten. Unfortunately for Ford, newspaper reporters and photographers witnessed the entire bloody melee, and the following day, the whole country knew of the gory "Battle of the Overpass." From that day forward, public opinion steadily shifted toward the UAW.

Ford continued to resist and scored a temporary victory in February 1939 when the United States Supreme Court ruled sit-down strikes illegal. In 1940, however, the courts ordered Ford to stop interfering with union organizing efforts, and in February 1941, he was forced by the courts to pay thousands of dollars in back wages to workers he had fired for being union sympathizers. He continued to release employees favoring unionization and refused to permit a referendum on the issue. Finally, on April 4, 1941, the UAW struck and picketed the Rouge plant. Ford appealed to Governor Murray D. VanWagoner and President Roosevelt for troops to break the strike, but both refused. A week later Ford agreed to hold an election on May 21 to determine whether or not his

This picture, taken by a *Detroit News* photographer, shows (l-r) Robert Kanter, a UAW organizer, Walter Reuther, the president of West Side Local, UAW, Richard Frankensteen, the organization director of the UAW, and J.J. Kennedy, an assistant to Frankensteen, being approached by three of Henry Ford's security police at River Rouge. Minutes later violence erupted and the bloody "Battle of the Overpass" took place.

workers favored union representation. When the results showed 70 percent in favor, Ford met with UAW officials and signed the most generous contract ever given the union to that time. He agreed to a closed (all union) shop, increased wages, seniority benefits, and replacement of his security force with uniformed guards. The UAW was now a permanent force in American labor.

Sit-downs spread to nonautomotive businesses as well, and by March 3, 1937, Detroit was experiencing over thirty work stoppages. Laundries, cigar factories, warehouses, department stores, meat packing houses, and even Woolworth's dime stores were affected. Amid these strikes the *Labor News* joyfully printed the banner headline, "We've got 'em on the run, Brothers, we've got 'em on the run."

Much to the chagrin of management, Murphy refused to summon troops to end the sit-ins, choosing instead to urge the opposing sides to bargain collectively. He told Michigan citizens that he would never use bullets to end a strike. Workers appreciated this attitude, but the general public grew to resent the governor's "softness toward labor" when the strikes began to affect their normal activities. While nearly all the strikes were settled to labor's advantage, Governor Murphy paid the price for his enlightened stance as he was defeated for reelection in 1938 by Frank Fitzgerald, who pledged that "there would be no mob rule."

Growth from Troubled Times

Even though the depression years were dominated by countless tales of personal tragedy, racism, and brutality, these years also brought tremendous advances in the physical development of the state. New Deal relief and recovery measures poured federal money into Michigan and gave jobs to thousands. Civilian Conservation Corps camps recruited unemployed youths to work at reforestation projects, cleaning rivers and streams, building parks and recreational areas, and constructing roads in rural areas. Many of the spots which are today enjoyed by campers, vacationers, and tourists are a result of work done

During the Great Depression many unemployed persons were hired by the federal Works Progress Administration to do jobs in light industry. These WPA workers are shoveling snow along Gratiot Avenue in Detroit.

Navin Field, Detroit
(Post–1924).

during the depression. The Works Progress Administration hired men to do civic improvement labor in urban areas. WPA jobs included leaf raking, sewer cleaning, tree trimming, and road repair. It also funded creation of playgrounds and hiring of recreational directors. In Flint in 1935, for example, sixteen new playgrounds were built and an estimated 54,000 children used them each week; in addition, lifeguards were hired to watch every local "swimming hole." As a result of these programs, both juvenile delinquency and child traffic fatalities drastically declined, and not a single drowning occurred while a lifeguard was on duty. Cultural life was uplifted as well by the WPA because it hired unemployed actors, actresses, entertainers, and artists to perform at government expense. The Public Works Administration provided funds for heavy construction, and many schools, auditoriums, theaters, libraries, campus buildings, and airports were either erected or improved with federal money. On a more personal level, the federal government built several housing projects and instituted medical programs which enabled hundreds of Michigan residents to visit a doctor for the first time. In terms of physical and human development, it is estimated that it would have taken twenty years for private funding to accomplish what the federal government did in three.

By 1936 times were improving, the federal government was turning over relief programs to local and state agencies, and the automobile industry produced nearly 5 million cars and trucks. Even a recession the following year could not dim state pride in having Detroit being known as sport's "City of Champions," with the Tigers winning the pennant in 1934 and 1935, the Lions capturing the National Football League crown in 1935, the Red Wings taking the Stanley Cup the same year, and the "Brown Bomber" Joe Louis pounding his way to the World Heavyweight Boxing championship in 1937.

As Michiganians' self-respect and pride increased, so did the threat of war in Europe. Ironically, the economic effects of the depression lingered on until American entry in World War II brought massive government contracts to industry, put men into the armed forces, and introduced large numbers of women to factory labor. The "City of Champions" was, by 1939, without knowing it, on the road to becoming the "Arsenal of Democracy."

For Further Reading

Two excellent volumes deal with general events in Detroit during the depression. Malcomb W. Bingay, *Detroit Is My Own Home Town* (New York: Bobbs-Merrill Co., 1946) offers personal insights from a leading newspaper columnist, while Frank B. and Arthur W. Woodford, *All Our Yesterdays* (Detroit: Wayne State University Press, 1969) is a lively account of the history of the Motor City.

Sidney Fine, *Frank Murphy: The Detroit Years* (Ann Arbor: University of Michigan Press, 1976) is a scholarly recital of Murphy's rise to power. The Murphy-Brucker struggle is recounted very well in Richard T. Ortquist, "Unemployment and Relief: Michigan's Response to the Depression During the Hoover Years," *Michigan History*, LVII (1973). The banking crisis is detailed in Gordon Thomas and Max Morgan-Witts, *The Day the Bubble Burst* (New York: Doubleday, 1979).

Henry Ford has always fascinated biographers, and among the best works on his life and personal beliefs are Anne Jardim, *The First Henry Ford* (Cambridge: MIT Press, 1970); Keith Sward, *The Legend of Henry Ford* (New York: Russell and Russell, 1948); and Alex Baskin, "The Ford Hunger March," *Labor History*, XIII (1972).

The Flint sit-down strike and its effects are portrayed vividly in Sidney Fine, *Sit Down* (Ann Arbor: University of Michigan Press, 1970); Walter Linder, *How Industrial Unionism Was Won: The Great Flint Sit Down Against General Motors* (Bromley: Solidarity, 1969) and Thomas A. Karman, "Flint Sit Down Strike," *Michigan History*, XLVI (1962). The company position was put forth by General Motors' President Alfred M. Sloan in *Story of the General Motors Strike* (Detroit: General Motors Corporation, 1967). The rise of the UAW is told in James R. Prickett, "Communists and the Automobile Industry in Detroit Before 1935," *Michigan History*, LVII (1973); Irving Howe and B. J. Widick, *The U. A. W. and Walter Reuther* (New York: Random House, 1949); and William H. Chafe, "Flint and the Great Depression, *Michigan History*, LIII (1969).

Father Coughlin has been the subject of two biographies, Charles J. Tull, *Father Coughlin and the New Deal* (Syracuse: Syracuse University Press, 1965) and Sheldon Marcus, *Father Coughlin: The Tumultuous Life of the Priest of the Little Flower* (Boston: Little, Brown, 1973).

16

Inequality in the Arsenal of Democracy

Michigan residents, like those throughout the entire nation, were shocked and angered by the Japanese attack on the United States naval base at Pearl Harbor, December 7, 1941. Because of its seemingly limitless industrial capacity, Michigan became an immediate critical factor in the struggle to prevent the Axis powers—Germany, Italy, and Japan—from gaining world domination. Within hours after the news of Pearl Harbor reached Washington, the Federal Bureau of Investigation and United States Army were dispatched to Detroit. Four truckloads of soldiers were assigned to guard the Ambassador Bridge and Windsor Tunnel. Police patrolled every radio station and transmitter in the city. Plans were formulated to prevent sabotage and, if necessary, to seize all foreign-born Japanese in the state. With speed and efficiency, the automobile capital of the world was transformed into the "armorer for the Allies"—the "Arsenal of Democracy."

Michigan in the War

Michigan's contributions to the war effort are legendary and began even before active American involvement in the conflict commenced. In 1940, the United States National Defense Council, headed by General Motors President William S. Knudsen, was created to coordinate industrial preparedness. Knudsen toured industrial centers across the country and devised a blueprint to convert automobile plants, and their suppliers, into producers of war materiel. In August 1941, the government decreed that domestic automobile production had to be curtailed, and the following February it ordered that all automobile manufacturing was to cease until the conclusion of the war. General Motors symbolized the unity of the automobile industry in the war effort with its slogan "Victory Is Our Business."

[EXTRA] THE KALAMAZOO GAZETTE [EXTRA]

JAPS OPEN WAR ON U.S.

Bombers Rain Death on Honolulu
Killing Many; Hitting Battleship

Surprise Attack Held Stroke to Avert Blockade

Sudden Assault Comes Without Warning While Hull Talks with Envoys

Shock and outrage over the Japanese attack on Pearl Harbor is evident by the front page of the December 7, 1941, *The Kalamazoo Gazette*.

Over $200 billion in federal war contracts were issued, of which Michigan received better than 10 percent, second only to that granted to New York. Of the state's total war contracts, over $13 billion in business was given to Detroit-based firms. Among automobile companies, General Motors manufactured engines and munitions at several plants. The Hudson Motor Company built naval artillery. Ford produced more than 8,500 B-24 Liberator bombers at its specially constructed Willow Run plant and joined with Willys-Overland in assembling Jeeps and jet-propelled "buzz bombs." Packard built Rolls-Royce airplane engines. The Chrysler Corporation put 25,000 Grant, Sherman, and Patton tanks into combat areas from its Warren assembly operations, which, at one time, produced 1000 units per month. Chrysler and Wolverine Tube also manufactured several components used in the first atomic bombs. In September 1942, President Roosevelt toured Detroit, praised the city's labor force, and urged even greater output. The President's plea was heeded as in 1943 Detroit's industries delivered a record $12 billion in armaments. By war's end, Detroit, with 2 percent of the nation's population, was producing 10 percent of its war materiel.

Areas outside Detroit also contributed mightily to the war effort. Genesee and Ingham counties each received more than $1 billion in war contracts, while nine other counties each received armament orders worth at least $100 million. The Buick plant in Grand Blanc constructed the famous "Hellcat" tank. Gliders were made at Iron Mountain and helicopter parts at Grand Rapids. Kalamazoo manufactured amphibious tanks, while Bay City produced submarine chasers, destroyer escorts, and landing craft. Dow Chemical created synthetic-based war products at its plants in Ludington, Marysville, and Midland. The Kellogg Company of Battle Creek processed K Rations to feed combat soldiers. By war's end, Michigan had sent more than 4,000,000 engines and 200,000 mobile units, as well as 613,542 of its men and women, to the armed forces. Of these, 10,263 lost their lives, and 29,321 suffered wounds.

Michigan's war production was all the more remarkable considering the number of work hours lost because of strikes. Labor unrest stemmed from fatigue, unsympathetic management, government restrictions on wage increases, union rivalries, and worker suspicion toward union leadership. In 1944, Michigan accounted for more than 10 percent of all the nation's strikes, more than 25 percent of its idled workers, and more than 20 percent of the total production time lost because of work stoppages. During 1944, the year of the greatest labor unrest, as many as 65 percent of Michigan's UAW members went on strike. Other workers, who refused to strike, often participated in production slow-downs. Nearly all the strikes were in Detroit, where, as Alan Clive noted in his book *State of War*, "militants believed that they were fighting a war against management autocracy at home that was at least as important as the battle against fascism being waged abroad." Even though strikes were short, usually lasting only three or four days, they undermined the government's attempt to maintain unbroken production of war materiel.

Michigan's agricultural communities also served the nation by increasing cultivated acreage. Crop yields reached a record level in 1942, but several factors prohibited production from going higher. First, the federal government rationed the amount of farm machinery which could be manufactured; consequently, farmers often had to use badly outmoded equipment. Second, weather conditions played havoc with crops. In 1942 and 1943, the state received too much precipitation, in 1944 not enough, and in 1945 there was a late spring killing frost. Third, rural electrification projects begun during the depression either were cancelled or delayed. Finally, until Congress passed the Agricultural Deferment Act (1942) for youths engaged in farming, there was an immense labor shortage.

Labor shortages, which initially plagued war production efforts, were alleviated somewhat by the use of women, dubbed "Rosie the Riveters," in manufacturing plants. However, the addition of women to the work force occurred only after federal intervention. In the summer of 1942 the War Production Commission determined that because of shortages in both housing and medical facilities, Detroit could no longer accept emigrants from southern states to work in its factories. The Commission warned the Michigan Manufacturers' Association that it would cancel the state's defense contracts unless it began "recruiting large numbers of women who do not consider themselves a part of the industrial labor supply." Consequently, the Michigan Director of the War Manpower Commission distributed 650,000 postcards requesting the state's women "to take their places on the production lines." Before the struggle concluded, women worked in hundreds of war-related occupations, and without their contribution the "Arsenal of Democracy" would not have flourished as it did.

Labor shortages were eased further in 1943 with the arrival of the first of nearly five thousand German and Italian prisoners of war assigned to work in Michigan's fields and food processing centers. Approximately twenty prisoner-of-war camps operated in Michigan during the years 1943-46. In the upper peninsula, five camps, Port, Sawyer, AuTrain, Raco, and Evelyn, housed nearly one thousand prisoners. Camps in the lower peninsula were located at Fort Custer in Battle Creek, which served as the state's central induction and prisoner-of-war base, Hart, Fremont, Grant, Allegan, Odessa, Coloma, Waterloo, Bliss-

The first M-3 medium 28-ton tank rumbled out of the Chrysler Tank Arsenal on April 12, 1941 and was presented by the Chrysler Corporation as a gift to the United States Army. The Army claimed that this tank was the most powerful weapon of its type in the world and was a rolling fortress.

field, Dundee, Grosse Ile, Owosso, Freeland, and Romulus. Prisoner-of-war camps were minimum security facilities, usually consisting of tents surrounded by wooden fences. Additional security was unnecessary because, as one prisoner said: "It's not the guards or snow fence that keeps us in—it's the Atlantic Ocean."

Federal guidelines were published and distributed encouraging farmers to contact county agricultural agents to receive details on how to avail themselves of the services of the prisoners. Having been hired to work in a group, usually of ten, prisoners, guarded by a single soldier, engaged in six-day, forty-eight hour work weeks. Farmers paid the government the prevailing wage for local farm labor and, in turn, the government gave each prisoner eighty cents per day in the form of coupons redeemable in the camp commissary.

Prisoners proved to be excellent laborers. The manager of an Owosso canning plant recalled:

At first we experienced a little difficulty with them because we didn't know how to handle them, and because we spoke different languages. But after we got things straightened out, everything worked out fine. We couldn't have operated this season if it had not been for the services of these prisoners. At the peak of our operations, 95% of our male help were prisoners. We were very well satisfied.

This source of reliable, efficient workers ended in late 1946 when all the prisoners of war in Michigan were repatriated.

The War Within Michigan

Not all of Michigan's contributions to the war effort were positive, however, as the Detroit race riot of 1943 provided grist for the Axis propaganda mills. Racial unrest was not new to Detroit. On March 6, 1863, a mob of whites opposed to President Lincoln's Emancipation Proclamation and conscription laws marched into the city's black sector shouting that they refused to be sent to the front lines to die so that blacks could take their jobs. Violence erupted and blacks were brutally beaten and kicked to death. Houses were torched and when the fire department arrived, howling rioters slashed the water hoses. Since Detroit had not yet established a police force, fighting and arson continued unabated throughout the day. Troops from the local Fort Wayne arsenal finally restored order that evening, but by then hundreds of blacks had fled to find shelter in either neighboring communities or Canada.

Detroit's black population continued to increase, and by 1920, the pace

German prisoners-of-war were detained at Camp Custer in Battle Creek. Many of these prisoners would be sent throughout the state to work on farms and in factories.

Pearl Harbor Avenged

DETROIT TIMES

C   Detroit 31, Mich., Tuesday, Aug. 14, 1945.   6 Cents

JAPS ANNOUNCE SURRENDER!

Acceptance by Japan of the Allied terms of surrender was reported today by Japan's Domei Agency. Washington did not immediately confirm the Japanese report. The Domei account, recorded by the FCC, said that the Japanese government had agreed to the surrender formula as transmitted to Tokyo by the U. S. State Department. The announcement had all the authoritative ring of the first reports from Tokyo last week that Japan was ready to capitulate.

Guns Roar 'til Big 4 Gets Tokyo Note

By WILLIAM R. HUTCHINSON

WASHINGTON, Aug. 14. (INS)—The second world war with its frightful toll of human carnage rolled haltingly to an end today as the Big Four awaited official confirmation of Radio Tokyo's declaration that Japan had accepted the Allied terms of unconditional surrender.

Truman to Act for Allies

It's Not V-J Day

Domei is the agency for transmission of official information and throughout the war was the principal propaganda outlet of Nippon.

Accepts Potsdam Proclamation

Pacific Yanks Wild With Joy Over Peace

Hirohito Accepts Allies' Demands

The pride and jubilation over the end of World War II is evident in the headlines of the *Detroit Times* and the faces of the people in Detroit's Cadillac Square.

of new arrivals was so rapid that the number of black residents was doubling every five years. During this period white resentment festered, and the Ku Klux Klan found fertile recruiting ground in automobile plants filled with workers who had recently relocated from the South.

In 1925, racial hatreds broke into violence and once again the nation's eyes turned upon Detroit. Dr. Ossian Sweet, a black physician, purchased a house in a predominantly white neighborhood. Residents warned him not to enter their community, and when he ignored their threats, an angry throng congregated outside his new home. Police arrived to protect Sweet and his family, but a fight broke out in the street when relatives of the doctor arrived. Suddenly a shot was fired from within the house, killing a white bystander sitting on his porch across the street. Sweet and all nine people in his house were arrested and charged with murder. Clarence Darrow, retained as Sweet's defense attorney by the National Association for the Advancement of Colored People, argued that the fatal shot had been fired by an excited policeman, not his client. After deliberating several days, the jury declared itself hopelessly deadlocked and Presiding Recorder's Court Judge Frank Murphy decreed that a new trial would be held. At the second hearing Darrow based his defense on civil liberties and cited legal abuses suffered by blacks throughout American history. Moved by Darrow's eloquence, and an admission by Sweet's brother that he, not the doctor, fired the shot to protect the property, the all-white jury acquitted Sweet.

During the 1930s blacks made painfully slow advances in civil rights, and many black leaders expressed hope that the pace of the gains would be quickened by the outbreak of World War II. Because government officials claimed that the war was a crusade to preserve democracy and assure personal freedoms, blacks joined the armed forces in an effort to end fascism and racism not only in Europe, but also at home. Quickly they realized that their goal for America was a dream, and black servicemen bitterly complained that they fought and died in a segregated military merely to preserve their right to remain second-class citizens.

National NAACP leaders warned of unrest among their people and urged President Roosevelt to speak out against discrimination. *New Republic* magazine editorialized that Roosevelt confronted "a race problem as grave as the one Lincoln faced," but refused to admit it. In fairness to Roosevelt, he deliberately chose to ignore the potentially explosive race issue for two reasons: 1) he believed that the domestic war effort would be irreparably damaged by a federal initiative for black rights; and 2) he could not afford to lose the political support of Southern senators and congressmen which would result from his promotion of civil-rights legislation. Consequently, racial strife in urban centers became common. In June 1943, a series of nationwide race riots erupted in Western and Northern cities, the worst of which was in Detroit.

Violence had been expected in Detroit for years. Between the years 1940 and 1943, more than five hundred thousand Southern whites and fifty thousand blacks poured into the city seeking jobs. As the war progressed, tempers of the overcrowded residents grew short. Rationing, rising prices, shortages of vital commodities, fatigue from working overtime, limited availability of recreation facilities, worry over loved ones in the military, and a desire among noncombatants to prove their masculinity combined to make Detroit an explosive city. *Life* magazine called Detroit "dynamite" which was capable of either destroying Hitler or the United States. To make matters worse, as more white workers arrived, trailer camps sprang up housing large numbers of illiterate, shiftless men who were described by city officials as "cruel, pitiable, negative young savages."

Detroit was a model of racial segregation. Blacks were herded into a thirty-block ghetto called Paradise Valley, and the Detroit Housing Commission and fifty "neighborhood improvement associations," aided by the Ku Klux Klan, kept them there. Outside observers commented that Detroit was not only racially divided, but also infested with fascism. The Ku Klux Klan and similar organizations claimed over twenty thousand members, while racist ministers such as Father Charles Coughlin and Gerald L. K. Smith made Detroit their spiritual home. The *New Republic*, commenting on the influence of these churchmen, said,

The Sunday broadcasts over Detroit's radio stations were a babble of racism, fundamentalism, ignorance, and guile. They stank of an undemocratic ferment going on below the city's surface. No city, North or South, could match this hellish symphony of the Detroit radio stations.

This sentiment was echoed by the acting British consul general at Detroit who wrote to his superiors in London that "lunatic organizations have their largest audiences here" and that the majority of the city's populace were apathetic toward the outcome of the war.

Hostility began in early 1942 when two hundred black families tried to enter a new low-cost housing project named after Sojourner Truth, a black woman who had been a leader in the Underground Railroad. The development foolishly had been placed in a white neighborhood, and when the blacks arrived, over one thousand whites, coming from as far as twenty-five miles away, armed with clubs, rifles, and knives, forced them to leave. One thousand state troopers then escorted the blacks into the project, but white hatred soon drove them out again. Throughout the remainder of 1942, blacks and whites clashed in high schools, factories, and streetcars. Conditions deteriorated to such an extent that the federal Office of Facts and Figures predicted that unless the President acted quickly "hell would be let loose" in Detroit, but no action was taken.

In April 1943, over one hundred teenagers brawled in a local playground, and in early June nearly twenty-five thousand Packard Motor Company workers went on strike to protest the promotion of three black employees. Leaders of this walkout, which was the most serious of a dozen similar "hate strikes" which occurred during the first half of the year, told reporters that it might be better to allow Hitler and Hirohito to win the war than to have to continue working next to Negroes. The walkout ended peacefully, but by then many Detroiters expected a riot to begin at any time.

On June 20 the city exploded. Over one hundred thousand Detroiters, black and white, thronged to Belle Isle seeking relief from a prolonged heat wave. A black youth organized a gang of teenagers to harass white picnickers and provoke violence. Fighting spread to the bridge linking Belle Isle to the city. Sailors from the nearby Broadhead Naval Arsenal entered the fray to avenge a beating given two white sailors by blacks the previous day. By eleven o'clock that night over five thousand people were fighting on the bridge, but within three hours police had restored order without firing a shot.

Early on the morning of the 21st, a hysterical black rushed into a Paradise Valley nightclub and told the patrons that whites had killed a black woman and her baby by throwing them over the Belle Isle bridge. Enraged by this entirely false story, blacks marched to the bridge. Finding it blocked by police, the mob turned their fury on the white-owned stores and houses in Paradise Valley. Burning and looting began, liquor and guns were distributed freely, and police were summoned to restore order.

While this was occurring, white gangs were formed in response to a false rumor that blacks were attacking white women on Belle Isle. Burning, looting, and distribution of guns and liquor began, and for several hours all along Woodward Avenue blacks were indiscriminately seized and beaten.

At nine o'clock in the morning, NAACP leaders met with Mayor Edward Jeffries and requested that federal troops enter the city to quell the insanity in the streets. The mayor ignored their plea and had them removed from his office. Within the hour, however, he changed his mind and made the request to Governor Harry Kelly, but no soldiers arrived for nearly twelve hours.

After twenty hours of fighting, a state of emergency was declared. By eight o'clock in the evening of the 21st, over 75 percent of Detroit had been affected by the rioting; over one hundred fires raged throughout the city; Detroit Receiving Hospital recorded wounded residents entering at the rate of one every two minutes. Finally, troops using rifle butts and tear gas cleared the streets and by midnight the riot was over.

The fighting resulted in thirty-four deaths, over seven hundred reported injuries, more than $2 million in property damage, and at least one million man hours lost in war production. Axis propagandists used the riot as an example of American democracy; the Ethiopian Pacific League urged blacks to support the Japanese as the only true champion of nonwhite races; and American journalists wrote that a succession of Detroits could mean the loss of the war and would certainly mean the loss of the peace. Analysis of the riot participants revealed shocking facts: nearly 70 percent were under twenty-one years of age, 25 percent were female, and 25 percent were illiterate. One study concluded that part of Detroit's problem was simply that, with men in the military and women in the factories, no parental influence over their youngsters existed.

Unbelievably, city officials seemed oblivious to their problems. All blame for the riot was placed unjustly upon blacks and no attempt was made to alleviate even part of the difficulties by attempting to acquire more federal housing projects for blacks. Factory workers armed themselves and awaited the next riot. Mayor Jeffries expressed the only lesson he learned by saying "We'll know what to do next time." Unfortunately, there was a "next time," but in 1967 the city still did not "know what to do." While Michigan has much of which to be proud concerning its role in crushing tyranny in Europe and Asia, the "Arsenal of Democracy" also has much of which to be ashamed by its failure to work equally hard to crush oppression at home.

For Further Reading

Michigan's role as the "Arsenal of Democracy" is well recounted in Carl Crow, *The City of Flint Grows Up* (New York: Harper & Brothers, 1945); Frank and Arthur Woodford, *All Our Yesterdays* (Detroit: Wayne State University Press, 1969); and Marion Wilson, *The Story of Willow Run* (Ann Arbor: University of Michigan Press, 1956). Alan Clive, *State of War: Michigan in WW II* (Ann Arbor: University of Michigan Press, 1979) is the most recent, and complete, analysis of Michigan's contributions to the war effort. Agricultural contributions are detailed in Alan Clive, "The Michigan Farmer in World War II," *Michigan History* (Winter 1976). Racial unrest in Detroit is brilliantly related in Robert Conot, *American Odyssey* (New York: Morrow, 1974) and August Meier and Elliott Rudwick, *Black Detroit and the Rise of the U.A.W.* (New York: Oxford University Press, 1979). The riot of 1863 is explained, albeit inadequately, in John C. Schneider, "Detroit and the Problem of Disorder: The Riot of 1863," *Michigan History* (Spring 1974). An insightful look into the Sweet case is offered in Sidney Fine, *Frank Murphy: The Detroit Years* (Ann Arbor: University of Michigan Press, 1975). The race riot of 1943 is masterfully analyzed in Harvard Sitkoff, "The Detroit Race Riot of 1943," *Michigan History* (Fall 1969). Another account of the events which rocked Detroit is Robert Shogan and Thomas Craig, *The Detroit Race Riot* (Philadelphia: Chilton Books, 1964). An excellent work on blacks in Detroit in the nineteenth century is David M. Katzman, *Before the Ghetto* (Urbana: University of Illinois Press, 1973).

17

Fears and Frustration in the Cold War Era

Following the Second World War, the nation underwent its usual period of unstable postwar economic conditions. Businessmen clamored for higher prices, labor demanded increased wages, and consumers, whose bank accounts had swollen through wartime savings, eagerly awaited an opportunity to purchase durable goods such as automobiles which had been unavailable during the war. Since money was plentiful and merchandise scarce, inflation threatened to ravage the country unless the federal government effectively controlled the economy. The Office of Price Administration was charged with stabilizing the marketplace. Despite strikes for higher pay by workers in the automobile, meat-packing, coal, steel, railroad, and electrical industries, and consumer indifference over inflation, the agency did a remarkable job. During the ten months following the conclusion of hostilities, prices rose only 7 percent, although this still left them 33 percent higher than in January 1942. After the original Price Administration charter expired on June 30, 1946, and a new, weaker version was instituted, prices soared 25 percent within a month.

Shortages continued and blackmarket sales were common. Demand was especially high for automobiles since, according to *Fortune* magazine, there were at least 9 million units ready to be traded for new models. Because demand greatly outstripped production, it was estimated in 1946 that 75 percent of all new car deliveries were to customers who had bribed salesmen to place their orders. Meat was also in short supply and distributors sold only to their regular patrons. In Detroit, a neighborhood butcher refused to sell to a stranger who entered his shop, saying only, "Let her starve!" Using shortages and rising prices as campaign issues, Republicans swept to a nationwide victory in 1946 and gained control of both Houses of Congress for the first time since 1930.

The Father of the Bipartisan Foreign Policy

The return of Republicanism occurred much earlier in Michigan, as the GOP had regained control of the legislature in 1934 and had held the governorship since 1942 when Harry F. Kelly defeated incumbent Democrat Murray D. Van-Wagoner. The most influential Republican officeholder was United States Senator Arthur H. Vandenberg, a former Grand Rapids newspaper editor, who had been appointed to the Senate in 1928 to fill the vacancy caused by the death of Woodbridge M. Ferris. His initial years in Washington saw Vandenberg become known for his backing of President Hoover's "rugged individualism" and then for his grudging support of several New Deal recovery measures, most notably the Federal Deposit Insurance Corporation. His foremost domestic achievement was sponsoring a bill which called for automatic reapportionment of the House of Representatives after each ten-year census. In 1936 he was offered, but refused, his party's vice-presidential nomination.

Vandenberg's fame, however, rested with his role in shaping American foreign policy. Like so many other Americans, following the First World War Vandenberg became disillusioned with Europe and turned toward isolationism as a means of preventing the United States from being drawn into another foreign misadventure. Throughout the 1930s he reigned as a leading Senate spokesman for nonintervention and urged complete American neutrality in all European and Asian conflicts. In 1940, he suggested that the United States abandon the Philippines if their retention might lead to a war with Japan. That same year Vandenberg led the opposition to a Conscription Act, saying that a peacetime draft would foster war hysteria. The following year, he vigorously argued against passage of a lend-lease act on the grounds that it would give Roosevelt a "blank check" to involve the United States in World War II. Even after the Japanese attack on Pearl Harbor made isolation impossible, Vandenberg lamented that the United States "might have driven her [Japan] needlessly into hostility through its dogmatic diplomatic attitudes."

As the struggle progressed, Vandenberg complained that Roosevelt was conducting a "private war" by keeping decisions made at wartime conferences secret from both Congress and the State Department. He did reluctantly move toward internationalism because he believed that "enlightened selfishness" would require the United States "to accept international responsibilities in the postwar world far beyond anything heretofore done in peacetime." In 1943 he joined with Democratic leaders to urge Senate passage of a resolution calling for American adherence to an international peace organization after the war. He insisted, however, that no action be taken on implementing the resolution until the actual fighting had ceased.

On January 19, 1945, Vandenberg made one of the most important speeches in the history of the United States Senate. He emphasized that the nation had to remain self-reliant, but that modern aircraft and missiles had made an isolated "Fortress America," protected by the vastness of the oceans, both impractical and impossible. In an impassioned plea for sanity in the postwar world he told his colleagues:

Flesh and blood now compete unequally with winged steel. . . . If World War III ever unhappily arrives, it will open new laboratories of death too horrible to contemplate. I propose to do everything within my power to keep those laboratories closed for keeps. I want maximum American cooperation consistent with legitimate American self interest . . . to make the basic idea of Dumbarton Oaks [the conference held to create the United Nations] succeed.

Three weeks later, Roosevelt requested that he serve as a delegate to the conference drafting the United Nations Charter. He agreed and thereby became the most important Republican advocate of the new world peace organization.

From 1945 until his death in 1951, Vandenberg used his influence to win Republican support for the Truman Doctrine, Marshall Plan, North Atlantic Treaty Organization, and United States participation in the Organization of American States. Despite failing to win his party's presidential nomination in 1940, 1944, and 1948, the Michigan statesman emerged as one of the most powerful and influential spokesmen in the nation for creating mechanisms which would allow antagonists to settle disputes through negotiation rather than war. When he entered the Senate, he said that he was idealistic enough to believe that reasonable men, even with marked philosophical and political differences, could work together for the common good. Constant application of that tenet made Vandenberg one of the great Americans of the twentieth century.

The Green and White Polka Dot Bow Tie

In 1946 "Cowboy Kim" Sigler, a former Democrat who had gained statewide fame as a crime fighter while serving as special prosecutor for a one-man grand jury investigating large-scale bribery of state legislators, was elected governor. During his administration, Sigler angered conservative Republicans with his personal flamboyance and political liberalism. Nevertheless, Democratic weakness made him seem unbeatable for reelection in 1948. Sigler's Democratic challenger was G. Mennen Williams, a thirty-seven-year-old Grosse Pointe socialite and heir to the Mennen toiletries fortune. Williams toured the state promising voters that he would work for better schools, improved unemployment and workmen's compensation benefits, civil liberties laws, higher pay for teachers, low-income housing projects, aid to the elderly, modernization of prisons, and construction of a bridge across the Straits of Mackinac.

Leaders of the anti-Sigler forces within the Republican Party contrived a scheme which ultimately affected their party and the state beyond all expectations. They urged their followers not to vote for Sigler and permit Williams to win. Then, they planned to reorganize the party around a conservative candidate who would recapture the governorship for the Republicans in 1950. The sacrifice of Sigler was made, but the cost of removing the governor proved to be excessive, as no one was able to topple the new Democratic governor. In five successive elections, "Soapy," always cheerful, vigorous, and sporting his famous trademark—a green and white polka dot bow tie—won reelection over popular Republicans Harry Kelly, Secretary of State Fred Alger, Jr., State Police Commissioner Donald S. Leonard, Detroit Mayor Albert E. Cobo, and Michigan State University Professor Paul D. Bagwell. When Williams stepped aside in 1961 to become President John F. Kennedy's Undersecretary of State for African Affairs, he had governed Michigan longer than anyone else in the state's history.

Aided by his law partner Hicks Griffiths, Ann Arbor businessman Neil Staebler, United Automobile Workers President Walter Reuther, and Congress of Industrial Organizations President August Scholle, Williams assembled a liberal-labor coalition to advise him on political issues. Their chief concern was Michigan's overreliance on the automobile industry to provide revenue and employment. Consequently, the new governor pledged to promote economic diversification through tourism, agriculture, and light industry. His motto became: "We must make Michigan a more pleasant place in which to live and we must make it a more profitable place." To help fund his new proposals in 1949, Williams requested a 4 percent corporate income tax. The conservative, probusiness Republican majority, which controlled both houses of the legislature throughout Williams' twelve years in office, refused to implement the levy not only in 1949, but also in every subsequent year when the governor reintroduced it. Despite monetary difficulties, before he left office Williams had fulfilled every promise made during his 1948 campaign.

One of the governor's primary concerns was quality education. When he assumed office, 40 percent of the state's school buildings had been constructed before 1900 and 65 percent before 1920. Not only were most schools outmoded and in need of modernization, but also they were overcrowded and understaffed. The postwar "baby boom" increased the state's school-age population 54 percent during the years 1950-58. To cope with this crisis, Williams urged a state-supported consolidation program which resulted in the reduction of the number of school districts from 5,200 to 2,100, construction of more than 30,000 new classrooms, and hiring of an additional 20,000 teachers.

Colleges, universities, and community colleges also benefited from the governor's programs. During his administration, enrollment in four-year colleges and universities increased from 90,000 to 165,000 and the number of students attending community colleges rose an astounding 227 percent. In response to public demands for expanded higher education facilities, the state authorized the creation of seven new community colleges to serve regional needs. In addition, in 1956 the University of Michigan opened a branch campus at Flint in a

Elkton-Pigeon-Bay Port's modern high school represents one of the many benefits small communities can gain through consolidation of school districts.

building furnished by philanthropist Charles Stewart Mott, and three years later established another branch at Dearborn, on land donated by the Ford Motor Company. In 1956, Michigan State, which had been granted university status the previous year by the legislature, established a campus at Oakland, near Rochester, on 2,100 acres given by Mr. and Mrs. Alfred G. Wilson. During the 1950s the legislature also designated Wayne College as a state-supported university and upgraded to university level Western Michigan, Eastern Michigan, and Central Michigan colleges. Two new colleges were proposed to meet anticipated regional growth. Grand Valley State College near Grand Rapids was to ease enrollment pressures at Western Michigan University and Delta College in Bay County was to serve Saginaw Valley students. By 1960, Michigan boasted of having thirty-one four-year colleges. Unquestionably, the educational goals of John D. Pierce and Isaac Crary were carried forward dramatically by Governor Williams.

The governor was also interested in prison reforms. During a 1950 visit to the correctional institution at Marquette, he was held hostage briefly by inmates attempting an escape. After his release and the recapture of his abductors, Williams asked for a list of inmate grievances. Based upon this information, and documents furnished by prison officials, the governor established several committees to investigate the operation of the state's penal institutions. Acting upon committee recommendations, the legislature passed the Model Corrections Act, which placed all prison administration under a state director and five-member commission. At the governor's insistence, the legislature also provided funds to construct ten outdoor work camps and vocational training centers for young offenders; create a medium-security youth reformatory at Ionia; build Camp Pugsley, the nation's first state-operated youth probation facility near Traverse City; establish a youth division in the State Corrections Department; and institute a reception-diagnostic center at the world's largest walled prison at Jackson to segregate mentally unstable inmates from other prisoners. During the 1950s, Michigan's incarceration centers became models of economy, efficiency, and progressive penal rehabilitation techniques.

Another of Williams' concerns was civil rights. His stated goal was the elimination of inequality in voting, housing, employment, and schools. In 1949 he appointed an advisory committee on civil rights and urged favorable action on his proposed Fair Employment Act. Finally, in 1955, the legislature passed the bill, which included a provision for establishing a commission to hear complaints of alleged job discrimination. The governor also appointed several members of racial minorities to fill state offices and judicial vacancies. Because of his constant pleas for the national Democratic Party to take a strong stand on civil liberties, Williams earned the enmity of every Southern governor, senator, and congressman, which, in turn, ultimately cost him his party's vice-presidential nomination in 1960.

Williams' efforts to increase tourism was rewarded, and as early as 1951, more than one million fishing and four hundred thousand hunting licenses were issued. Tourist-related businesses flourished and throughout the country Chamber of Commerce advertisements touted Michigan as the nation's "water wonderland." To foster state unity and boost tourism in the upper peninsula, which had become a $50 million annual bonanza for that area by 1950, Williams urged creation of a seven-member Mackinac Bridge Authority, headed by former United States Senator Prentiss M. Brown of St. Ignace, to study the feasibility of building a span from Mackinaw City to St. Ignace. After receiving a favorable report, in 1954 the legislature authorized construction of the $100 million project. In November 1957, the 26,444 foot, four-lane "miracle bridge," the country's longest suspension span over open water carried traffic for the first time.

Aiding in the expansion of tourism was a phenomenal growth in the state's population. During the years 1950-60, Michigan's population rose 22.8 percent, making it the seventh largest state. However, 90 percent of the growth occurred in the southern two-thirds of the state, and every upper peninsula county, as well as thirty-three in the northern lower peninsula, lost residents. Also evident was a trend of whites leaving the cities. Wayne County, for example, lost 220,000 residents, nearly all from Detroit, while neighboring Oakland, Macomb, and Washtenaw gained. Most of the state's population remained clustered near urban, industrial centers. Another discernible trend was that nearly 95 percent

Senator Patrick McNamara,
Governor G. Mennen Williams and
Democratic Presidential candidate
John F. Kennedy on Mackinac
Bridge, 1960.

of newly arriving nonwhites settled in urban centers, which made inner cities a haven for minorities.

As the middle classes moved to the suburbs, new economic and social demands arose. In response to complaints about lack of safety and parking problems in downtown Detroit, in 1950 J. L. Hudson pioneered the concept of large, regional shopping centers. "Northland," a $20 million shopping mall ten miles from the center of Detroit, contained seventy stores, theaters, a baby-sitting service, and a parking lot so vast that shoppers were cautioned to remember their posted lane number to avoid losing their automobiles. Angry employers in Detroit complained that their workers who lived in suburbia arrived late for work because of traffic conditions. To prevent businessmen from moving their companies from the city, the Detroit Common Council authorized construction of the nation's first sunken expressway. The city's director of Public Works predicted that the proposed 105-mile John C. Lodge-Edsel Ford expressway system would not only eliminate forever traffic congestion, but also would save gasoline by ending slow, stop-and-go driving situations. Upon completion of the expressways in 1954, *Fortune* magazine praised Detroit for "meeting the critical problem created by its own prodigious output." The cost of this concrete network was $840 million, which included the expense of removing 5,532 houses, 401 businesses, and 39 apartment buildings. When the city began work on the Chrysler Expressway in the late 1950s, Detroit trailed only Los Angeles in miles

The Lodge-Ford Interchange in Detroit is typical of the maze of interstate highways which ribbon Michigan.

of freeway. Tourist-related businesses clamored for better roads to facilitate
travel and, as a result, Michigan became the nation's leader in interstate highways, with work either being completed or in progress on I-94, I-96, and I-75.
Finally, motorists demanded increased safety on the new roads, and in 1956
Michigan became the first state to require successful completion of a driver education class as a prerequisite for obtaining an operator's license. Not all social
and economic demands were positive, as Michiganians were gripped by irrational
fears during the postwar "Red Scare" and sought unnecessary protection
through restrictions on civil liberties.

Red Baiting

Justice Department officials had long considered Michigan a hotbed of Communist activity. During the "Red Scare" of 1919-20 Detroit, because of its
nearly 25 percent foreign-born population, was the target of a major anti-Communist raid. In August 1922, the American Communist Party held its first na-

tional convention on a farm near St. Joseph. Based on information provided by a federal agent who had infiltrated the gathering, the meeting was raided, seventeen arrests made, and party documents confiscated. Five years later a known Communist organizer was elected general secretary of the Auto Workers Union and soon afterward Communist newspapers were circulated regularly among workers. Strikes and protest marches at Flint's Fisher Body plant in 1930, Ford's Dearborn Assembly plant in 1932, and Detroit's Briggs' Manufacturing Company in 1933 all were either organized, or participated in, by Communists. The United Automobile Workers union was suspected of being pro-Communist because its leader, Walter Reuther, had visited Russia, and in 1937 General Motors executives charged that the Flint sit-down strike was Communist inspired. In 1940 the Federal Bureau of Investigation made another anti-Communist raid in Detroit, this time as a result of an unfounded rumor that a foreign army either was being, or had been, raised in the city. Because of events such as these, not only were federal intelligence agencies watching Michigan for subversive activities, but so too were concerned Michiganians.

In the years immediately following World War II, the spread of communism abroad and at home worried many Americans. Our wartime ally, Russia, was not only breaking its Yalta promise to allow free elections in its East European satellite nations, but also was encouraging, financing, and arming Communist rebels in an attempt to overthrow the governments of Greece and Turkey. In Asia, Communist forces under Mao Tse Tung were on the verge of seizing power in China. To the north in Canada, a spy ring was uncovered which had passed secret military information to the Soviet Union throughout the war. In New York City the headquarters of a Communist magazine was raided and more than two thousand stolen State Department documents were found.

Fearing further domestic subversion, the House Un-American Activities Committee (HUAC) began a series of hearings which resulted in allegations that Communists were employed in the federal government, labor unions, the media, public schools, and universities. President Harry S Truman, in an effort to forestall another "Red Scare," established a Loyalty Review Board to investigate the more than three million federal employees and recommend removal of all bad security risks. In 1948 the Justice Department prosecuted eleven leaders of the American Communist Party. During the trial, government attorneys made it appear that the defendants headed a large, dangerous, well-financed, well-structured subversive organization, which was not true. That same year, Americans were stunned when Whittaker Chambers, a senior editor of *Time* magazine and self-proclaimed former Communist, accused Alger Hiss, a respected former State Department official under Franklin Roosevelt, of being a Soviet agent. During Hiss's trials, which culminated in 1951 with his conviction for perjury, an anti-Communist hysteria swept the nation. Another "Red Scare" had begun.

In 1950 Congress passed the McCarran Act, which required all Communists and their organizations to register with the attorney general and furnish names of their publications. This act made it a crime to participate in any activity that might aid in creating a dictatorship in America and banned Communists from working in defense-related industries. The Michigan legislature expanded upon the federal law and authorized life imprisonment for anyone who either wrote or spoke subversive sentiments.

Detroit Mayor Eugene Van Antwerp and Police Commissioner Harry S. Toy urged voters in early 1950 to repeal the section of the city charter which forbade investigations into the private lives of city employees. Voters complied by a 4-1 margin and shortly thereafter full security checks into the background of every worker were begun by a newly created Loyalty Commission. Van Antwerp's primary target was the United Public Workers, which he alleged had at least 150 Communist members. Even though fewer than twenty union members resigned to avoid scrutiny, it was enough to encourage HUAC to put all of Detroit, and especially the automobile industry, under investigation.

HUAC reported in mid-1950 that Ford Local 600, with fifty-five thousand United Automobile Workers members, was opposed to fighting communism. It also claimed that twenty-seven Communist automobile workers had been placed at Flint's Buick plant to spread militancy among their colleagues. Using this unsubstantiated charge as fact, General Motors officials fired six of the reputed militants and began to purge the assembly lines of other suspected Communists—men who also happened to be the most active supporters of the unionization movement.

The question of communism even entered the 1950 gubernatorial race. Harry Kelly, the Republican candidate, claimed that Governor Williams was dominated by labor bosses, especially "Red Walter" Reuther, and ultraliberal pressure groups such as the Americans for Democratic Action. The former governor cryptically warned that it was "a short jump from the methods used by the Americans for Democratic Action to capture control of the Democratic party to the teaching of un-American philosophies in our schools." Williams, a founder of the organization in question, hinted that his opponent was a Communist dupe, saying that "everywhere when the chips are down Communists team up with the extreme right in an effort to defeat those who follow the middle course." Initial returns had Kelly the victor, but Williams sought a recount. Retabulation showed several errors and after five weeks of tension and uncertainty Williams was certified as the winner by slightly more than 1,100 votes.

As McCarthyism covered the nation with its black cloud, the Michigan legislature struck blindly at the invisible Communist enemy. In 1952 it passed both a Communist Control Act and, despite protests from the governor, a bill giving the State Police Commissioner broad powers to create a secret, antisubversive police squad. Commissioner Toy not only supported the state "Red Squad," but also established one of his own in Detroit, saying that "un-American citizens ought either to be shot, thrown out of the country, or put in jail." Toy added that vigilance was needed because Soviet agents were entering the country "disguised as Jewish rabbis," and were infiltrating the state's automobile plants. During its twenty-five-year existence the state "Red Squad," whose primary duty was to spy on members of the Socialist Workers Party, compiled a five thousand page file on thousands of Michigan residents. Over the years not only Socialists, but also civil-rights activists, liberal politicians, and antiwar demonstrators were investigated as possible subversives. In 1975, two lawsuits were filed charging that the squad suppressed dissent and violated the civil rights of persons belonging to minority political parties. The courts agreed and ordered that the squad be disbanded. While it was in operation, however, it had the power to ruin the lives of those in its files by citing lies, rumors, and innuendo as fact.

In 1952, Charles E. Potter, a member of HUAC, ran for the United States Senate against incumbent Democrat Blair Moody, Sr., who had been appointed by Williams to fill Vandenberg's unexpired term. Potter, who had been instrumental in the committee's investigations into the automobile industry, claimed that Moody was a "tool of Moscow trained" Walter Reuther and told an audience that they had to choose between "a man who believes in fighting Communism and destroying it, and a man who would destroy the committee [HUAC] which is fighting Communism." Despite extensive campaigning by Williams for Moody, Potter won. Williams also triumphed, but only after another recount, which led a disgruntled Republican to remark: "To beat Williams, you've got to beat him twice, once in the election and again at the recount."

In October 1953, local anti-Communist fervor reached a new high when six Michigan Communist Party leaders went on trial in Detroit. After four months of testimony, the jury found all six guilty. Presiding Judge Frank Pickard offered the defendants free transportation to Russia as an alternative to $10,000 fines and five years in prison, but all refused.

The following year HUAC visited Michigan in an effort to boost the reelection hopes of one of its members, Kit Clardy of Lansing. Hearings were held, and, as usual, men were accused on the basis of rumor and gossip of being Communist sympathizers. Clardy even made the constitutional right of protection against self-incrimination seem un-American and an admission of guilt, saying that he "didn't know of any innocent man that has ever appeared before this committee and invoked the Fifth Amendment." By the conclusion of the state hearings, those accused had been threatened and beaten by coworkers, had their houses stoned or burned, and lost their jobs. A jubilant Clardy exclaimed that such events were "the best kind of reaction there could have been to our hearings."

Fortunately, following the abortive Army-McCarthy hearings, the "Red Scare" waned by mid-1954 and in November fear-mongers such as Clardy were defeated in their bids for reelection. Great damage had been done, however, as thousands of innocent Michiganians had suffered the effects of irresponsible emotionalism, hatred, and hysteria.

The End of an Era

In 1959 Michigan had recovered from a lingering economic recession and businessmen were anticipating increased revenues accruing from the long-awaited opening of the St. Lawrence Seaway, which allowed direct water commerce between Michigan and European markets. Governor Williams, with an eye on a presidential bid the following year, submitted a record budget to the legislature and for the tenth consecutive year requested passage of a corporate income tax. Republicans responded by voting to increase the sales tax from three to four cents on a dollar. To dramatize that revenues from a sales tax increase would be insufficient to balance the state budget, Williams announced that state employees would not be paid for several days' labor. This ploy backfired, as Republicans blamed the governor for "payless paydays" and putting "Michigan on the rocks." Industries threatened to move to a better economic climate and the state's bond rating fell to its lowest level in history. Williams' career was ruined and, to avoid his first defeat, he announced that he would not seek a seventh term. An era in Michigan's political history had ended.

For Further Reading

The career of Senator Vandenberg is partially recounted in several volumes dealing with American foreign policy, and C. David Tompkins, *Senator Arthur Vandenberg: The Evolution of a Modern Republican* (East Lansing: Michigan State University Press, 1970) discusses his political career. However, the only book mentioning his entire career is Arthur Vandenberg, Jr., *The Private Papers of Senator Vandenberg* (Boston: Houghton Mifflin, 1951). The best biography on Governor Williams is Frank McNaughton, *Mennen Williams of Michigan* (New York: Oceana Publications, 1960), but since it is a campaign biography it must be read with care. Williams gave insight into his views of how to run a state in *A Governor's Notes* (Ann Arbor: Institute of Public Administration, University of Michigan, 1961). Creation of the Mackinac Bridge is extensively detailed by its chief engineer, David Steinman, in *Miracle Bridge at Mackinac* (Grand Rapids: Eerdmans, 1957). Michigan's role in the "Red Scare" is recounted in David Caute, *The Great Fear* (New York: Simon & Schuster, 1978), Richard M. Fried, *Men Against McCarthy* (New York: Columbia University Press, 1976), Charles E. Potter, *Days of Shame* (New York: Coward-McCann, 1965), and James R. Prickett, "Communists and the Automobile Industry in Detroit Before 1935," *Michigan History* (Fall 1973).

18

The Turbulent Sixties

During the 1960s, Michigan's population increased 13 percent, approximately the same as the national average for the decade. Nearly all the state's growth came from the suburbs, whose population swelled by 946,000, or 27 percent, to reach a total of 4,380,000. By 1970, 77 percent of Michigan's populace resided in metropolitan areas compared to a national total of 69 percent. Nonmetropolitan population accounted for a mere 10 percent of state growth during the decade.

Several trends can be detected by comparing census figures from 1970 with those compiled ten years earlier. First, the population in central cities declined from 2,570,000 to 2,468,000. Two major exceptions were Ann Arbor and the Lansing-East Lansing area which had growth rates well in excess of 40 percent, reflecting enrollment booms at the University of Michigan and Michigan State University. A more typical story was that of Detroit which lost 159,000 residents, or 10 percent of its population, while its neighboring suburbs grew by 596,000, or 28 percent. Second, rural counties such as Clare, Roscommon, and Oscoda had growth patterns exceeding 30 percent, which led some analysts to conclude that many Michiganians were opting for a slower, less complicated style of life. If that were true, it must also be concluded that the new rural populace sought solitude near urban centers, because Iron and Gogebic counties, the most remote areas in the western upper peninsula, suffered population losses of 18 percent and 17 percent, respectively. Third, white population in the state declined from 91 percent to 88 percent. In the central cities the number of whites decreased by 17 percent, while nonwhite residents increased by 41 percent. Nonwhites comprised slightly less than 5 percent of suburban growth. White flight from the inner cities was a problem which would cause serious economic, political, and social unrest as the decade progressed.

Economic Growth and Stagnation

Michigan's "boom or bust" economy is dependent upon the automobile industry, whose production output and financial well-being are dependent, in turn, upon the ever-changing whims of the buying public. The recession of 1958 had a tremendous impact upon the automobile industry and by the end of the year more than 400,000 workers were unemployed. Tragically, four years later industry analysts estimated that nearly 75 percent of those laid off in 1958 had not been recalled to their jobs. To further complicate this problem, during that four-year period over 100,000 jobs in the industry had been lost to automation.

In 1962, the state's economy began to soar as new car purchases reached record levels and unemployment, which had neared 10 percent in 1960, had fallen to 4.7 percent in 1967. Michigan's economic rebound was so great that by 1966 its Gross Product exceeded the Gross National Product of all but ten countries in the world. By the end of the decade, personal income for Michigan residents totalled $29.3 billion, which meant that an average household of four persons had an annual income of nearly $12,000.

Agriculture remained an important aspect of the state's financial growth. In 1967, Michigan ranked nineteenth in the nation in value of farm products sold, with $2.5 billion of the state's produce and dairy goods being marketed. As the 1970s drew near, Michigan ranked fifth or better in twenty farm-production categories, including first place in dry edible beans, red tart cherries, cucumbers for pickles, and eastern winter wheat. Slightly over half of farm income was derived from livestock sales and nearly 30 percent came from sales of dairy products.

Educational Advances

Educational facilities in Michigan greatly expanded at all levels as a result of the postwar "baby boom." By 1969 Michigan contained more than 4,500 public elementary and secondary schools and was expending an average of $800 per pupil in state aid. The number of community colleges had grown to 28, with an enrollment approaching 100,000 students, while 54 private colleges and universities served another 53,000 people higher education. Attendance at the state's eleven public institutions of advanced learning neared 200,000, and, in 1967 alone, these colleges and universities granted 22,000 bachelor of arts and bachelor of science degrees, 11,000 master's degrees, and 1,200 doctorates. By the end of the decade, Michigan ranked third in the output of master's degrees and fifth in doctorates. In fact, Michigan, by 1969, could claim credit for putting forth 10 percent of the nation's doctoral recipients in engineering and science.

In the late 1950s, the Detroit School Needs Committee was active in seeking new ways to finance education. Shown here are committee members Dr. Remus G. Robinson, George Romney, president of American Motors Corporation, and Detroit Superintendent of Schools Samuel Brownell.

More state assistance did not guarantee better educational opportunities, however, as local revenues were still the financial cornerstone of the schools. The problems of local financing were especially apparent in Detroit. A massive white exodus from the city had left Detroit with a nonwhite majority. As many as 20 percent were unemployed. Consequently, the ability to pay for needed additional millage for support of schools was rapidly dissolving. Vandalism, racial incidents, assaults, and poorly educated graduates combined to drive even more whites and affluent nonwhites from the inner city, which in turn diminished the tax base further. Education of high quality in Detroit, and other large industrial cities such as Flint, Lansing, and Saginaw, was becoming almost an "impossible dream" as teachers also sought more favorable surroundings.

Nor did bigger always assure a better learning environment for the thousands of students at the large state universities. In an attempt to bring professors closer to their students, Wayne State University instituted Monteith College, and Michigan State University created the residential colleges of Lyman Briggs, Justin Morrill, and James Madison. The purpose of these colleges was to offer highly specialized training to a limited and select group of students in a particular field of study. To counter the student complaint that no one listened to them because they were "just a number," in 1967 Michigan State University became the first school in the Big Ten to hire an ombudsman to hear student views, assist in problem solving, and generally "cut the red tape" which confounded many students. Education made great strides during the 1960s, but it had many new crises to face as the decade progressed.

The most perplexing question confronting university administrators during the mid-1960s was how to control student unrest without stifling academic freedom and free speech. Radical groups such as the Students for a Democratic Society not only spoke against the Vietnam War, conscription, and Reserve Officer Training Corps programs on campus, but also began to recruit members still in high school in order to assure a continuation of radical activism in the future. Many angry young black students recklessly charged that the state's universities practiced racial discrimination and sought to perpetuate segregationist policies. Calls arose for affirmative action programs to force universities to recruit more minorities both as students and faculty. Women's organizations echoed the cry for affirmative action and demanded the hiring of more female faculty. In 1969, amid rampant campus disorders, protest marches, student demands, and threats by radical groups to overthrow the "establishment" through violence, the Michigan legislature passed a law whereby any student convicted of violating city or university rules while participating in campus violence would be deemed ineligible for state scholarships and tuition grants.

Because the killing in Vietnam showed no signs of abating and overt racism was on the rise throughout the nation, "end the war" societies flourished and Black Power groups such as the Black Panthers and the Student Nonviolent Coordinating Committee attracted hundreds of new members. Even though Michigan's universities did not experience student takeovers and destruction which plagued several Eastern schools, it was clear that the days of quiet contemplation on a college campus were numbered—and it was equally evident that administrators and faculty were uncertain of the best method to meet the challenge and change in education which loomed ahead.

Another New Constitution

In 1960, Michigan's thirty-five-year-old lieutenant governor, John B. Swainson, with solid support from the United Automobile Workers union, defeated popular Secretary of State James M. Hare in the Democratic gubernatorial primary. Swainson then won a narrow triumph in the November general election over his Republican challenger, Paul D. Bagwell. The new chief executive immediately angered many Democratic leaders by removing all his predecessor's advisers except Neil Staebler and by his unwillingness to match Williams' zest in championing liberal causes and battling the Republican legislature. In fact, had it not been for the convening of a convention to revise the state constitution, Swainson's term would have been remarkably uneventful.

Dissatisfaction with Michigan's constitution and the governance structure it provided reached new heights after continuous friction between Governor Williams and the Republican legislature culminated with the infamous "payless paydays" of April 1959. Under the direction of the Junior Chamber of Commerce, League of Women Voters, and Citizens for Michigan, an organization founded in 1959 by American Motors Corporation President George W. Romney, a drive was instituted to revise the outdated constitution. The constitution had been last revised in 1908 but since then had been amended sixty-nine times. Ironically, the reason that the 1908 document survived for so long was because it contained a clause which said that even though the question of calling a constitutional convention had to come automatically before the voters every sixteen years, in order for the question to pass it had to receive a majority of the total votes cast in the election, not merely a majority of those cast on the proposal itself. Because so many voters ignore ballot proposals, a call for a constitutional convention won approval in 1948 and 1958 but was not implemented because in each instance a majority of local votes cast was not achieved. On November 8, 1960, Michigan voters remedied this problem by passing the so-called "Gateway Amendment" to the constitution. This amendment changed the requirements for calling a constitutional convention so that a majority of those voting on the proposal would decide the issue. In April 1961, voters approved the convening of a convention to revise Michigan's constitution, although the margin of victory was a mere 23,481 votes. The narrowness of this margin is more significant in light of the fact that seventy-nine of the state's eighty-three counties voted against the proposal, but proponents of the measure in Macomb, Oakland, Washtenaw, and Wayne counties turned out in sufficient numbers to provide the margin of victory.

There were 144 delegates chosen to the convention, one for each state senatorial and representative district, and, of that number, 99 were Republicans and 45 Democrats. Among the latter, forty-one came from metropolitan Detroit and the remainder from the upper peninsula. Stephen Nisbet was elected president and George Romney, Edward Hutchinson, and Thomas Downs were made vice-presidents. The delegates met for nearly eight months and the document they put forth for public approval at the polls made several notable alterations in the state government. First, to allay criticism that under the existing constitution terms for elected officials were too short and elections too frequent, it was proposed that the governor, lieutenant governor, secretary of state, attorney general, and state senators stand for election, in nonpresidential years, to four-year terms. Second, to shorten the ballot, the positions of state treasurer, superintendent of public schools, highway commissioner, and auditor general were to be filled by appointment of the governor. Third, to eliminate political unrest caused by having the governor and lieutenant governor run independently, which often resulted in members of different parties being chosen to fill the positions, beginning in 1964 the governor and lieutenant governor would run as a team. Fourth, a state ban was placed on graduated income taxes and deficit spending. Fifth, the bureaucracy was streamlined with the reduction of the number of state boards and agencies from 120 to 20. Sixth, the judiciary was modernized with the abolition of the position of justice of the peace and requirements that all judges have legal training and stand for election, rather than be appointed by the governor. Finally, the legislature was to be reapportioned according to district population rather than population and area.

Governor Swainson, Highway Commissioner John Mackie, August Scholle, and other prominent Democrats opposed the new constitution primarily because of the reorganization of the bureaucratic structure and executive branch. Most Republicans supported the new document, as did the League of Women Voters, Junior Chamber of Commerce, citizens' groups, educators, and many local organizations throughout the state. On April 1, 1963, the new constitution was approved by the slender margin of just over seven thousand votes.

A Citizen for Michigan

The constitutional convention gave Michigan not only a new constitution but also its next governor. George Romney had become well known to Michigan residents by personally rejuvenating American Motors and bringing the corporation from the brink of disaster to profitability through reliance on the compact economical Rambler. Among automobile executives Romney was considered a dangerous, crusading maverick because of his 1955 testimony before a Senate subcommittee in which he attacked his industry's insistence on putting "dinosaurs in our driveways" and convincing the public that they needed "cars nineteen feet long and weighing two tons . . . to run a 118-pound housewife three blocks to the drugstore for a two-ounce package of bobby pins and lipstick." He further proposed that the federal government should consider breaking monopolies such as General Motors in order to increase competition in the automotive market.

In 1957, Romney turned his attention to securing tax reform legislation and two years later he formed Citizens for Michigan to act as a "people's lobby" to further that cause. As the most prominent and vocal member of the constitutional convention, Romney was accused by Democrats of using that body to foster his own political and economic beliefs. His influence on the convention was so great that the new constitution was called by some critics "Romney's Charter" and its passage was viewed by political analysts as a "victory for Romney in the face of the Democrats, organized labor, and the National Association for the Advancement of Colored People."

In February 1962, while serving as a delegate to the constitutional convention, Romney announced his candidacy for the Republican gubernatorial nomination. Using the slogan "Let's Get Michigan on the Move," Romney turned the campaign into a personal crusade, ignoring other Republican candidates and earning the enmity of party leaders who dubbed him "Lonesome George." Handsome, athletic, silver-haired, and jut-jawed, the dynamic and indefatigable Romney captivated audiences throughout the state.

Romney's opponent, incumbent Governor Swainson, was hampered by a deep split between the liberal-labor and conservative elements of the Democratic Party. The governor was further weakened by his veto of a bill which would have prohibited Detroit from assessing an income tax on suburbanites who were employed within the city. State Senator John Bowman, a Roseville Democrat who sponsored the bill, predicted that Swainson's action would cost him eighty thousand votes in November. In an effort to counter the definite swing to his adversary, Swainson agreed to meet Romney in a series of statewide debates. The governor's attempt was to no avail as Romney triumphed by eighty thousand votes—a cruel irony for Swainson in light of Bowman's earlier comment. Republicans had little reason for jubilation, however, because except for Romney, the entire party slate had been defeated.

In 1964 Romney again separated himself from the Republican ticket and refused to support conservative Senator Barry M. Goldwater, the party's presidential nominee, lest he alienate his liberal and independent backers. Romney's opponent was Neil Staebler, who was considered by many to be the most influential and astute Democrat in the state. Staebler's campaign suffered because Michigan was in the midst of a period of economic prosperity; however, party leaders hoped that if President Lyndon B. Johnson received a 500,000 vote majority in the state, his "coattails" would carry Staebler to victory as well. Johnson did better than expected, beating Goldwater by more than one million votes in Michigan, but, to the surprise of political observers, Romney trounced Staebler by almost 400,000 votes.

Two years later Romney ran for a third term against Zolton Ferency, the liberal chairman of the Democratic State Central Committee. For the first time, Romney made an effort to be a "team player" and campaigned for other Republican candidates, especially Robert Griffin, the newly appointed United States senator who was running for a full term against former Governor Williams. Throughout the campaign, Ferency tried to exploit the governor's previous independence by joking that Romney had accused him of starting a smear campaign because he had called the governor a Republican! Despite Ferency's wit, the Republicans won a smashing victory with Romney triumphing by well over 500,000 votes while Griffin amassed an unexpectedly large 220,000 vote margin over Williams. Moreover, Republicans gained eighteen seats in the state legislature.

By 1967, Romney's record of achievement and impressive victories at the polls made him the forerunner in the quest for the 1968 Republican presidential nomination. Ironically, the governor's candid honesty cost him that prize. In October 1965, Romney had made a four-day tour of South Vietnam and returned convinced that Johnson's Asian policies were correct. During the next two years the governor came to believe that while in Vietnam he had been lied to by high-ranking American civilian and military personnel, and that the harsh reality was that the United States' war effort had become a source of humiliation abroad and demoralization at home. On September 4, 1967, the governor appeared on a Detroit television interview program and said that when he visited Vietnam he had received "the greatest brainwashing that anybody can get." Newsmen seized upon this statement and portrayed Romney as being too gullible and naive to be President. For all practical purposes, that single honest remark removed Romney from serious presidential consideration. During the campaign the governor vigorously stumped Michigan and other states on behalf of the Republican nominee Richard M. Nixon. As a reward for his service to the party and in recognition of his remarkable record as Michigan's chief executive, Romney was appointed to serve in Nixon's cabinet as secretary of Housing and Urban Development. On January 22, 1969, Romney resigned as governor and was succeeded by Lieutenant Governor William G. Milliken.

During Romney's administration Michigan's economy rebounded and the governor basked in the relative ease by which state services could meet expanding needs and still achieve the constitutionally mandated balanced budget. In 1963 and 1965 the governor sent a tax reform program to the legislature, but each time it was defeated by a coalition of Democrats and conservative Republicans. The election of more liberal Republicans to the state senate in 1966 enabled Romney's 1967 tax reform package, which imposed levies of 2.6 percent on individual income, 5.6 percent on corporate earnings, and 7 percent on financial institutions, to be enacted into law. Romney also pushed for improved civil rights and mental health legislation, upward revision of the minimum wage law, strengthened unemployment and workmen's compensation benefits, reorganization of the state department of labor, and passage of the state's first construction safety bill. Under Romney's leadership Michigan escaped the economic darkness of the 1950s and moved forward with progressive social legislation; only the tragedy which befell Detroit in the summer of 1967 marred his years in office.

Playing Politics While a City Burned

Because of its large and growing black population, Detroit was active in the strong civil rights impulse which swept the nation during the early 1960s. In June 1963, approximately 250,000 blacks and whites assembled outside Cobo

Reverend Martin Luther
King, Jr. and Governor
John B. Swainson.

Hall to hear speeches by former Governor Swainson, Detroit's Mayor Jerome
Cavanagh and Police Commissioner George Edwards, Walter Reuther, and Reverend Martin Luther King, Jr., the "Black Apostle of Nonviolence." King told
the enthusiastic throng that they represented the "largest and greatest demon-
stration ever held in the United States" and that their message was ringing clearly
throughout the country: "We want all of our rights. We want them here and we
want them now."

Detroit had been selected for the 1963 civil-rights conclave partly because
Mayor Cavanagh, the thirty-five-year-old liberal attorney who had scored a stun-
ning upset victory over the incumbent mayor in 1961, had pledged to make his
city a model of harmonious race relations and to eradicate hunger, substandard
housing, and high levels of minority unemployment. By 1967, Cavanagh had
obtained for his city more than $42 million in federal antipoverty funds. Of this
sum, $10 million was used for special training and placement programs for the
unskilled and illiterate, $4 million for medical clinics, and $3 million for summer Head Start and recreational programs for children. Detroit seemed to be
handling its problems so efficiently that the director of the Congress of Racial

Equality, Floyd McKissick, excluded it from a list of twelve cities he thought likely to experience racial unrest in 1967.

Despite the money spent and effort expended, Detroit still simmered with discontent. Unemployment reached 11 percent in mid-1967, and the total was even higher among black youths. Inner-city blacks demanded more jobs, better housing, quality education, an end to alleged police harassment, and respect. In late June 1967, Black Panther leader H. Rap Brown addressed a Black Arts Convention in Detroit and urged the black community to "Let white America know that the name of the game is tit-for-tat, an eye for an eye, a tooth for a tooth, and a life for a life." His final warning proved prophetic: "Motown, if you don't come around, we're going to burn you down."

July 1967 was oppressively hot and humid, causing tempers to grow short. On July 23, Detroit police made an early morning raid on the United Community League for Civil Action, an illegal after-hours drinking establishment in the dilapidated, predominantly black, 12th Street area, and arrested the bartender and eighty-two customers. Within minutes, hundreds of jeering spectators gathered and someone heaved a bottle through the squad car's windshield. The crowd quickly was transformed into an uncontrollable mob engaged in looting, vandalism, and arson.

Mayor Cavanagh had two socially and politically sound options. First, he could remove all police from the area in hopes that the mob would disperse of its own volition. Second, he could send in massive numbers of riot police to prevent the unrest from spreading. Unfortunately, he did neither. He ordered police to the scene, but instructed them not to forcibly disperse the rioters. When the mob realized that the police were mere spectators, looting increased, especially against white-owned shops. Over 1,600 fires were set, but the fire department was unable to respond effectively because rioters pelted the fire-fighters with bricks, rocks, and bottles. Even Congressman John Conyers and City Councilman Nicholas Hood, two of Detroit's most popular and influential black leaders, were stoned when they tried to calm the mob. Just as twenty-four years earlier, "all Hell had broken loose" in the Motor City.

At nine in the evening of the twenty-third, Governor Romney declared a state of emergency in Detroit, Highland Park, and Hamtramck, and dispatched the first of 7,300 National Guardsmen to the riot scene. Meanwhile, reports of violence in Flint, Saginaw, Grand Rapids, Benton Harbor, Muskegon, Kalamazoo, Mt. Clemens, and Pontiac reached the governor's office. Shortly after three o'clock in the morning of the twenty-fourth, Romney, with the support of such prominent Democrats as Walter Reuther and black Detroit Congressman Charles Diggs, telephoned United States Attorney General Ramsey Clark asking for federal troops to be sent to Detroit. The attorney general asked the governor to formally "request" soldiers to quell the "insurrection." Romney angrily refused and reminded Clark that no insurance companies would pay for damages incurred through an insurrection. The governor asked, "Who's going to rebuild this place after the troops go home?" and slammed down the receiver. By mid-morning Romney's temper had cooled and he made the required formal request, but omitted any reference to an insurrection. In response, President Johnson ordered the 82nd and 101st Airborne Divisions to Selfridge Air Force Base near Mt. Clemens. The paratroopers were instructed, however, not to enter the riot scene until the President's personal emissary, Cyrus Vance, had met with Romney, toured the area, and reported to Johnson.

Romney's fury raged anew when the President made a nationwide television address in which he stated that he had sent soldiers into Detroit "with the greatest regret" and "only because of the clear, unmistakable, and undisputed evidence that Governor Romney and local officials have been unable to bring the situation under control." The governor, a leading candidate for the 1968 Republican presidential nomination, charged that Johnson "played politics with the riot" merely to discredit a potential challenger. Finally, twenty-four hours after Romney's initial request for federal assistance, paratroopers entered the ravaged city and the violence soon abated.

By July 28, the most costly riot in the nation's history was over. Property damage exceeded $50 million; 44 people lost their lives and another 1,000 were injured seriously enough to require medical attention; 5,000 residents of Detroit were left homeless; and 7,331 arrests had been made. Another tragic aspect of the riot's aftermath was the appearance of profiteers who sought to take advantage of the plight of the needy by charging one dollar for a twenty-five cent quart of milk and equally exorbitant amounts for other necessary commodities.

The underlying causes of the riot were never pinpointed, but the blame for its spread was placed squarely with President Johnson. The *Detroit News* editorialized that: "The President seemed to go out of his way to blame Mr. Romney, a Republican presidential contender, for failing to handle the Detroit situation. This newspaper does not believe that politics was played in Detroit or Lansing.

During the Detroit riot of 1967 entire city blocks were leveled by fire.

But it strongly believes it was played in Washington and perhaps even prolonged the riot." *The New York Times* said that Johnson "shilly-shallied" and
was grossly partisan in trying to "place the entire political responsibility on
Governor Romney."

Following the disorders, many Detroiters asserted that the events were not
a race riot. Richard Emrick, Episcopal bishop of Michigan and chairman of the
Detroit Citizens' Committee for Equal Opportunity, noted that "This was not a
race riot. The looting and sniping were integrated. The major part of the riot
was a criminal attack upon property. . . . But there was no racial warfare, which
means that we can assume the basic unity of the city and look forward to re-
building and working together." A "New Detroit Committee," headed by Joseph
L. Hudson, Jr., was established to bring together community leaders to discuss
the city's problems and plan for its future. Working as a united, concerned citizenry, it was hoped that Detroit could be reborn and undergo a spiritual and
cultural renaissance which would recapture the dream of racial harmony and
prosperity.

For Further Reading

Michigan's political structure during the 1960s is excellently analyzed in
Carolyn Stieber, *The Politics of Change in Michigan* (East Lansing: Michigan
State University Press, 1970). The making of the new constitution is recounted
in Albert L. Sturm, *Constitution Making in Michigan* (Ann Arbor: Institute of
Public Administration, University of Michigan, 1963) and James K. Pollock,
Making Michigan's New Constitution, 1961-1962 (Ann Arbor: University of
Michigan Press, 1962). Eugene Finegold (ed.), *Michigan Writes a New Consti-
tution* (Detroit: Proceedings of the 1961 MCEP faculty workshop, 1962) contains addresses made by prominent citizens active in the movement for calling a
constitutional convention.

Governor Romney's career is covered in several biographies, but all are
campaign oriented and must be read as such. Among the best are Dan Angel,
Romney: A Political Biography (New York: Exposition Press, 1966); Richard
Fuller, *George Romney and Michigan* (New York: Vantage Press, 1966); and T.
George Harris, *Romney's Way: A Man and an Idea* (Englewood Cliffs: Prentice-
Hall, 1967).

Campus unrest is discussed in minute detail in the *Final Staff Report, State
of Michigan Senate Committee to Investigate Campus Disorders and Student
Unrest* (Lansing: State of Michigan, 1970).

The Detroit riot is the subject of many superb studies. The most insightful
are Robert Conot, *American Odyssey* (New York: Morrow, 1974); James H. Lincoln, *The Anatomy of a Riot* (New York: McGraw-Hill, 1968); John Hershey,
The Algiers Motel Incident (Alfred A. Knopf, 1969); and Sidney Fine, *Violence
in the Model City* (Ann Arbor: University of Michigan Press, 1989).

19

Challenges of the 1970s

The 1970s brought challenge and change to Michigan. Effects of the "counterculture revolution" in which "hippies" made nonconformity a symbol of freedom to restless youths, Watergate, the Arab oil embargo, continued fighting in Vietnam, and the P.B.B. crisis profoundly affected state residents, while beads, long hair, short skirts, drug usage, increasing "crime in the streets," and antiwar protest marches became part of Michigan's social scene. As the decade neared its end, congressional insistence on stringent automobile emission standards and improved gasoline mileage, coupled with the aggressive recruiting of industries by Southern municipalities promising cheaper labor costs and lower taxes, raised the haunting question of whether Michigan could maintain its industrial economic base. Rising uncertainty concerning the future seemed to be the only common factor among Michiganians as they faced the 1980s.

Crime and Urban Blight

Perhaps the greatest problems Michigan confronted during the 1970s were a 300 percent increase in violent crime and the erosion of urban centers, both of which were especially evident in Detroit. Michigan's largest city lost 100,000 residents during the 1960s and another 100,000 departed between the years 1970 and 1975. Loss of industries to the suburbs and to other states, combined with a decline in the number of available jobs because of increased automation in manufacturing plants, created high unemployment, ranging close to 50 percent for black teenagers, in the inner city. Neighborhoods deteriorated, vacant houses and shops became common, and crime grew rampant.

Statistics for 1971 indicated that illegal narcotic activities represented a $350 million annual operation in Detroit and that "drug warfare" during the first six months of that year had resulted in forty deaths. In 1973 *Time* magazine featured an article naming Detroit the "Murder City" and "Crime Capital of the Nation" because during the preceding year the city had recorded 601 homicides, the highest per capita murder rate in the country.

To reduce the crime rate, a plainclothes police unit known as STRESS—Stop The Robbers, Enjoy Safe Streets—was established. Despite an admirable record of success, the unit was forced to disband because of allegations of brutality and racism from the black community. Crime, usually drug related, escalated dramatically. By 1975, Detroit averaged three murders per day and led the nation with 44.5 homicides for every 100,000 residents. The following year Detroit received further national notoriety when black gangs attacked patrons of a rock concert at Cobo Hall. The melee which followed resulted in several shootings, stabbings, and rapes.

In 1977 Detroit began to reverse its crime statistics. A new police commissioner, William Hart, a black who had worked his way through the ranks, was chosen and given authority to reorganize the department. More officers were hired, local police substations were opened, the *Detroit News* instituted a "silent witness" program by which informers could pass tips anonymously to the authorities, a "war on narcotics" was begun, and neighborhood protective associations were formed. Although property crimes continued to rise, by 1979, Detroit's murder rate was down to 1.5 homicides per day and other serious personal crimes were reduced in frequency.

Decreasing crime rates were not the only signs of Detroit's revival. In 1973 state senator Coleman Young was elected as that city's first black mayor. An analysis of the election disclosed extreme racial polarization, with 90 percent of blacks voting for Young and a like percentage of whites casting their ballots for his white opponent, Police Commissioner John Nichols. Young worked hard to reduce crime and racial antagonisms in order to improve Detroit's image. During his administration the city instituted summer festivals to promote ethnic pride, constructed the Renaissance Center, with its 73-story Detroit Plaza hotel surrounded by four 39-story business complexes, erected the riverfront Joe Louis Sports Arena, won the right to host the 1980 Republican National Convention, and lured many young, middle-class people back into the inner city through a program of neighborhood revitalization in which older houses were renovated and sold at low cost. Mayor Young's efforts to rebuild Detroit into a growing, dynamic metropolis were so successful that in 1979 he was named by his fellow mayors as one of the nation's most effective urban executives.

Areas other than Detroit also have been engaged in massive renewal projects. In the early 1970s Flint embarked upon a long-range program of revitalizing its inner city by establishing a downtown shopping mall, renovating the banks of the Flint River, removing dilapidated structures, erecting a convention center, and supporting construction of a new 48-acre campus along the riverfront for the Flint branch of the University of Michigan. In 1978, Governor William G. Milliken cited Flint as a model of successful urban renewal. Smaller communities underwent changes as well. St. Clair and Algonac, located along the St. Clair River, completely razed and rebuilt their downtown business districts, thereby creating entirely new, modern central cities. Regardless of size the desire to preserve the economic and social life of the inner city is a major goal of every community in the state.

Automobile Economics

Another serious problem faced by Michigan was the economic devastation caused by the effects of the October 1973 Arab oil embargo. Gasoline shortages, combined with threats of rationing, led to a rapid reduction in new car sales. By early 1974, huge inventories of unsold automobiles filled General Motors, Ford, and Chrysler lots. In addition, Michigan's billion-dollar-a-year tourist industry, which is crucial to the economic stability of the upper peninsula and northern lower Michigan, was crippled because potential unavailability of gasoline kept would-be travelers home.

Reduced automobile production resulted in soaring unemployment. Detroit's unemployment rate in February 1975 reached 18 percent and in the six-county Detroit metropolitan area it was estimated that 27 percent of the work force was idled. The number of jobless grew to such immense proportions that the Michigan Employment Security Commission had to hire 1,040 new employees and open forty temporary offices to service the crush of aid applications.

By 1978, automobile production and sales had increased greatly, but soon another crisis developed. In mid-1979, Lee Iacocca, president of Chrysler Corporation, announced that the company was on the verge of bankruptcy. Chrysler's continued emphasis on manufacturing large "gas guzzling" automobiles had driven away economy-minded consumers and a $1 billion deficit was projected for 1979 by company executives. To rescue the corporation, Iacocca sought a $1.5 billion guaranteed loan package from the federal government. After lengthy deliberations, during which it was demonstrated that Chrysler's collapse would result in unemployment for 140,000 company workers and for another 360,000 workers in subsidiary industries, Congress agreed to the loan. This action reflected not only congressional belief that Chrysler should be saved, but also that in the long term the loan would be less expensive for the government than the cost of unemployment compensation and welfare which would follow the company's collapse.

The message of the 1970s was clear. If Michigan persisted in clinging to the automobile industry for its economic well-being in a period of steadily dwindling supplies of fossil fuels, an economic downswing was inevitable. In January 1980, University of Michigan researchers predicted a major financial crisis before the year 2000 unless the state reoriented its economic base and established an energy program based on conservation and development of solar and nuclear power sources.

Traditionally, Michigan's economy has centered around automobiles, agriculture, and tourism, all of which are vulnerable to interruptions in fuel supplies. Within the past several years an attempt at economic diversity has occurred and one of the state's newest growth industries is the production of wine. Vineyards in the Hartford and Paw Paw area take advantage of the perfect climatic conditions for growing grapes, and by 1979 Michigan had emerged as the fourth largest wine-producing state in the nation. In September 1979, the state commerce commission started broadcasting television advertisements which proudly proclaimed that "Michigan doesn't make all the wine in the world, but it does make some of the best." This claim was not a mere idle boast. Bronte Vineyards won a gold medal in 1979 for its Baco Noir burgundy in competition featuring wines from throughout the world. Bronte also won a gold medal for its champagne and received national acclaim for originating the popular sparkling "Cold Duck." State encouragement of new industries, such as wine production, is essential for economic growth and stability.

The "Ghetto Governor"

During the 1970s, both major political parties vigorously fought for the

Harvesters, such as this, reap grapes in Michigan's several vineyards.

opportunity to shape the future direction of the state. With Romney out of office, Democrats anticipated recapturing the governorship in 1970. The new governor, William G. Milliken, of Traverse City, had served three years as state senator before being elected lieutenant governor in 1964. Milliken charmed voters with his boyish appearance and pledged to keep Michigan on the move through progressive leadership. In 1970, his Democratic opponent, former state senator Sander Levin, attacked the governor for his support of state aid to parochial schools. As the election grew near, Levin's opposition to parochiaid seemed to weaken, which cost him the endorsement of the politically potent Michigan Education Association. His apparent switch gave voters the impression that not only was Milliken's position correct, but also that Levin had demonstrated uncertainty in making a decision. This issue overshadowed Levin's call for reform of the state's taxation and welfare structures, and it carried the governor to a narrow 44,409 vote victory.

Four years later, in a rematch of the 1970 gubernatorial contestants, Levin accused Milliken of causing Michigan's high unemployment and of being a Republican like the "band of politicians" who had been responsible for the Watergate burglary. Even though Watergate resulted in Michigan Republicans losing four congressional seats and control of the state senate, Milliken was returned to office by a 114,618 vote margin.

During the governor's second term, he established himself as a friend of minorities and educators. His close working relationship with Mayor Young and his support for increased state aid for Detroit earned Milliken the title "Ghetto Governor." One of the governor's quests was reorganization of public school financing. Although he had not yet succeeded in achieving his goal of state-funded public education to replace the existing system based on local property taxes, Milliken persisted in sending his proposal to the legislature. In 1978 Michigan voters demonstrated their appreciation of the governor's efforts and gave him a 300,000 vote victory over Democratic state senator William B. Fitzgerald.

Cattlegate

During the 1978 campaign, one of Senator Fitzgerald's most serious allegations was that the governor had mishandled the P.B.B. crisis. Since the effects of P.B.B. may prove to be among the most tragic in the state's history, its story is of interest to all Michiganians. In 1973, the Michigan Chemical Corporation ran out of color-coded bags used to differentiate between two of its products, Firemaster, the trade name for the highly toxic chemical fire retardant polybrominated biphenyl (P.B.B.), and Nutrimaster, a food supplement for dairy cattle. Rather than stop manufacture, the company placed each substance in plain brown bags with the appropriate trade name stenciled on them. Through a human error, bags of Firemaster and Nutrimaster were stacked close together and sacks of each were sent to the Michigan Farm Bureau Services. At the Farm Bureau, the contents of the sacks were combined with the bureau's standard feed mix, repackaged, and dispersed throughout the state.

Farmers who used the mixture noticed an almost immediate decline, often reaching 50 percent, in their herd's milk production. After months of testing at various laboratories throughout the country, in April 1974, the United States Agricultural Research Center at Beltsville, Maryland, announced that feed samples showed traces of P.B.B. and that public safety dictated that all contaminated cattle should be destroyed.

Following this revelation, farmers demanded assistance from the state, but until medical reports linked P.B.B. with serious illness and a purported increase in the incidence of cancer, little was done. In 1976, Governor Milliken, who had come under attack from Democrats who charged that he sought to cover up the incident in order to maintain sales of the state's dairy products, established a P.B.B. Scientific Advisory Panel to determine the effects of the "unfortunate error" on Michigan residents. Meanwhile, the state legislature passed a P.B.B. Reform Bill to lower the admissible levels of the chemical in dairy products and to provide for disposal of diseased cattle in burial pits near Kalkaska. Reimbursement for slain livestock was also allowed, but lengthy court battles caused delays in payment. In 1977, Congress passed a bill sponsored by Senator Griffin which allowed Michigan to receive federal reimbursement for 75 percent of the money, to a maximum of $150 million, which the state had to pay farmers to cover livestock losses and medical expenses incurred from P.B.B. contamination.

By 1979, the dispute over P.B.B. and its effects on humans still raged. Irate citizens protested a new burial site near Mio, in Oscoda County, and claimed that P.B.B. would be released into the soil as the carcasses decayed. No new legislation provided assurance that another "Cattlegate" would not occur in the future, and no new medical evidence disproved the contention that nearly all Michiganians face higher chances for developing cancer because of ingestion of tainted dairy products. The potentially catastrophic results of the P.B.B. incident may not be fully realized for generations.

A Ford in the White House

While P.B.B. caused Michigan residents the most concern during the 1970s, the selection of Gerald R. Ford to be Vice-President, and his subsequent elevation to the presidency, brought the greatest sense of pride. Ford, a Grand Rapids Republican who had served in the House of Representatives for twenty-four years, including twelve as minority leader, won the respect of a nation wearied by the corruption of Watergate through his refreshing honesty, modesty, sincerity, and informality. Under Ford's leadership the nation's sagging economy surged forward as more than 4 million new jobs were created in the private sector, unemployment declined from 9.2 percent to 6.8 percent, the Dow Jones Industrial Stock Average soared past the 1,000 mark, and inflation was pared from 12 percent to 5 percent. In foreign affairs, during Ford's administration the policy of détente with the Soviet Union was continued, a basis for a lasting Middle East peace was established, and the Soviet Union agreed on strategic arms limitation talks. Even though popular dissatisfaction against the Republican Party deprived the President of victory in 1976, Michiganians, like all Americans, could reflect with satisfaction upon the record achieved by Gerald Ford.

The Conscience of the Senate

Despite the nationwide acclaim given Ford for restoring honesty to the White House, Michigan's best known and most beloved public figure during the 1960s and 1970s was Philip A. Hart. A graduate of the University of Michigan Law School, Hart became the political protégé of his classmate G. Mennen Williams and was the governor's handpicked running mate in 1954 and 1956. In 1958 Hart successfully challenged Republican incumbent Charles Potter and was sent to Washington to begin what was to become an illustrious eighteen-year career in the United States Senate.

As a senator, Hart became nationally famous for his leadership in shaping almost every major piece of legislation favoring civil rights, consumer protection, and regulation of big business. He was the floor manager for the Voting Rights Act of 1965 and its extension in 1970 and for the Open Housing Act of 1968. Hart also was the chief sponsor of the Drug Safety Act (1962), the Truth-in-Packaging Act (1965), the Truth-in-Lending Act (1966), the Motor Vehicle Information and Cost Saving Act (1972), and the Anti-Trust Act of 1976 which gave state attorneys general power to bring antitrust suits on behalf of individual citizens.

Always willing to risk his political career in support of an issue which he believed was right, even when his constituents were in opposition, Hart backed busing for school desegregation, strict antipollution and safety legislation for the automobile industry, and gun control. His dedication to the American people and their protection was unwavering, and he was a tireless worker against all forms of injustice. Mike Mansfield, the majority leader of the Senate, labeled Hart the most outstanding senator he had ever known and said that he was "a man of great courage, great compassion, and great determination" who, in the pursuit of justice, was "a man of steel."

Seriously ill and suffering the effects of cancer, Hart summed up his Senate career in a farewell speech shortly before his death in December 1976. He concluded by saying simply that "I leave as I arrived, understanding clearly the complexity of the world into which we were born and optimistic that if we give it our best shot, we will come close to achieving the goals set for us 200 years ago." Philip Hart, a man of gentleness and kindness, truly deserved the title given him by his colleagues—"the Conscience of the Senate."

For Further Reading

Few books have been published on Michigan in the 1970s. An excellent biography of Governor Milliken is Dan Angel, *William G. Milliken: A Touch of Steel* (New York: Public Affairs Press, 1974). Joyce Braitwaite and George Weeks, *The Milliken Years* (Traverse City: The Village Press, 1988) offers a pictorial history filled with many quotations from Milliken's speeches. Gerald Ford's autobiography, *A Time to Heal* (New York: Harper and Row, 1979) offers insight into the political happenings in Michigan and the nation during the years 1972-76.

20

Toward the Twenty-First Century

Reeling from the crises of the 1970s, Michiganians hoped that the new decade of the 1980s would bring them more stability and security, but the unresolved issues of the 1970s precluded any chance for rapid improvement in the state's economic and social climate. Over the years Michigan's once-abundant natural resources had been depleted, but mining, lumbering, and shipping continued to provide wealth to businesses, and the state's many lakes, rivers, and streams still afforded recreational opportunities to residents and tourists. However, fish rendered inedible by high levels of toxic mercury, ground water supplies infected by waste disposal dumps, and state parks littered with garbage from thoughtless campers provided ample proof that Michigan's environment required ever-increasing protection from both corporate and individual exploitation and pollution. As prices for automobiles and fuel moved upward, calls arose, especially from residents in large metropolitan areas, for creation of a statewide mass transit system to meet the needs of both inner-city residents and commuting suburbanites. The urgency of this requirement was intensified by studies showing that the state's expressway system, designed in the 1950s to meet the needs of residents for at least the next fifty years, was already overburdened by traffic, in turn causing an unanticipated need for costly and inconvenient roadway resurfacing.

Culturally, the Detroit Institute of Arts, Michigan Council for the Arts, the Interlochen Arts Academy, which boasted such artists as pianist Van Cliburn on its faculty, and a host of privately financed summer stock theaters throughout the state, attested to the quality of and interest in the arts in Michigan. Yet each time state and local budgets faced a deficit, the arts were the first to fall victim to reduced funding, while government officials defended the cuts by asserting that cultural activities were a luxury appreciated only by a small percentage of the population. Ironically, this occurred at a time when many unions were negotiating shorter work weeks, which resulted in more leisure time for people to patronize the arts.

Sports remained one of the major activities in the state, with attendance growing every year at events of all descriptions. Yet, violence at sporting events on the high-school level continued to force many urban schools to restrict their games to daytime hours for increased security.

The state's schools, both public and private, continued to be a source of pride to Michiganians, but test scores revealed that despite increased funding, reading, writing, and mathematics skills among the student body were declining, while school vandalism cost taxpayers hundreds of thousands of dollars annually. Certain state services, such as welfare and prison construction, expanded, but with them came increased taxes and rebellious taxpayers. Thus, Michigan truly remained a state in turmoil.

The Republican Convention of 1980

In 1980, Detroit hosted the Republican National Convention, which not only gave the Motor City's economy a $44,000,000 infusion but also afforded Michigan a chance to improve its "Rust Belt" image in the nation. George Bush, a Yale University classmate of Governor Milliken, had gained his lone victory over former California governor Ronald Reagan in the Michigan presidential primary, but his poor showing elsewhere forced him to drop out of the race prior to the convention. Milliken and twelve other moderate Republican del-

Governor William Milliken, former President Gerald Ford, and Republican presidential nominee Ronald Reagan, 1980.

egates refused to abide by Bush's urging to support Reagan, and this so-called "Michigan Thirteen" acquired the dubious distinction of casting the only votes for Bush. After a brief period of speculation that Michigan's favorite son, former President Gerald Ford, might accept the second spot on the ticket, Reagan selected Bush to placate moderates and achieve party harmony. In November, the national Republican ticket carried Michigan, although Democrats retained control of the state legislature.

The Eighties' Disastrous First Year

In his 1980 State of the State Address, Governor William Milliken said that the state's future was "exciting, but frightening." Unfortunately, the year proved to be more of the latter than the former. Nearly forty years of relative prosperity for Michigan and its citizens came to an abrupt end as inflation, soaring interest rates, and an influx to America of Asian-made automobiles caused a decline in domestic car sales. Subsidiary automotive industries soon began to suffer as well, and by mid-year more than 620,000 Michigan workers were jobless—the most people out of work since the Great Depression. The city of Flint became world famous as its 24 percent unemployment rate was cited repeatedly by Republican presidential nominee Ronald Reagan as proof that, despite the efforts of Republican governors such as George Romney and William Milliken, the national Democratic Party ultimately was responsible for the automobile industry's plight because of its failure to institute high protective tariffs to reduce foreign competition.

As automobile sales declined and unemployment increased, state revenues from income, sales, and business taxes plummeted. Consequently, requests for state unemployment assistance increased and by mid-1980 10 percent of the state's residents received some form of welfare benefits. To meet these demands for government resources, tax increases were necessary, but 1980 was a year of calls for tax reduction, not raises. In November, voters narrowly defeated a ballot proposal which would have devastated public services by cutting state spending by 40 percent. Fearful of an expanded tax revolt, Governor Milliken and legislative leaders, working together, attempted to prevent what seemed to be imminent economic catastrophe, while, at the same time, avoiding both a raise in taxes and excessive hardship among those most in need.

To accomplish this goal, severe budget slashing was necessary. Consequently, in 1981 Michigan residents were told to expect less public transportation, reduced road repairs, an end to school breakfast programs, reduced care for the mentally ill, cutbacks in recreational facilities, fewer state police patrols, drastically diminished aid to public schools and state-supported universities, and cuts in welfare.

Further compromising Michigan's future, Chrysler Corporation had to request even more federal loans to avoid bankruptcy, violent crime increased, and the federal government cited the state as hazardous for its residents' health because of its high level of toxic waste material. Legislative Majority Leader Bobby Crim summarized Michigan's dilemma well when he said: "We're not going to make a recovery in one year. Michigan at this time in history has more problems than ever before, more problems than any other state."

The Newest "Boy Governor"

In early 1982 Michigan maintained for the third consecutive year the dubious distinction of having the highest unemployment rate in the nation. Moreover, state officials and the general populace were embarrassed and angry when it was revealed that after no domestic bank would back a proposed sale of $500,000,000 in short-term notes to ease the state's debt crisis, five Japanese banks consented to save Michigan from fiscal collapse. This economic stress, coupled with Governor Milliken's announcement that he would not seek reelection, gave Democrats hope that they could capture the governorship for the first time in twenty years. Expectations of a Democratic victory were buoyed further when James J. Blanchard, the thirty-nine-year-old suburban Detroit congressman who had been credited with assembling the so-called "Chrysler bailout package," emerged triumphant in the primary election.

Blanchard expected his Republican opponent to be popular, moderate lieutenant governor James Brickley, who had the tacit backing of Governor Milliken and the Republican state party organization. Republican voters in the primary election, however, shocked political pundits by selecting as their candidate Richard H. Headlee, a conservative insurance company executive who had the support of former governor George Romney.

The campaign devolved into vilification. Conservative Republicans labeled Blanchard and his running mate, former ten-term congresswoman Martha Griffiths, as big-spending, high-taxing, New Deal liberals, whose only experience came from Washington, not Lansing. Democrats and moderate Republicans accused Headlee of being insensitive to the needs of the poor, minorities, and cities. Furthermore, Headlee's speeches against passage of the Equal Rights Amendment and state-supported abortion funding earned him the enmity of women's groups across the state. To muddy the waters even more, a third candidate, Robert Tisch, a vocal tax-cut advocate and political gadfly, entered the race as an independent. On election day, Blanchard, backed by a coalition of Democrats and moderate Republicans, rolled to an easy 200,000 vote victory.

The new governor inherited a $1.7 billion deficit from his predecessor. Because the state constitution mandated a balanced budget, Blanchard proposed a temporary 38 percent increase in the state income tax, as well as a $225 million cut in state services. After a bitter legislative battle, the tax bill passed, and Michigan edged back from the brink of fiscal disaster. Bond ratings were upgraded, funding for state programs and education increased, and a Michigan Youth Corps established to give temporary summer jobs to more than 60,000 young people. By early 1983, domestic automobile sales, aided by imposition of a federal import quota on foreign cars, began to rise, unemployment dipped to 14 percent, and Michigan appeared to be on the road to recovery.

Despite the brighter economic picture, the governor's popularity sank to 34 percent in the polls because of the tax increase. Angry voters instituted a recall drive in 1983 against politicians who had supported the tax increase. It proved unsuccessful, but voters pledged to renew their efforts the following year. Assurances by Blanchard that the tax bill, as passed, provided for automatic phasing out of the levy did little to calm his foes. Nor were the critics silenced when former governor Milliken praised Blanchard, saying: "If I were governor, I would have taken substantially the same steps. He did what he had to do, and I commend him for it." Recalls were begun against individual lawmakers who had supported the tax legislation, and these proved successful enough to defeat two Democratic state senators and give control of Michigan's upper house to the Republicans.

In late 1983 Blanchard outlined a program of economic strategies stressing diversification of industry, retraining of workers for high-technology jobs, and regional cooperation among the Great Lakes states to attract new industry. While Michigan's growth still was tied closely to the return of a healthy automobile industry and the stemming of the exodus of workers and business from the state, a new optimism was being felt by most Michiganians. By mid-1985, Michigan was hailed as the "comeback state." The tax increase was being rolled back, the state's credit rating hovered just beneath the top investment grade, and a prominent national management and accounting firm cited Michigan's business climate as the best in the country.

Even in the midst of economic difficulties, Blanchard demonstrated his commitment to quality education. During his first term, state support for K-12 education increased by 50 percent and test scores in the state's educational assessment program reached an all-time peak. Nor was higher education neglected by the governor. When he took office, approximately 60 percent of Michigan's residents were high school graduates and 14.3 percent had completed at least four years of college. Michigan was unusual in that nearly 75 percent of its college students were in public, rather than private, institutions of higher learning, nearly 20 percent above the national average. To meet the future needs of a populace fearful of the spiraling costs of college education, Blanchard proposed the Michigan Educational Trust Fund (MET) in which parents could make a one-time investment of $3,000 per child and be guaranteed that child would receive a four-year education at any of Michigan's fifteen state-supported colleges beginning in the year 2005. Although critics questioned the financial ability of the state to fulfill these contracts, the measure was passed into law as a majority of legislators believed MET was in keeping with Michigan's tradition of assuring educational opportunities to all its citizens.

Basking in these successes, Blanchard won an unexpectedly easy 1986 re-election bid over Wayne County executive William Lucas, who previously had served as that county's sheriff. Much of Blanchard's impressive victory margin of 69 to 31 percent must be attributed more to Republican factionalism than public favor with the governor. Lucas, the first black to be nominated for the state's highest office, had been a lifelong Democrat until late 1985 and had not earned the trust of the Republican faithful, even though he was an outspoken, articulate conservative who had cut Wayne County's debt through such strict measures as laying off workers and selling a publicly owned hospital.

Unfortunately, the tone for Blanchard's second term was set within a week after the election when General Motors chairman Roger Smith announced the closing of seven plants in Michigan, including the company's oldest factory, the Cadillac Fleetwood plant in Detroit, which would idle 17,450 workers. Since the governor had denounced rumors of the closings as baseless during the campaign, he lost credibility with the electorate once again despite his truthful assertion that he had been misled by Smith.

Another damaging trend for the state was the continued decline in the number of residents engaged in agriculture, the state's third largest industry. During the 1980s, the number of Michigan farms diminished from 66,000 to 55,000, while cultivated acreage fell from 11.4 million to 10.8 million. Even though the state retained its ranking as the nation's number one cherry producer and as one of the top in apple production, family-run dairy and grain farms were being sold at an alarming rate either to agribusinesses or land developers.

The Women's Hall of Fame

On June 10, 1987, an important part of Michigan's population received long overdue recognition with the opening of a Women's Historical Center and Hall of Fame. Located in Lansing, the center contained exhibits honoring more than thirty initial inductees, among whom were abolitionist Sojourner Truth, Lieutenant Governor Martha Griffiths, former first lady Helen Milliken, and civil rights activist Rosa Parks. Nominations for future induction were to be collected annually by the Michigan Women's Study Association, which would then select the honorees. The museum features exhibits of the art, photography, crafts, and literature of Michigan women, as well as displays relating the contributions of Michigan women to science, politics, and law.

The Election of 1990

Confident of a third term in 1990 despite a lackluster previous four years, Blanchard destroyed his re-election bid by unexpectedly dropping his seventy-eight-year-old lieutenant governor, Martha Griffiths, from the ticket for what he called "the best interests of the state." Infuriated, Griffiths lambasted the governor, saying: "The biggest problem in politics is that you help some S.O.B. get what he wants, and then he throws you off the train." Immediately women's and senior citizens' organizations attacked Blanchard for sex and age discrimination, and the assaults did not diminish even when he named Olivia Maynard, the Director of the State Office of Services to the Aging, as his new running mate. Republican gubernatorial nominee John Engler, the Majority Leader of the State Senate, immediately seized upon the opportunity to win over the angry electorate and selected sixty-six-year-old state senator Connie Binsfeld, a former Michigan Mother of the Year, to run with him at the head of the ticket.

To compound the governor's woes, traditional Democrats were upset at Blanchard's efforts to attract middle-class and business support by proposing property tax relief and setting forth a "hard line" anticrime package, including military-style boot camps for young offenders. Especially critical were labor, blacks, and women. Detroit Mayor Coleman Young chided the governor for not giving "enough attention to the problems of minorities and cities," while state representative Morris Hood of Detroit was even more blunt, stating that the entire Democratic party, including Blanchard, was "guilty of forgetting its roots." Prophetically, Hood warned that "many of the working people I know have talked about sitting this election out." If all this was not enough, three months before the election Blanchard's ex-wife published a book portraying the governor as a neglectful husband and father.

One other issue worked against Blanchard's re-election chances. In 1990, anti-abortion groups were beginning a parental consent petition drive, but the governor was not only a supporter of Medicare-funded legal abortions but also a spokesman for the National Abortion Action League. Conversely, his opponent, John Engler, worked diligently to win support from Right to Life of Michigan. Abortion rights thus became not only a major issue in the race but perhaps, as many pundits argue, the key factor in Engler's narrow 17,595-vote victory.

Years of Reform

In an economic situation similar to that of his predecessor, the new governor inherited a $1.8 billion deficit. Unlike Blanchard, Engler opted to reduce it through systematic cost-cutting and government reorganization rather than to increase taxes. Engler's reforms revitalized the fiscal climate so successfully that in 1993 Michigan led the nation in new business growth and had the most robust economic development of all industrial states. In 1993, a state record of 4,350,000 men and women were employed, an increase of nearly 400,000 since 1991, and unemployment was at its lowest level (7 percent) in fifteen years. Furthermore, the growth in personal income for Michigan citizens was nearly three times the national average.

Michigan's turnaround was based on three factors. First came welfare reform, aimed at ending dependency on the state. In 1991 general assistance welfare payments were stopped for 84,000 single, able-bodied adults. Despite allegations made by Democratic lawmakers, social service employees, and labor union leaders that Engler was insensitive to the poor, and polls showing a high disapproval rating, the governor remained steadfast about reducing welfare. He assured residents that this was merely the initial step in a program which would result in more than mere cost savings, because it was in conjunction with new employment retraining programs and community service alternatives to welfare. To the surprise of many of his critics, the program worked so well that in 1993 Michigan led the nation in the number of welfare recipients who were also employed and moving toward self-sufficiency. In mid-1994, Engler announced the second stage of his welfare reform program, which required that able-bodied welfare recipients either become employed or enroll in a job training program, or their state assistance would be reduced by 25 percent after one year and eliminated after two years.

Even as prosperity returned for many Michigan residents, poverty remained a major issue in urban centers. Detroit, for example, with a minority population of 76 percent, had the unfortunate distinction of being the nation's poorest major metropolitan center, ranking last among the country's largest one hundred cities in median home value and first in the number of households receiving welfare. Thirty-three percent of the city's households were beneath the federal poverty line, an increase of 8 percent from 1979. In keeping with the governor's initiative, Detroit's "Focus: HOPE" established retraining programs for the unemployed, in an effort to reduce the city's social and economic ills.

A second element of the governor's financial recovery plan was put into effect: a tax relief program including a property-tax freeze, a cut in the state small business tax, and elimination of inheritance taxes. Michigan ended the 1993 fiscal year with nearly one billion dollars in surplus. A government program for privatization of state services, such as competitive bidding for health insurance and government partnerships with private industries, was begun, resulting in significant benefits. Such a partnership with a pharmaceutical company has made it possible for the state to supply free vaccines to virtually all children. The government also made a contract with the Salvation Army to provide shelter for more than 5,000 homeless persons.

Another of Engler's primary goals was education reform. Initially, the Michigan Educational Trust Fund was eliminated from the budget due to its high cost. However, education was spared from budget slashing; in fact, it received increases of more than $500 million. In a bold bipartisan initiative, Engler endorsed a 1993 proposal introduced by Democratic state senator Debbie Stabenow calling for ending reliance on property taxes for school funding, and in March 1994, voters approved reducing state property taxes on primary residences by an average of 83 percent. To replace the lost revenue, the state sales tax was increased by 50 percent to six cents on a dollar, and an increase on cigarettes of fifty cents per package was instituted. The latter proviso led critics to point out derisively that the state's residents had placed themselves in a dilemma: if they chose to reduce their risk of lung cancer by not smoking cigarettes, they were cutting revenue for schools as well. Also in 1994, the governor signed into law a bill establishing the most comprehensive charter school act in the nation, enabling outside entities, such as public universities, community colleges, teachers, or other school districts, to open competing schools within a school district. Shortly thereafter an Ingham county circuit court judge ruled charter schools unconstitutional on the grounds that they were private institutions and as such not entitled to state aid. The governor ordered the state to file a countersuit, and a lengthy legal battle was begun which will end only when a supreme court decision is rendered. Other elements of Michigan's "education revolution" included legislation for the minimum number of hours in a school year to be increased from 900 hours to 1080 hours beginning in 1999 and the addition of $230 million for teaching "at-risk" students. School administrators throughout the nation are watching the results of the "Michigan Model," and if it proves successful Michigan will regain its historic place as an innovative leader in public education.

Solving the Mystery of the "Fitz"

The Great Lakes have been for Michigan not only a source of commercial and recreational benefits but also of tragedy. Gale-force winds and waves have sunk hundreds of ships. Historically, November has been the most treacherous month for sailing on the Great Lakes, with major storms claiming more than twenty vessels in 1842, ninety-seven in 1869, and eighty-one during the years 1900-1966. Twentieth-century November disasters alone caused the death of more than seven hundred seamen, including all but two on the *Carl D. Bradley,* which went down November 18, 1958, and one from the *Daniel J. Morrell* which sank November 28, 1966.

None of these maritime calamities, however, captured the public imagination as did the loss of the 729-foot ore carrier *Edmund Fitzgerald,* with all of its twenty-nine crewmen, on November 10, 1975. Partly because the tragedy was popularized by Gordon Lightfoot's ballad, "The Wreck of the *Edmund Fitzgerald,*" and partly because the exact cause of its sinking had never been determined, the sinking of the *Fitzgerald* became an event of fascination, even

The *Edmund Fitzgerald*, which sank on November 10, 1975, with all of its twenty-nine member crew.

luring world-renowned oceanographer Jacques Cousteau to examine the site of the wreckage.

In the early 1990s, an underwater video of the wreckage tended to discredit the earlier Coast Guard theory that the *Fitzgerald* had broken in two after being lifted simultaneously by two waves. The new pictures indicated that the ship had taken water through unsecured hatch covers, had sunk in one piece, and had then broken into three parts upon crashing into the lake bottom 550 feet below the surface.

In July, 1994, "Expedition 1994," headed by a Michigan diver, Fred Shannon, came to another conclusion. When new photographs showed all hatch bolts in their proper position, Shannon blamed the tragedy on an undisclosed "structural failure." Even with this new evidence, the exact cause of the *Fitzgerald* sinking remains a mysterious chapter in the lore of the Great Lakes.

Birth and Death

While Michigan made headlines throughout the early 1990s primarily because of its political and economic climate, it became the focus of the nation's social consciousness because of a small child and a retired pathologist. In mid-

1993, national media attention focused on a custody battle over "Baby Jessica," whose unwed mother had signed away all rights to her daughter at the time of the baby's birth in 1991. When she was six days old, Jessica was adopted by Jan and Roberta DeBoer, who took the infant from Iowa to their home in Ann Arbor, Michigan. However, the biological parents, having married, changed their minds about the adoption and demanded custody of the child. Throughout the first seven months of 1993, a legal battle raged, which culminated in the Michigan Supreme Court ruling that Jessica had to be returned to her natural parents. When the United States Supreme Court refused to overturn the Michigan ruling, the "Baby Jessica" case became a focus for children's advocacy groups who sought legislation protecting rights of adopted children from unjust custody rules. By 1994, the crusade had become a national movement with the formation of the DeBoer Committee for Children's Rights, which boasted fifty-one chapters, with 2,000 members, in thirty-six states.

At the same time as Michigan's movement for children's rights, came Dr. Jack Kevorkian's campaign for the rights of the dying. From 1990 through 1994, Kevorkian, a retired pathologist, used a simple carbon monoxide delivery system, which he named the "Mercitron," to assist twenty terminally ill persons to commit suicide. Although each of the victims and their families had sought

Jessica DeBoer as she left her adoptive parents. *Courtesy* The Detroit News, *Alan Lessig, photographer.*

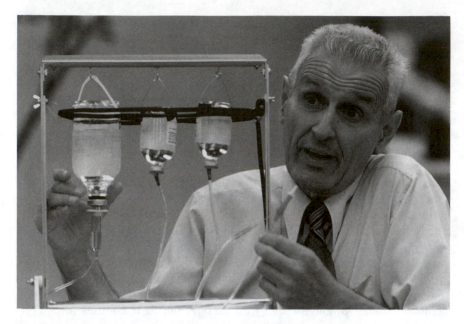

Dr. Jack Kevorkian and his suicide machine. *Courtesy* The Detroit News, *W. Gary Porter, photographer.*

Kevorkian's aid in gaining "death with dignity," his opponents charged that Kevorkian was abetting in murder and dubbed him "Dr. Death."

As his notoriety grew, Kevorkian came under attack not only from Right-to-Life groups who tried unsuccessfully to bring him to trial for murder, but also from Governor Engler and the Michigan legislature. In February 1993, Engler signed into law legislation declaring assisted suicide a felony punishable by a $2,000 fine and a maximum of four years in jail, but three months later the law was declared unconstitutional.

In 1994, Kevorkian, who referred to himself as an "obitiarist" (specialist in death), began to collect petition signatures to place assisted suicide on the ballot for a statewide referendum. Buoyed by polls showing Michigan residents favored assisted suicide by more than a two-to-one margin, Kevorkian predicted his ultimate triumph, saying: "It may not happen in my lifetime, but my opponents are going to lose."

The Election of 1994

As Michigan neared its opportunity to have a referendum on Governor Engler's policies in the November 1994 election, several significant facts dominated the state's political and economic environment. During fiscal years 1990 to 1995, the general fund budget had decreased by $10,100,000, but spending for higher education had increased 14.35 percent, allocations for mental health had gone up by 22.2 percent, funding for the Department of Corrections had soared 62 percent (with the opening of seven new prisons and three prison camps), money for the State Police had risen by 36.6 percent, and welfare spending had been increased 45.5 percent. In short, essential state services had received more funding, while the overall budget had declined.

As a result of these policies and a strong economy which had created a $1,000,000,000 surplus in the state treasury, the electorate gave Engler an over-whelming vote of confidence. The governor garnered 61 percent of the vote and carried all but two of the state's eighty-three counties in defeating his Democratic opponent, former congressman Howard Wolpe. Moreover, the governor's coattails enabled not only Spencer Abraham to become the first Republican elected to the United States Senate from Michigan since 1972 but also Candice Miller to oust veteran Secretary of State Richard Austin, giving Republicans that office after forty years of Democratic control. In addition, Republicans retained their 22-16 margin in the state senate, gained a 56-54 majority in the state house, and achieved a majority on the State Board of Education for the first time in Michigan's history.

Being returned to office was not the only reason for the governor to rejoice. Five days after the election, the state's first lady, Michelle Engler, gave birth to triplets, making her husband the first Michigan governor since Austin Blair in 1864 to become a father while serving in the executive office. Flashing a broad smile, Engler told reporters: "Four years ago, I was single, a state senator, and looking for 17,000 votes. Today, I'm governor, married, and looking for 17,000 diapers."

Looking Ahead

Because of events in the early 1990s, Michigan seemed well on the road to reclaiming its former position as a national leader in economic growth, progressive social reform, and education. The automobile industry had rebounded, but reliance on automobile manufacturing as the sole bulwark of the state's economy had diminished. Michigan's business community began to look to the world market by establishing Business Development Offices in Canada, Mexico, Europe, Japan, and Africa. In addition, by joining with other Great Lakes states, Michigan became part of a consortium to work for preservation of natural resources and regional growth based on cooperation rather than competition.

Despite the promising economic outlook and the success of social and educational innovations, many challenges remained. Polls in 1994 revealed that more than three-fourths of the state's residents favored women having the right to choose an abortion, but divisive debates between Right-to-Life and Pro-choice factions raged on, stressing not legal but, rather, moral issues. While new black leaders emerged, including Mayors Dennis Archer of Detroit and Woodrow Stanley of Flint, and others such as Detroit congressman John Conyers and twenty-four-year veteran Secretary of State Richard Austin continued to serve, nonwhites remained underrepresented in the state's political system. Despite women in both major parties running strong, but unsuccessful, primary races in 1994 to fill the United States Senate seat vacated by eighteen-year-incumbent Donald Riegle, women's voice in politics still did not reflect their numerical strength. Minorities continued to suffer both rates of unemployment at least twice those for whites and unequal opportunities in education and housing. Crime remained the number one issue with Michigan residents. Legislation reducing the age of juvenile offenders for trial as adults from sixteen to fourteen years of age was proposed, and bills for "truth in sentencing," increased hiring of state police troopers, and new prison construction were signed into law.

The final steps toward the new century are filled both with hope and anxiety. If Michigan can use its economic and natural resources wisely and meet the needs of its citizens, the state will continue in the social vanguard of the nation. Judging from their response to past challenges, clearly Michigan residents will not shirk from meeting the challenges of the future.

For Further Reading

While little has been written as yet concerning the Blanchard years, basic information on his first term may be obtained in Neil Staebler, *Out of the Smoke-Filled Room* (Ann Arbor: George Wahr Publishing Co., 1990) and George Weeks, *Stewards of the State* (Ann Arbor: Historical Society of Michigan, 1987). Roger Martin, et al., *The Journey of John Engler* (West Bloomfield: Altwerger & Mandel Publishing Co., 1991) offers a reasonably balanced account of the 1990 gubernatorial race as set forth by reporters from the Lansing Bureau of the *Detroit News*. Current public policy issues facing Michigan are set forth in Phyllis T. H. Grummon and Brendan Mullan (ed.), *Policy Choices: Framing the Debate for Michigan's Future* (East Lansing: Michigan State University Press, 1993) and *Policy Choices: Creating Michigan's Future* (East Lansing: Michigan State University Press, 1995).

Appendix A

GOVERNORS OF THE TERRITORY AND STATE OF MICHIGAN

Territorial Governors	Term of Office	Political Party
William Hull	1805-1813	Democrat
Lewis Cass	1813-1831	Democrat
George B. Porter	1831-1834	Democrat

State Governors	Term of Office	Political Party
Stevens T. Mason	1835-1839	Democrat
William Woodbridge	1840-1841	Whig
John W. Gordon	1841	Whig
John S. Barry	1842-1846	Democrat
Alpheus Felch	1846-1847	Democrat
William L. Greenly	1847-1848	Democrat
Epaphroditus Ransom	1848-1850	Democrat
John Barry	1850-1851	Democrat
Robert McClelland	1852-1853	Democrat
Andrew Parsons	1853-1855	Democrat
Kinsley S. Bingham	1855-1859	Republican
Moses Wisner	1859-1861	Republican
Austin Blair	1861-1865	Republican
Henry H. Crapo	1865-1869	Republican
Henry P. Baldwin	1869-1873	Republican
John J. Bagley	1873-1877	Republican
Charles M. Croswell	1877-1881	Republican
David H. Jerome	1881-1883	Republican
Josiah Begole	1883-1885	Fusion
Russell A. Alger	1885-1887	Republican
Cyrus G. Luce	1887-1891	Republican
Edwin B. Winans	1891-1893	Democrat

John T. Rich	1893-1897	Republican
Hazen S. Pingree	1897-1901	Republican
Aaron T. Bliss	1901-1905	Republican
Fred M. Warner	1905-1911	Republican
Chase S. Osborn	1911-1913	Republican
Woodbridge N. Ferris	1913-1917	Democrat
Albert E. Sleeper	1917-1921	Republican
Alexander J. Groesbeck	1921-1927	Republican
Fred W. Green	1927-1931	Republican
Wilbur M. Brucker	1931-1933	Republican
William A. Comstock	1933-1935	Democrat
Frank D. Fitzgerald	1935-1937	Republican
Frank Murphy	1937-1939	Democrat
Frank D. Fitzgerald	1939	Republican
Luren D. Dickinson	1939-1941	Republican
Murray D. VanWagoner	1941-1943	Democrat
Harry F. Kelly	1943-1947	Republican
Kim Sigler	1947-1949	Republican
G. Mennen Williams	1949-1961	Democrat
John B. Swainson	1961-1963	Democrat
George W. Romney	1963-1969	Republican
William G. Milliken	1969-1983	Republican
James J. Blanchard	1983-1991	Democrat
John Engler	1991-	Republican

Appendix B

Counts, Dates of Organization, and Origins of County Names

ALCONA	1869	Believed to have been coined by Henry Rowe Schoolcraft to mean "the excellent prairie."
ALGER	1885	Named for Governor Russell Alger.
ALLEGAN	1835	Thought to be a name derived by Schoolcraft from the Chippewa words for "fine lake" or "fine river."
ALPENA	1857	A Schoolcraft word which loosely translated into "the bird."
ANTRIM	1863	Several Michigan counties had substantial numbers of Irish Catholic settlers who sought to preserve some of their native heritage. Thus, this county is named for County Antrim in Ireland.
ARENAC	1883	A combination of the Latin "arena" and the Indian "ac," which means "the sandy place."
BARAGA	1875	Named for the Catholic bishop of northern Michigan, Frederic Baraga.
BARRY	1839	Several Michigan counties were named for members of President Andrew Jackson's cabinet as a means of honoring the administration under which statehood was first sought and then achieved. William T. Barry was Jackson's postmaster general.
BAY	1857	So named because it nearly encompasses Saginaw Bay.
BENZIE	1869	Originally derived from a French river title "aux-Bec-Scies." In later years, the name was changed to Betsey and finally Benzie.
BERRIEN	1831	Named for Jackson's attorney general, John Berrien.
BRANCH	1833	Named for Jackson's secretary of the Navy, John Branch.

CALHOUN	1833	Named for Jackson's first Vice-President, John C. Calhoun.
CASS	1829	Named for Michigan's Territorial Governor Lewis Cass.
CHARLEVOIX	1869	Named for the Jesuit missionary Pierre Charlevoix.
CHEBOYGAN	1853	Taken from the Indian name for the major river in the area.
CHIPPEWA	1826	Named to honor the Chippewa Indians who inhabited much of the state before the arrival of Europeans.
CLARE	1871	Named for County Clare in Ireland.
CLINTON	1839	Named to honor New York Governor DeWitt Clinton, whose administration financed construction of the Erie Canal, which brought thousands of settlers to Michigan.
CRAWFORD	1879	Named for Colonel William Crawford.
DELTA	1861	Originally the county contained parts of the later counties of Menominee, Dickinson, Iron, and Marquette, and formed a triangle, or delta, shape.
DICKINSON	1891	Named for Don M. Dickinson, attorney general under President Grover Cleveland.
EATON	1837	Named for Jackson's secretary of war, John Eaton.
EMMET	1853	Named for Irish patriot Robert Emmet.
GENESEE	1836	Many settlers came from the Genesee Valley in western New York and settled in the Flint area. To honor their former residence, they named their new home Genesee, the Iroquois word for "beautiful valley."
GLADWIN	1875	Named for Major Henry Gladwin, commander of Fort Detroit during Pontiac's uprising.
GOGEBIC	1887	Thought to mean "rock," the derivation is unknown.
GRAND TRAVERSE	1851	From the French "grande travers," meaning "great crossing" or "long crossing."
GRATIOT	1855	Named for Captain Charles Gratiot, who built and commanded the garrison bearing his name at Port Huron.
HILLSDALE	1835	Named for the beautiful hills and fields in the area.

HOUGHTON	1846	Reorganized in 1848. Named in honor of geologist Douglass Houghton.
HURON	1859	Named to honor the Huron Indians.
INGHAM	1838	Named for Jackson's secretary of the treasury, Samuel D. Ingham.
IONIA	1837	Named for the Greek province.
IOSCO	1857	Derived from the Indian word for water "osco."
IRON	1885	Named for the ore abundant in the area.
ISABELLA	1859	Named for the Spanish queen who financed the voyage of Columbus to the New World.
JACKSON	1832	Named for President Andrew Jackson.
KALAMAZOO	1830	Supposedly an Indian word for "boiling water." Other translations include "reflected river" and "otter tail."
KALKASKA	1871	A Schoolcraft creation. Originally spelled Calcasca, in honor of Schoolcraft's family name Calcraft, the Ks were substituted to make the title seem more like an Indian word.
KENT	1836	Named for the noted New York judge, Chancellor Kent.
KEWEENAW	1861	An Indian word meaning "portage place."
LAKE	1871	Many small lakes dot the region.
LAPEER	1835	Purportedly from the French "La Pierre," meaning "flint" or "stone."
LEELANAU	1863	A sentimental creation of Schoolcraft, whose wife used the word as one of her several literary pen names.
LENAWEE	1826	An Indian term for "man."
LIVINGSTON	1836	Named for Jackson's secretary of state, Edward Livingston.
LUCE	1887	Named for Governor Cyrus G. Luce.
MACKINAC	1849	Originally organized in 1818 as Michilimackinac, it was reorganized in 1849 under the shortened title given the former fort at the Straits.
MACOMB	1818	Named for General Alexander Macomb.
MANISTEE	1855	Named for the primary river in the county.
MARQUETTE	1846	Reorganized in 1848. Named for the Jesuit missionary and explorer Jacques Marquette.
MASON	1855	Named for the state's first governor, Stevens T. Mason.
MECOSTA	1859	Named for Chief Mecosta.

MENOMINEE	1861	Originally named Bleeker, it was reorganized in 1863. It is named for the Menominee Indians.
MIDLAND	1850	So named because it is near the geographical center of the state.
MISSAUKEE	1871	Named for a local Indian chief, although he was better known as Nesaukee.
MONROE	1822	Named for President James Monroe.
MONTCALM	1850	Named for the French general, Louis Montcalm.
MONTMORENCY	1881	Named for one of the many Counts Montmorency.
MUSKEGON	1859	An Ojibwa word for "swamp."
NEWAYGO	1851	Allegedly named for an Indian chief.
OAKLAND	1820	Abundant stands of oak trees were found in the area.
OCEANA	1851	Reorganized in 1855. It received its name because of its nearness to Lake Michigan.
OGEMAW	1873	Reorganized in 1875. Named for Chief Ogemaw-ki-keto of the Chippewa of Saginaw, Swan Creek, and Black River.
ONTONAGON	1846	Reorganized in 1848 and declared legal by the state legislature in 1853. It derives its name from the Ojibwa word for "dish" or bowl."
OSCEOLA	1869	Named for the Seminole Indian chief Osceola.
OSCODA	1881	A combination of two Schoolcraft words "ossin," meaning "stone," and "muskoda," meaning "prairie."
OTSEGO	1875	Iroquois for "clear water" or "meeting place."
OTTAWA	1837	Named to honor the Ottawa Indians who inhabited much of the state before the arrival of Europeans.
PRESQUE ISLE	1871	From the French for "narrow peninsula" or "almost an island."
ROSCOMMON	1873	Named for County Roscommon in Ireland.
SAGINAW	1875	Derived from the Indian terms "Sac-e-nong," meaning "Sauk Town" or "sag ong," meaning "place of the opening."
ST. CLAIR	1821	Named for General Arthur St. Clair.
ST. JOSEPH	1829	Named for the patron saint of New France.
SANILAC	1848	Named for Chief Sanilac.
SCHOOLCRAFT	1846	Named for Henry Rowe Schoolcraft.
SHIAWASSEE	1837	Exact meaning is unknown. Some possibilities include "straight running water" and "twisting river."

TUSCOLA	1850	A Schoolcraft word meaning "level lands."
VAN BUREN	1850	Named for Jackson's second Vice-President, Martin Van Buren.
WASHTENAW	1826	Reorganized in 1829. Its name comes from the Ojibwa words for "land beyond the Grand Rivers."
WAYNE	1815	Named for General Anthony Wayne.
WEXFORD	1869	Named for County Wexford in Ireland.

Index